Lydia Maria Francis Child, Wendell Phillips

Letters of Lydia Maria Child

With a Biographical Introduction

Lydia Maria Francis Child, Wendell Phillips

Letters of Lydia Maria Child
With a Biographical Introduction

ISBN/EAN: 9783337016142

Printed in Europe, USA, Canada, Australia, Japan

Cover: Foto ©Thomas Meinert / pixelio.de

More available books at **www.hansebooks.com**

LETTERS OF LYDIA MARIA CHILD

WITH

A BIOGRAPHICAL INTRODUCTION

By JOHN G. WHITTIER

AND

AN APPENDIX

By WENDELL PHILLIPS

BOSTON
HOUGHTON, MIFFLIN AND COMPANY
New York: 11 East Seventeenth Street
The Riverside Press, Cambridge
1883

L. Maria Child.

PREFATORY NOTE.

WHEN the friend whom Mrs. Child would have chosen above all others consented to write a biographical introduction to this volume, solely as a labor of love, the compiler, though an entire novice at such work, could not refuse his urgent request — seconded by one of Mrs. Child's nearest relations, to whom she had left her papers — to select and arrange her letters.

Her life was so much richer in thought and sentiment than in events, and so devoted to the progressive movements relating to human weal and woe, that it is thought her letters, given in chronological order, will almost tell her whole story.

If any correspondents miss some favorite letter in the collection, we would remind them of the embarrassment of riches; for her correspondence extended over sixty years; and of the impossibility of suiting all tastes; and we cordially thank them all for the abundant supply of material.

PUBLISHERS' NOTE.

THE portrait of Mrs. Child which is prefixed to this volume, while failing to satisfy some of her nearest relatives and friends, who would have preferred not to have it appear, is yet so much liked by other friends who knew her well that the Publishers do not feel justified in withholding it from the public. Mrs. Child herself was always averse to being photographed, and there is no thoroughly good and satisfactory portrait of her in existence, so that the engraver's task has necessarily been a difficult one, and his success greater than could reasonably have been anticipated.

CONTENTS.

	PAGE
INTRODUCTION	V–XXV
LETTERS	1–261

APPENDIX.

Remarks of Wendell Phillips at the Funeral of Mrs. Child   263

"Within the Gate," by *John G. Whittier*   .   .   . 269

List of Mrs. Child's Works   272

INDEX   275

INTRODUCTION.

IN presenting to the public this memorial volume, its compilers deemed that a brief biographical introduction was necessary; and as a labor of love I have not been able to refuse their request to prepare it.

Lydia Maria Francis was born in Medford, Massachusetts, February 11, 1802. Her father, Convers Francis, was a worthy and substantial citizen of that town. Her brother, Convers Francis, afterwards theological professor in Harvard College, was some years older than herself, and assisted her in her early home studies, though, with the perversity of an elder brother, he sometimes mystified her in answering her questions. Once, when she wished to know what was meant by Milton's "raven down of darkness," which was made to smile when smoothed, he explained that it was only the fur of a black cat, which sparkled when stroked! Later in life this brother wrote of her, "She has been a dear, good sister to me: would that I had been half as good a brother to her." Her earliest teacher was an aged spinster, known in the village as "Marm Betty," painfully shy, and with many oddities of person and manner, the never-forgotten calamity of whose life was that Governor Brooks once saw her drinking out of the nose of her tea-kettle. Her school was in her bedroom, always untidy, and she was a constant chewer of tobacco; but the children were fond of her, and Maria and her father always carried her a good Sunday dinner. Thomas W. Higginson, in "Eminent Women of the Age," mentions in this connection that, according to an established custom, on the night before Thanksgiving "all the humble friends of the Francis household — Marm Betty, the washerwoman, wood-sawyer, and journeymen, some twenty or thirty in all — were summoned to a preliminary entertainment. They there partook of an immense chicken pie, pumpkin pie made in milk-pans, and heaps of doughnuts. They feasted in the large, old-fashioned kitchen; and went away loaded with crackers and bread and pies, not forgetting 'turnovers' for the children. Such plain application of the doctrine that it is more blessed to give than receive may have done more to mould the character of Lydia Maria Child of maturer years than all the faithful labors of good Dr. Osgood, to whom she and her brother used to repeat the Assembly's catechism once a month."

Her education was limited to the public schools, with the exception of one year at a private seminary in her native town. From a note by her brother, Dr. Francis, we learn that when twelve years of age she went to Norridgewock, Maine, where her married sister resided. At Dr. Brown's, in Skowhegan, she first read "Waverley." She was greatly excited, and exclaimed, as she laid down the book, "Why cannot I write a novel?" She remained in Norridgewock and vicinity for several years, and on her return to Massachusetts took up her abode with her brother at Watertown. He encouraged her literary tastes, and it was in his study that she commenced her first story,

INTRODUCTION.

"Hobomok," which she published in the twenty-first year of her age. The success it met with induced her to give to the public, soon after, "The Rebels: a Tale of the Revolution," which was at once received into popular favor, and ran rapidly through several editions. Then followed in close succession "The Mother's Book," running through eight American editions, twelve English, and one German, "The Girl's Book," the "History of Women," and the "Frugal Housewife," of which thirty-five editions were published. Her "Juvenile Miscellany" was commenced in 1826.

It is not too much to say that half a century ago she was the most popular literary woman in the United States. She had published historical novels of unquestioned power of description and characterization, and was widely and favorably known as the editor of the "Juvenile Miscellany," which was probably the first periodical in the English tongue devoted exclusively to children, and to which she was by far the largest contributor. Some of the tales and poems from her pen were extensively copied and greatly admired. It was at this period that the "North American Review," the highest literary authority of the country, said of her, "We are not sure that any woman of our country could outrank Mrs. Child. This lady has been long before the public as an author with much success. And she well deserves it, for in all her works nothing can be found which does not commend itself, by its tone of healthy morality and good sense. Few female writers, if any, have done more or better things for our literature in the lighter or graver departments."

Comparatively young, she had placed herself in

the front rank of American authorship. Her books and her magazine had a large circulation, and were affording her a comfortable income, at a time when the rewards of authorship were uncertain and at the best scanty.

In 1828 she married David Lee Child, Esq., a young and able lawyer, and took up her residence in Boston. In 1831–32 both became deeply interested in the subject of slavery, through the writings and personal influence of William Lloyd Garrison. Her husband, a member of the Massachusetts legislature and editor of the "Massachusetts Journal," had, at an earlier date, denounced the project of the dismemberment of Mexico for the purpose of strengthening and extending American slavery. He was one of the earliest members of the New England Anti-Slavery Society, and his outspoken hostility to the peculiar institution greatly and unfavorably affected his interests as a lawyer. In 1832 he addressed a series of able letters on slavery and the slave-trade to Edward S. Abdy, a prominent English philanthropist. In 1836 he published in Philadelphia ten strongly written articles on the same subject. He visited England and France in 1837, and while in Paris addressed an elaborate memoir to the Société pour l'Abolition d'Esclavage, and a paper on the same subject to the editor of the "Eclectic Review," in London. To his facts and arguments John Quincy Adams was much indebted in the speeches which he delivered in Congress on the Texas question.

In 1833 the American Anti-Slavery Society was formed by a convention in Philadelphia. Its numbers were small, and it was everywhere spoken against. It was at this time that Lydia Maria Child startled the country by the publication of her noble "Appeal in behalf of that Class of Americans called Africans." It is quite impossible for any one of the present generation to imagine the popular surprise and indignation which the book called forth, or how entirely its author cut herself off from the favor and sympathy of a large number of those who had previously delighted to do her honor. Social and literary circles, which had been proud of her presence, closed their doors against her. The sale of her books, the subscriptions to her magazine, fell off to a ruinous extent. She knew all she was hazarding, and made the great sacrifice, prepared for all the consequences which followed. In the preface to her book she says, "I am fully aware of the unpopularity of the task I have undertaken; but though I *expect* ridicule and censure, I do not *fear* them. A few years hence, the opinion of the world will be a matter in which I have not even the most transient interest; but this book will be abroad on its mission of humanity long after the hand that wrote it is mingling with the dust. Should it be the means of advancing, even one single hour, the inevitable progress of truth and justice, I would not exchange the consciousness for all Rothschild's wealth or Sir Walter's fame."

Thenceforth her life was a battle; a constant rowing hard against the stream of popular prejudice and hatred. And through it all — pecuniary privation, loss of friends and position, the painfulness of being suddenly thrust from "the still air of delightful studies" into the bitterest and sternest controversy of the age — she bore herself with patience, fortitude, and unshaken reliance upon the justice and ultimate triumph of the cause she had espoused. Her pen was never idle. Wherever there was a brave word to be spoken, her voice was heard, and never without effect. It is not exaggeration to say that no man or woman at that period rendered more substantial service to the cause of freedom, or made such a "great renunciation" in doing it.

A practical philanthropist, she had the courage of her convictions, and from the first was no mere closet moralist, or sentimental bewailer of the woes of humanity. She was the Samaritan stooping over the wounded Jew. She calmly and unflinchingly took her place by the side of the despised slave and free man of color, and in word and act protested against the cruel prejudice which shut out its victims from the rights and privileges of American citizens. Her philanthropy had no taint of fanaticism; throughout the long struggle, in which she was a prominent actor, she kept her fine sense of humor, good taste, and sensibility to the beautiful in art and nature.[1]

[1] The opposition she met with from those who had shared her confidence and friendship was of course keenly felt, but her kindly and genial disposition remained unsoured. She rarely spoke of her personal trials, and never posed as a martyr. The nearest approach to anything like complaint is in the following lines, the date of which I have not been able to ascertain: —

THE WORLD THAT I AM PASSING THROUGH.

Few in the days of early youth
Trusted like me in love and truth.
I've learned sad lessons from the years,
But slowly, and with many tears;
For God made me to kindly view
The world that I am passing through.

Though kindness and forbearance long
Must meet ingratitude and wrong,
I still would bless my fellow-men,
And trust them though deceived again.
God help me still to kindly view
The world that I am passing through.

While faithful to the great duty which she felt was laid upon her in an especial manner, she was by no means a reformer of one idea, but her interest was manifested in every question affecting the welfare of humanity. Peace, temperance, education, prison reform, and equality of civil rights, irrespective of sex, engaged her attention. Under all the disadvantages of her estrangement from popular favor, her charming Greek romance of " Philothea" and her Lives of Madame Roland and the Baroness de Staël proved that her literary ability had lost nothing of its strength, and that the hand which penned such terrible rebukes had still kept its delicate touch, and gracefully yielded to the inspiration of fancy and art. While engaged with her husband in the editorial supervision of the " Anti-Slavery Standard," she wrote her admirable "Letters from New York;" humorous, eloquent, and picturesque, but still humanitarian in tone, which extorted the praise of even a pro-slavery

> From all that fate has brought to me
> I strive to learn humility,
> And trust in Him who rules above,
> Whose universal law is love.
> Thus only can I kindly view
> The world that I am passing through.
>
> When I approach the setting sun,
> And feel my journey well-nigh done,
> May earth be veiled in genial light,
> And her last smile to me seem bright.
> Help me till then to kindly view
> The world that I am passing through.
>
> And all who tempt a trusting heart
> From faith and hope to drift apart,
> May they themselves be spared the pain
> Of losing power to trust again.
> God help us all to kindly view
> The world that we are passing through!

community. Her great work, in three octavo volumes, " The Progress of Religious Ideas," belongs, in part, to that period. It is an attempt to represent in a candid, unprejudiced manner the rise and progress of the great religions of the world, and their ethical relations to each other. She availed herself of, and carefully studied, the authorities at that time accessible, and the result is creditable to her scholarship, industry, and conscientiousness. If, in her desire to do justice to the religions of Buddha and Mohammed, in which she has been followed by Maurice, Max Müller, and Dean Stanley, she seems at times to dwell upon the best and overlook the darker features of those systems, her concluding reflections should vindicate her from the charge of undervaluing the Christian faith, or of lack of reverent appreciation of its founder. In the closing chapter of her work, in which the large charity and broad sympathies of her nature are manifest, she thus turns with words of love, warm from the heart, to Him whose Sermon on the Mount includes most that is good and true and vital in the religions and philosophies of the world: —

"It was reserved for Him to heal the brokenhearted, to preach a gospel to the poor, to say, 'Her sins, which are many, are forgiven, for she loved much.' Nearly two thousand years have passed away since these words of love and pity were uttered, yet when I read them my eyes fill with tears. I thank Thee, O Heavenly Father, for all the messengers thou hast sent to man; but, above all, I thank Thee for Him, thy beloved Son! Pure lily blossom of the centuries, taking root in the lowliest depths, and receiving the light and warmth of heaven in its golden heart! All that the pious have felt, all that poets have said, all that artists have done, with their manifold forms of beauty, to represent the ministry of Jesus, are but feeble expressions of the great debt we owe Him who is even now curing the lame, restoring sight to the blind, and raising the dead in that spiritual sense wherein all miracle is true."

During her stay in New York, as editor of the "Anti-Slavery Standard," she found a pleasant home at the residence of the genial philanthropist, Isaac T. Hopper, whose remarkable life she afterwards wrote. Her portrayal of this extraordinary man, so brave, so humorous, so tender and faithful to his convictions of duty, is one of the most readable pieces of biography in English literature. Thomas Wentworth Higginson, in a discriminating paper published in 1869, speaks of her eight years' sojourn in New York as the most interesting and satisfactory period of her whole life. "She was placed where her sympathetic nature found abundant outlet and occupation. Dwelling in a house where disinterestedness and noble labor were as daily breath, she had great opportunities. There was no mere alms-giving; but sin and sorrow must be brought home to the fireside and the heart; the fugitive slave, the drunkard, the outcast woman, must be the chosen guests of the abode,— must be taken, and held, and loved into reformation or hope."

It would be a very imperfect representation of Maria Child which regarded her only from a literary point of view. She was wise in counsel; and men like Charles Sumner, Henry Wilson, Salmon P. Chase, and Governor Andrew availed themselves of her foresight and sound judgment of men and measures. Her pen was busy with correspondence, and whenever a true man or a good cause needed encouragement, she was prompt to give it. Her donations for benevolent causes and beneficent reforms were constant and liberal; and only those who knew her intimately could understand the cheerful and unintermitted self-denial which alone enabled her to make them. She did her work as far as possible out of sight, without noise or pretension. Her time, talents, and money were held not as her own, but a trust from the Eternal Father for the benefit of His suffering children. Her plain, cheap dress was glorified by the generous motive for which she wore it. Whether in the crowded city among the sin-sick and starving, or among the poor and afflicted in the neighborhood of her country home, no story of suffering and need, capable of alleviation, ever reached her without immediate sympathy and corresponding action. Lowell, one of her warmest admirers, in his " Fable for Critics " has beautifully portrayed her abounding benevolence: —

"'There comes Philothea, her face all aglow,
She has just been dividing some poor creature's woe,
And can't tell which pleases her most, to relieve
His want, or his story to hear and believe;
No doubt against many deep griefs she prevails,
For her ear is the refuge of destitute tales;
She knows well that silence is sorrow's best food,
And that talking draws off from the heart its black blood."

"The pole, science tells us, the magnet controls,
But she is a magnet to emigrant Poles,
And folks with a mission that nobody knows,
Throng thickly about her as bees round a rose;
She can fill up the *carets* in such, make their scope
Converge to some focus of rational hope,
And, with sympathies fresh as the morning, their gall
Can transmute into honey, — but this is not all;
Not only for those she has solace; O, say,

Vice's desperate nursling adrift in Broadway,
Who clingest, with all that is left of thee human,
To the last slender spar from the wreck of the woman,
Hast thou not found one shore where those tired drooping feet
Could reach firm mother-earth, one full heart on whose beat
The soothed head in silence reposing could hear
The chimes of far childhood throb back on the ear?
Ah, there's many a beam from the fountain of day
That, to reach us unclouded, must pass, on its way,
Through the soul of a woman, and hers is wide ope
To the influence of Heaven as the blue eyes of Hope;
Yes, a great heart is hers, one that dares to go in
To the prison, the slave-hut, the alleys of sin,
And to bring into each, or to find there, some line
Of the never completely out-trampled divine;
If her heart at high floods swamps her brain now and then,
'T is but richer for that when the tide ebbs agen,
As, after old Nile has subsided, his plain
Overflows with a second broad deluge of grain;
What a wealth would it bring to the narrow and sour,
Could they be as a Child but for one little hour!"

After leaving New York her husband and herself took up their residence in the rural town of Wayland, Mass. Their house, plain and unpretentious, had a wide and pleasant outlook; a flower garden, carefully tended by her own hands, in front, and on the side a fruit orchard and vegetable garden, under the special care of her husband. The house was always neat, with some appearance of unostentatious decoration, evincing at once the artistic taste of the hostess and the conscientious economy which forbade its indulgence to any great extent. Her home was somewhat apart from the lines of rapid travel, and her hospitality was in a great measure confined to old and intimate friends, while her visits to the city were brief and infrequent. A friend of hers, who had ample opportunities for a full knowledge of her home-life, says, " The domestic happiness of Mr. and

Mrs. Child seemed to me perfect. Their sympathies, their admiration of all things good, and their hearty hatred of all things mean and evil were in entire unison. Mr. Child shared his wife's enthusiasms, and was very proud of her. Their affection, never paraded, was always manifest. After Mr. Child's death, Mrs. Child, in speaking of the future life, said, 'I believe it would be of small value to me if I were not united to him.'"

In this connection I cannot forbear to give an extract from some reminiscences of her husband, which she left among her papers, which, better than any words of mine, will convey an idea of their simple and beautiful home-life : —

"In 1852 we made a humble home in Wayland, Mass., where we spent twenty-two pleasant years entirely alone, without any domestic, mutually serving each other, and dependent upon each other for intellectual companionship. I always depended on his richly stored mind, which was able and ready to furnish needed information on any subject. He was my walking dictionary of many languages, my Universal Encyclopedia.

"In his old age he was as affectionate and devoted as when the lover of my youth ; nay, he manifested even more tenderness. He was often singing, —

"'There's nothing half so sweet in life
As Love's *old* dream.'

"Very often, when he passed by me, he would lay his hand softly on my head and murmur, 'Carum caput.' . . . But what I remember with the most tender gratitude is his uniform patience and forbearance with my faults. . . . He never would see anything but the bright side of my character. He always insisted upon thinking that whatever I said was the wisest and the wittiest, and that whatever I did was the best. The simplest little *jeu d'esprit* of mine seemed to

him wonderfully witty. Once, when he said, 'I wish for your sake, dear, I were as rich as Crœsus,' I answered, 'You *are* Crœsus, for you are king of Lydia.' How often he used to quote that!
"His mind was unclouded to the last. He had a passion for philology, and only eight hours before he passed away he was searching out the derivation of a word."

Her well-stored mind and fine conversational gifts made her company always desirable. No one who listened to her can forget the earnest eloquence with which she used to dwell upon the evidences from history, tradition, and experience, of the superhuman and supernatural; or with what eager interest she detected in the mysteries of the old religions of the world the germs of a purer faith and a holier hope. She loved to listen, as in St. Pierre's symposium of "The Coffee-House of Surat," to the confessions of faith of all sects and schools of philosophy, Christian and pagan, and gather from them the consoling truth that our Father has nowhere left his children without some witness of himself. She loved the old mystics, and lingered with curious interest and sympathy over the writings of Böhme, Swedenborg, Molinos, and Woolman. Yet this marked speculative tendency seemed not in the slightest degree to affect her practical activities. Her mysticism and realism ran in close parallel lines without interfering with each other. With strong rationalistic tendencies from education and conviction, she found herself in spiritual accord with the pious introversion of Thomas à Kempis and Madame Guion. She was fond of Christmas Eve stories, of warnings, signs, and spiritual intimations, her half belief in which sometimes seemed like credulity to her auditors. James Russell Lowell, in his tender tribute to her, playfully alludes to this characteristic: —

> "She has such a musical taste that she'll go
> Any distance to hear one who *draws a long bow*.
> She will swallow a wonder by mere might and main."

In 1859 the descent of John Brown upon Harper's Ferry, and his capture, trial, and death, startled the nation. When the news reached her that the misguided but noble old man lay desperately wounded in prison, alone and unfriended, she wrote him a letter, under cover of one to Governor Wise, asking permission to go and nurse and care for him. The expected arrival of Captain Brown's wife made her generous offer unnecessary. The prisoner wrote her, thanking her, and asking her to help his family, a request with which she faithfully complied. With his letter came one from Governor Wise, in courteous reproval of her sympathy for John Brown. To this she responded in an able and effective manner. Her reply found its way from Virginia to the New York "Tribune," and soon after Mrs. Mason, of King George's County, wife of Senator Mason, the author of the infamous Fugitive Slave Law, wrote her a vehement letter, commencing with threats of future damnation, and ending with assuring her that "no Southerner, after reading her letter to Governor Wise, ought to read a line of her composition, or touch a magazine which bore her name in its list of contributors." To this she wrote a calm, dignified reply, declining to dwell on the fierce invectives of her assailant, and wishing her well here and hereafter. She would not debate the specific merits or demerits of a man whose body was in charge of the courts, and whose reputation was sure to be in charge of poster ity. "Men," she continues, "are of small consequence in comparison with principles, and the principle for which John Brown died is the question at issue between us." These letters were soon published in pamphlet form, and had the immense circulation of 300,000 copies.

In 1867 she published "A Romance of the Republic," a story of the days of slavery; powerful in its delineation of some of the saddest as well as the most dramatic conditions of master and slave in the Southern States. Her husband, who had been long an invalid, died in 1874. After his death her home, in winter especially, became a lonely one; and in 1877 she began to spend the cold months in Boston.

Her last publication was in 1878, when her "Aspirations of the World," a book of selections, on moral and religious subjects, from the literature of all nations and times, was given to the public. The introduction, occupying fifty pages, shows, at threescore and ten, her mental vigor unabated, and is remarkable for its wise, philosophic tone and felicity of diction. It has the broad liberality of her more elaborate work on the same subject, and in the mellow light of life's sunset her words seem touched with a tender pathos and beauty. "All we poor mortals," she says, "are groping our way through paths that are dim with shadows; and we are all striving, with steps more or less stumbling, to follow some guiding star. As we travel on, beloved companions of our pilgrimage vanish from our sight, we know not whither; and our bereaved hearts utter cries of supplication for more light. We know not where Hermes Trismegistus lived, or who he was; but his voice sounds plaintively human, coming up from the depths of the ages, calling out, 'Thou art God! and thy man crieth these things unto Thee!' Thus closely allied in our sorrows and limitations, in our aspirations and hopes, surely we ought not to be separated in our sympathies. However various the names by which we call the Heavenly Father, if they are set to music by brotherly love, they can all be sung together."

Her interest in the welfare of the emancipated class at the South and of the ill-fated Indians of the West remained unabated, and she watched with great satisfaction the experiment of the education of both classes in General Armstrong's institution at Hampton, Va. She omitted no opportunity of aiding the greatest social reform of the age, which aims to make the civil and political rights of woman equal to those of men. Her sympathies, to the last, went out instinctively to the wronged and weak. She used to excuse her vehemence in this respect by laughingly quoting lines from a poem entitled "The Under Dog in the Fight":—

"I know that the world, the great big world,
Will never a moment stop
To see which dog may be in the wrong,
But will shout for the dog on top.

"But for me I never shall pause to ask
Which dog may be in the right;
For my heart will beat, while it beats at all,
For the under dog in the fight."

I am indebted to a gentleman who was at one time a resident of Wayland, and who enjoyed her confidence and warm friendship, for the following impressions of her life in that place:—

… "On one of the last beautiful Indian summer afternoons, closing the past year, I drove through Wayland, and was anew impressed with the charm of our friend's simple existence there. The tender beauty of the fading year seemed a reflection of her own gracious spirit; the lovely autumn of her life, whose golden atmosphere the frosts of sorrow and advancing age had only clarified and brightened.

"My earliest recollection of Mrs. Child in Wayland is of a gentle face leaning from the old stage window, smiling kindly down on the childish figures beneath her; and from that moment her gracious motherly presence has been closely associated with the charm of rural beauty in that village, which until very lately has been quite apart from the line of travel, and unspoiled by the rush and worry of our modern steam-car mode of living.

"Mrs. Child's life in the place made, indeed, an atmosphere of its own, a benison of peace and good-will, which was a noticeable feature to all who were acquainted with the social feeling of the little community, refined, as it was too, by the elevating influence of its distinguished pastor, Dr. Sears. Many are the acts of loving kindness and maternal care which could be chronicled of her residence there, were we permitted to do so; and numberless are the lives that have gathered their onward impulse from her helping hand. But it was all a confidence which she hardly betrayed to her inmost self, and I will not recall instances which might be her grandest eulogy. Her monument is builded in the hearts which knew her benefactions, and it will abide with 'the power that makes for righteousness.'

"One of the pleasantest elements of her life in Wayland was the high regard she won from the people of the village, who, proud of her literary attainment, valued yet more the noble womanhood of the friend who dwelt so modestly among them. The grandeur of her exalted personal character had, in part, eclipsed for them the qualities which made her fame with the world outside.

"The little house on the quiet by-road overlooked broad green meadows. The pond behind it, where bloom the lilies whose spotless purity may well symbolize her gentle spirit, is a sacred pool to her townsfolk. But perhaps the most fitting similitude of her life in Wayland was the quiet flow of the river, whose gentle curves make green her meadows, but whose powerful energy, joining the floods from distant mountains, moves, with resistless might, the busy shuttles of a hundred mills. She was too truthful to affect to welcome unwarrantable invaders of her peace, but no weary traveler on life's hard ways ever applied to her in vain. The little garden plot before her door was a sacred inclosure, not to be rudely intruded upon; but the flowers she tended with maternal care were no selfish possession, for her own enjoyment only, and many are the lives their sweetness has gladdened forever. So she lived among a singularly peaceful and intelligent community as one of themselves, industrious, wise, and happy; with a frugality whose motive of wider benevolence was in itself a homily and a benediction."

In my last interview with her, our conversation, as had often happened before, turned upon the great theme of the future life. She spoke, as I remember, calmly and not uncheerfully, but with the intense earnestness and reverent curiosity of one who felt already the shadow of the unseen world resting upon her.

Her death was sudden and quite unexpected. For some months she had been troubled with a rheumatic affection, but it was by no means regarded as serious. A friend, who visited her a few days before her departure, found her in a comfortable condition, apart from lameness. She talked of the coming election with much interest, and of her plans for the winter. On the morning of her death (October 20, 1880) she spoke of feeling remarkably well. Before leaving her chamber she complained of severe pain in the region of the heart. Help was called by her companion, but only reached her to witness her quiet passing away.

The funeral was, as befitted one like her, plain and simple. Many of her old friends were present, and Wendell Phillips paid an affecting and eloquent tribute to his old friend and anti-slavery coadjutor. He referred to the time when she accepted, with serene self-sacrifice, the obloquy which her "Appeal" had brought upon her, and noted, as one of the many ways in which popular hatred was manifested, the withdrawal from her of the privileges of the Boston Athenæum. Her pall-bearers were elderly, plain farmers in the neighborhood; and, led by the old white-haired undertaker, the procession wound its way to the not distant burial-ground, over the red and gold of fallen leaves, and under the half-clouded October sky. A lover of all beautiful things, she was, as her intimate friends knew, always delighted by the sight of rainbows, and used to so arrange prismatic glasses as to throw the colors on the walls of her room. Just after her body was consigned to the earth, a magnificent rainbow spanned, with its arc of glory, the eastern sky.[1]

[1] The incident at her burial is alluded to in a Sonnet written by William P. Andrews: —

> "Freedom! she knew thy summons, and obeyed
> That clarion voice as yet scarce heard of men;
> Gladly she joined thy red-cross service when
> Honor and wealth must at thy feet be laid:
> Onward with faith undaunted, undismayed
> By threat or scorn, she toiled with hand and brain
> To make thy cause triumphant, till the chain
> Lay broken, and for her the freedmen prayed.
> Nor yet she faltered; in her tender care

The letters in this collection constitute but a small part of her large correspondence. They have been gathered up and arranged by the hands of dear relatives and friends as a fitting memorial of one who wrote from the heart as well as the head, and who held her literary reputation subordinate always to her philanthropic aim to lessen the sum of human suffering, and to make the world better for her living. If they sometimes show the heat and impatience of a zealous reformer, they may well be pardoned in consideration of the circumstances under which they were written, and of the natural indignation of a generous nature in view of wrong and oppression. If she touched with no very reverent hand the garment hem of dogmas, and held to the spirit of Scripture rather than its letter, it must be remembered that she lived in a time when the Bible was cited in defense of slavery, as it is now in Utah in support of polygamy; and she may well be excused for some degree of impatience with those who, in the tithing of mint and anise and cummin, neglected the weightier matters of the law of justice and mercy.

Of the men and women directly associated with the beloved subject of this sketch, but few are now left to recall her single-hearted devotion to apprehended duty, her unselfish generosity, her love of all beauty and harmony, and her trustful reverence, free from pretence and cant. It is not unlikely that the surviving sharers of her love and friendship may feel the inadequateness of this brief memorial, for I close

> She took us all; and wheresoe'er she went,
> Blessings, and Faith and Beauty, followed there,
> E'en to the end, where she lay down content:
> And with the gold light of a life more fair,
> Twin bows of promise o'er her grave were blent."

it with the consciousness of having failed to fully delineate the picture which my memory holds of a wise and brave, but tender and loving woman, of whom it might well have been said, in the words of the old Hebrew text, "Many daughters have done virtuously, but thou excellest them all."

LETTERS.

TO REV. CONVERS FRANCIS.

NORRIDGEWOCK [Maine], June 5, 1817.

MY DEAR BROTHER,[1] — I have been busily engaged in reading " Paradise Lost." Homer hurried me along with rapid impetuosity; every passion that he portrayed I felt: I loved, hated, and resented, just as he inspired me! But when I read Milton, I felt elevated "above this visible diurnal sphere." I could not but admire such astonishing grandeur of description, such heavenly sublimity of style. I never read a poem that displayed a more prolific fancy, or a more vigorous genius. But don't you think that Milton asserts the superiority of his own sex in rather too lordly a manner? Thus, when Eve is conversing with Adam, she is made to say, —

> "My author and disposer, what thou bid'st
> Unargu'd I obey; so God ordained.
> God is thy law, thou mine: to know no more
> Is woman's happiest knowledge, and her praise."

Perhaps you will smile at the freedom with which I express my opinion concerning the books which I have been reading. I acknowledge it might have the appearance of pedantry, if I were writing to any one but a brother; when I write to you, I feel perfectly

---

[1] This letter, the earliest received by the compilers, was written when Miss Francis was fifteen years old.

unrestrained; for I feel satisfied that you will excuse a little freedom of expression from a sister, who willingly acknowledges the superiority of your talents and advantages, and who fully appreciates your condescension and kindness.

TO THE SAME.

NORRIDGEWOCK, September, 1817.

I perceive that I never shall convert you to my opinions concerning Milton's treatment to our sex.

Whether the ideas I have formed of that author be erroneous or not, they are entirely my own. I knew Johnson was a violent opponent to Milton, both in political and religious concerns; but I had never seen, or heard, of any of his remarks upon his poetical productions. Much as I admire Milton, I must confess that Homer is a much greater favorite with me. "Paradise Lost" is unquestionably the sublimest effort of human genius. It fixes us in a state of astonishment and wonder; but it is not characterized by that impetuosity and animation which, I think, gives to poetry its greatest charm.

TO THE SAME.

February 3, 1819.

I have been reading "Guy Mannering." I admire it for its originality. Dominie Sampson is certainly a character that never had a precedent. Meg Merrilies has something of that wild enthusiasm which characterizes the wife of MacGregor; and there is a nameless something in her character which corresponds with the awful grandeur of Highland scenery.

Don't you think that the spells of the gypsy and the astrology of Mannering might have considerable effect upon the superstitious mind by being left entirely unaccounted for? I should be almost tempted to leave sober history, and repair to these Scottish novels for instruction, as well as amusement, were not the historical views which they afford almost entirely confined to Scotland. The author seems to possess great versatility of talent. Almost all the sciences seem to have had a share of his attention ; and his observations on human nature seem to be peculiarly accurate. I think I shall go to Scotland (you see that my head is full of rocks and crags and dark blue lakes ; however, you know that I mean Portsmouth) very soon. I always preferred the impetuous grandeur of the cataract to the gentle meanderings of the rill, and spite of all that is said about gentleness, modesty, and timidity in the heroine of a novel or poem, give *me* the mixture of pathos and grandeur exhibited in the character of Meg Merrilies ; or the wild dignity of Diana Vernon, with all the freedom of a Highland maiden in her step and in her eye ; or the ethereal figure Annot Lyle, — " the lightest and most fairy figure that ever trod the turf by moonlight ; " or even the lofty contempt of life and danger which, though not unmixed with ferocity, throws such a peculiar interest around Helen MacGregor.

In *life* I am aware that gentleness and modesty form the distinguished ornaments of our sex. But in *description* they cannot captivate the imagination, nor rivet the attention.

Do you know you have a great many questions to answer me? Do not forget that I asked you about the " flaming cherubims," the effects of distance, horizontal or perpendicular, " Orlando Furioso," and Lord Byron.

TO THE SAME.

NORRIDGEWOCK, November 21, 1819.

I have long indulged the hope of reading Virgil in his own tongue. I have not yet relinquished it. I look forward to a certain time when I expect that hope, with many others, will be realized. . . . I usually spend an hour, after I retire for the night, in reading Gibbon's "Roman Empire." The pomp of his style at first displeased me; but I think him an admirable historian. There is a degree of dignified elegance about this work which I think well suited to the subject.

TO THE SAME.

NORRIDGEWOCK, December 26, 1819.

I am aware that I have been too indolent in examining the systems of great writers; that I have not enough cultivated habits of thought and reflection upon any subject. The consequence is, my imagination has ripened before my judgment; I have quickness of perception, without profoundness of thought; I can at one glance take in a subject as displayed by another, but I am incapable of investigation. What time I have found since I wrote you last has been pretty much employed in reading Gibbon. I have likewise been reading Shakespeare. I had before taken detached views of the works of this great master of human nature; but had never before *read* him. What a vigorous grasp of intellect; what a glow of imagination he must have possessed; but when his fancy droops a little, how apt he is to make low attempts at wit, and introduce a forced play upon words. Had he been an American, the reviewers, in spite of his genius, would have damned him for his contempt of the unities. It provokes me to see these critics with their pens "dipped in scorpion's gall," blighting the embryo buds of native genius. Neal must be condemned forsooth, without mercy, because his poem was one of genius' wildest, most erratic flights. Were every one as devout a worshipper at the shrine of genius as I am, they would admire him, even in his wanderings. I have been looking over the "Spectator." I do not think Addison so good a writer as Johnson, though a more polished one. The style of the latter is more vigorous, there is more nerve, if I may so express it, than in the former. Indeed, Johnson is my favorite among all his contemporaries. I know of no author in the English language that writes like him.

TO THE SAME.

WINSLOW [Maine], March 12, 1820.

I can't talk about books, nor anything else, until I tell you the good news; that I leave Norridgewock, and take a school in Gardiner, as soon as the travelling is tolerable. When I go to Gardiner, remember to write often, for "'t is woman alone who truly feels what it is to be a stranger." Did you know that last month I entered my nineteenth year?

I hope, my dear brother, that you feel as happy as I do. Not that I have formed any high-flown expectations. All I expect is, that, if I am industrious and prudent I shall be *independent*. I love to feel like Malcolm Græme when he says to Allan Bane,

"Tell Roderick Dhu I owe him naught."

Have you seen "Ivanhoe"? The "Shakespeare of novelists" has struck out a new path for his versatile and daring genius, I understand. Does he walk with such elastic and lofty tread as when upon his own mountain heath? Have his wings expanded since he left the hills of Cheviot? Or was the torch of fancy, lighted with the electric spark of genius, extinguished in the waters of the Tweed? I have never seen it. Indeed "I have na ony speerings" about the literary world, except through the medium of the newspapers. I am sorry to see the favored son of genius handled with such unmerciful, though perhaps deserved, severity in the review of "Don Juan." "Lalla Rookh" is the last I have seen from the pen of "Imagination's Charter'd Libertine." I hope we shall have another collection of gems as splendid, and more pure, than his former collections.

TO THE SAME.

WINSLOW, April 10, 1820.

I yesterday received your affectionate letter. You are too generous, my dear Convers. Ever since I entered my nineteenth year I have received nothing but presents and attention. I never was more happy in my life. I never possessed such unbounded elasticity of spirit. It seems as if my heart would vibrate to no touch but joy. Like old Edie Ochiltree "I wuss it may bode me gude." "An high heart goeth before destruction," but I never heard the same of a light one.

In one of your last letters you promise to send me "Don Juan." Do not send it, I beseech you. I can give you no idea of the anguish I felt when I read this shocking specimen of fearless and hardened depravity. I felt as if a friend had betrayed me. A sensation somewhat similar to what I should have felt, had you, my dear brother, committed an action unworthy of humanity. I have long cherished an enthusiastic admiration of this great man; I have long indulged the hope that when the blazing solstice of youth was over, autumnal reflection would shed a lovelier, though less brilliant, light upon his character; and that some tie might be found, sacred and tender enough to sooth the bitter misanthropy of his feelings. But with deep regret I relinquish the hope forever. Still I cannot but admire the bold efforts of his genius that flash through this work like the horrid glare of the lightning amid the terrors of a midnight storm. What a pity that one who might have shone, the most brilliant star in the flaming zodiac of genius, should only be held out as a blazing beacon to warn others from the road to wretchedness and guilt. It is intolerable to think that his Pegasus has still to gallop over twelve more cantos of such hellish ground.

TO THE SAME.

GARDINER [Maine], May 31, 1820.

You need not fear my becoming a Swedenborgian. I am in more danger of wrecking on the rocks of skepticism than of stranding on the shoals of fanaticism. I am apt to regard a system of religion as I do any other beautiful theory. It plays round the imagination, but fails to reach the heart. I wish I could find some religion in which my heart and understanding could unite; that amidst the darkest clouds of this life I might ever be cheered with the mild halo of religious consolation. With respect to Paley's system, I believe I said in my last that if I admitted your position, the next step was to acknowledge the spontaneous growth of goodness in the human heart. Is this what you did not understand? In your answer to my first letter on the subject, you say, "Is it always possible to foresee all the remote consequences of an action, so as to judge whether it is expedient or not? And even if it were, would not the time for action be past before we came to the decision?" In answer to that I made the above mentioned remark. If we oftentime commit good actions without time to reflect on their tendency, does it not argue a natural impulse to good which takes root in the heart before we have time to calculate its growth? And now tell me plainly what system would you build on the ruins of Paley's?

EXTRACTS FROM THE JOURNAL OF MISS FRANCIS, KEPT WHEN SHE FIRST MET MR. CHILD.

December 2, 1824. Mr. Child dined with us at Watertown. He possesses the rich fund of an intelligent traveller without the slightest tinge of a traveller's vanity. Spoke of the tardy improvement of the useful arts in Spain and Italy. They still use the plough described by Virgil. . . .

January 26, 1825. Saw Mr. Child at Mr. Curtis's. He is the most gallant man that has lived since the sixteenth century and needs nothing but helmet, shield, and chain armor to make him a complete knight of chivalry.

May 3, 1825. One among the many delightful evenings spent with Mr. Child. I do not know which to admire most, the vigor of his understanding or the ready sparkle of his wit. Talked of the political position of England. Laughed as he mentioned the tremendous squirearchy of America.

TO REV. DOCTOR ALLYN, DUXBURY, MASS.

WATERTOWN, September 28, 1826.

DEAR AND RESPECTED SIR, — Many times hath the spirit moved me to address thee by letter, but much fear of thy wisdom hath hitherto prevented. It is not that my reverence for thee hath at all decreased, that I now take up my pen to follow my own inclinations, but because thine absent daughter hath imposed it upon me as a duty. Thou knowest well that *Si Possum* is not always more heedful of the voice of conscience than of her own will, and therefore thou wilt conclude, and very justly withal, that personal affection and respect for thyself doth greatly move her thereunto.

A plague on Quaker style. It gives my pen the numb palsy to write in thees and thous. You have no doubt heard from Abba often, since she began her journey. I miss them sadly. I come home from school, tired to death with nouns and verbs, and I find the house empty, swept, and garnished, with not a single indication of animated existence except the cat, who sits in the window from morning till night, winking at the sun. That is to say, when the sun is to be winked at; for during the whole of this equinoctial week, the skies have looked like a tub of cold suds. The only variety is to go to church on Sunday, and hear the young Cambridgians talk of "the turpitude of vice, and the moral dignity of virtue."

Do I not remember your sayings well? By the way, have you determined yet whether there is the most of good or evil about me? . . .

What do you do with yourself in these days? Hold high converse with Plato, or feed your sheep with turnips? Snarl with Diogenes, or laugh at neighbor Paris and his Sampson's riddle? I wish I could pop down upon you, and enjoy one or two quiet days, but quiet does not seem to be in reserve for me. "How can you expect it," you will say, "when you are always engaged on some mad-cap enterprise or other? When Hobomoks, Rebels, Miscellanies, succeed each other, thick as hail?"

Do you remember, Doctor Allyn, that four years ago you promised me a long letter? An honest man will never refuse to pay an outlawed debt.

My Miscellany succeeds far beyond my most sanguine expectations. That is, people are generous beyond my hopes.

TO DAVID LEE CHILD.

PHILLIPS BEACH [Mass.], Sunday evening, August 8, 1830.

DEAREST HUSBAND,[1] — Here I am in a snug little old-fashioned parlor, at a round table, in a rocking-chair, writing to you, and the greatest comfort I have is the pen-knife you sharpened for me just before I came away. As you tell me sometimes, it makes my heart leap to see anything you have touched. The house here is real old-fashioned, neat, comfortable, rural, and quiet. There is a homespun striped carpet upon the floor, two profiles over the mantle-piece, one of them a soldier placed in a frame rather one-sided, with a white shirt ruffle, a white plume, and a white epaulette; a vase of flowers done in water colors, looking sickly and straggling about as if they were only neighbors-in-law, and Ophelia with a quantity of "carrotty" hair, which is thrown

Miss Francis was married to David Lee Child, of Boston, October 19, 1828.

over three or four rheumatic trees, and one foot ankle deep in water, as if she were going to see which she liked best, hanging or drowning.

These, with an old-fashioned table and desk, form a schedule of the furniture. The old lady is just like your good mother, just such honest shoulders, just such motions, a face very much like hers, and precisely the same kind motherly ways. I am sure you would be struck with the resemblance. I like the whole family extremely. They are among the best specimens of New England farmers, as simple and as kind as little children. The food is excellent. . . . In the stillness of the evening we can hear the sea dashing on the beach, "rolling its eternal bass" amid the harmony of nature. I went down to a little cove between two lines of rocks this morning, and having taken off my stockings, I let the saucy waves come dashing and sparkling into my lap. I was a little sad, because it made me think of the beautiful time we had, when we washed our feet together in the mountain waterfall. How I do wish you were here! It is nonsense for me to go a "pleasuring" without you. It does me no good, and every pleasant sight makes my heart yearn for you to be with me. I am very homesick for you; and my private opinion is, that I shall not be able to stand it a whole week. As for the place itself, it is exactly what I wanted to find. Oh, how I do wish we had a snug little cottage here, and just income enough to meet very moderate wants. I have walked about a mile to-day, and got well mudded by plunging into a meadow after that brightest of all bright blossoms, the cardinal flower. My dear husband, I *cannot* **stay** away a week.

TO MISS SARAH SHAW, UPON RECEIVING A DONATION TO
THE ANTI-SLAVERY CAUSE.

1833.

Your very unexpected donation was most gratefully received, though I was at first reluctant to take it, lest our amiable young friend had directly or indirectly begged the favor.

I am so great an advocate of individual freedom that I would have everything done voluntarily, nothing by persuasion. But Miss S—— assures me that you gave of your own accord, and this, though very unexpected, surprised me less than it would if I had not so frequently heard your brother speak of the kindness of your disposition.

We have good encouragement of success in the humble and unostentatious undertaking to which you have contributed. The zeal of a few seems likely to counterbalance the apathy of the many.

Posterity will marvel at the hardness of our prejudice on this subject, as we marvel at the learned and conscientious believers in the Salem witchcraft. So easy is it to see the errors of past ages, so difficult to acknowledge our own!

With the kindest wishes for your happiness and prosperity.

TO REV. CONVERS FRANCIS.

BOSTON, November 22, 1833.

That most agreeable of all agreeable men, Mr. Crawford of London, was here last night.

He tells harrowing stories of what he has seen at the South during his inspection of prisons there. Slaves kept in readiness to join their coffle were shut up in places too loathsome and horrid for the worst of criminals.

He says had any one told him such things as he has seen and heard, he should have considered it excessive exaggeration. Yet we talk of mild epithets, and tenderness toward our Southern brethren. Curse on the " smooth barbarity of courts." Of the various cants now in fashion, the cant of charity is to me the most disagreeable. Charity, which thinks to make wrong right by baptizing it with a sonorous name; that covers selfishness with the decent mantle of prudence; that glosses over iniquity with the shining varnish of virtuous professions; that makes a garland bridge over the bottomless pit, and calls the devil an " Archangel ruined."

If evil would manifest itself as it really is, how easy it would be to overcome it; but this it cannot do, simply because it *is* evil.

TO THE SAME.

Boston, July 27, 1834

I have at last obtained the " Christian Examiner," and read your article. As the old Quaker wrote me about the " Mother's Book," " I am free to say to thee, it is a most excellent thing." I think I never read a better article in my life; not even excepting the " Edinburgh." I was delighted with it.

You bow most reverently to Wordsworth, " that great poet," that confidant of angels," as Lavater says of Klopstock. Did not your conscience twinge you for throwing Peter Bell and the Idiot Boy in my teeth so often, and for laughing me to scorn when I said Milton's fame was the sure inheritance of Wordsworth?

I was glad for what you said concerning the state of the affections with regard to the perception of elevated truths.

I believe the more you look inward the more you will be convinced of the truth of what you advanced on that point, and that, too, not merely in a general point of view, but as applied to your own mind, and the different states of your own mind. When wishing to defend a truth merely from the love of intellectual power, or for the sake of appearing superior to some other person, I have felt my mind darkened, a thick fog arose, and scarcely one fine edge of light gave token of the glories I had hidden from myself: but while sitting in my own apartment, looking out upon the water or the heavens, or, in childish mood, watching the perpetual motion of the doves opposite my window, unconscious (as the "Edinburgh" says) of the existence of any of the little passions and impure motives which at once blind and harass the intellect, in such a state of feeling, the same truth, that I had before lost in darkness, is written on the mind with the power and certainty of a sunbeam; and to doubt it would appear to me as insane as to require proof that the moon is not an optical delusion.

I believe there can be no real religion where reason does not perform her high and very important office, but here again comes the important point, reason cannot do her perfect work unless the affections are pure. If we wish a thing to be true, or to make it appear true, for the sake of our party or our theory, or because it gives us an apparent superiority in morals, in intellect, — in a word, if self mingles with the motive, "the tree of knowledge is not the tree of life." We may imagine that it makes us as gods, knowing good from evil, "but the moment we eat thereof, we shall surely die."

I believe it is more safe and useful to dwell upon the necessity of keeping the heart pure, than of enlightening the understanding. An uneducated man can more safely trust to his conscience than to his understanding.

TO MRS. ELLIS GRAY LORING.

NEW YORK, August 15, 1835.

I am at Brooklyn, at the house of a very hospitable Englishman, a friend of Mr. Thompson's. I have not ventured into the city, nor does one of us dare to go to church to-day, so great is the excitement here. You can form no conception of it. 'Tis like the times of the French Revolution, when no man dared trust his neighbors. Private assassins from New Orleans are lurking at the corners of the streets, to stab Arthur Tappan; and very large sums are offered for any one who will convey Mr. Thompson into the Slave States. I tremble for him, and love him in proportion to my fears. He is almost a close prisoner in his chamber, his friends deeming him in imminent peril the moment it is ascertained where he is. We have managed with some adroitness to get along in safety so far; but I have faith that God will protect him, even to the end. Yet why do I make this boast? My faith has at times been so weak that I have started and trembled and wept, like a very child; and personal respect and affection for him have so far gained the mastery over my trust in Providence, that I have exclaimed in anguish of heart, "Would to God, I could die for thee!" Your husband could hardly be made to realize the terrible state of fermentation now existing here. There are 7,000 Southerners now in the city; and I am afraid there are not 700 among them who have the slightest fear of God before their eyes. Mr. Wright was yesterday barricading his doors and windows with strong bars and planks an inch thick. Violence, in some form, seems to be generally expected. Alas poor fools! They are building up the very cause they seek to destroy.

TO REV. CONVERS FRANCIS.

NEW ROCHELLE [N. Y.], September 25, 1835.

We are boarding in the family of an honest Hicksite Quaker, in this quiet secluded village, which we chose both for economy and safe distance from cities. There is nothing in the neighborhood worthy of a traveller's attention except the grave of Tom Paine, in the corner of a field, near the road-side. It is surrounded by a rough stone wall, two or three feet high. In one place the stones are broken down and lying loose, where Cobbett entered to carry off his bones. He was buried in this lonely manner, because all the churches, and even the Quakers, refused him admittance into their burying-grounds. And we who boast of living in a more liberal age, are carrying on the same petty persecution under different forms!

I agree with you most cordially that man, without a "principle of reverence for something higher than his own will, is a poor and wretched being;" but I would have that reverence placed on principles, not on persons; and this in a true republic would, I believe, be the case. I believe our difficulties grow out of the fact that we have in reality very little republicanism. A principle of despotism was admitted in the very formation of our government, to sanction which our consciences have been continually silenced and seared. In our social institutions, aristocracy has largely mingled. The opinion of a great man stands in the place of truth; and thus the power of perceiving truth is lost. We should be little troubled with mobs if people called respectable did not give them their sanction. But you will say a true republic never can exist. In this, I have more faith than you. I believe the world will be brought into a state of order through manifold revolutions. Sometimes we may be tempted to think it would have been better for us not to have been cast on these evil times; but this is a selfish consideration; we ought rather to rejoice that we have much to do as mediums in the regeneration of the world. . . .

You ask me to be prudent, and I will be so, as far as is consistent with a sense of duty; but this will not be what the world calls prudent. Firmness is the virtue most needed in times of excitement. What consequence is it if a few individuals do sink to untimely and dishonored graves, if the progress of great principles is still onward? Perchance for this cause came we into the world.

I have examined the history of the slave too thoroughly, and felt his wrongs too deeply, to be prudent in the worldly sense of the term. I know too well the cruel and wicked mockery contained in all the excuses and palliations of the system.

TO THE SAME.

NEW ROCHELLE, December 19, 1835.

In your last letter you charge democracy with being the mother of evil. I do not wonder at it; for these are times when its best friends have need of faith. But I believe the difficulty ever is in a lack of republicanism. The aristocratic principle, unable to act openly, disguises itself, and sends its poison from under a mask. What is the root of the difficulty on this great question of abolition? It is not with the farmers, it is not with the mechanics. The majority of their voices would be on the right side if the question were fairly brought before them; and the consciousness that such would be the result creates the earnest desire to stop discussion. No, no! It is not these who are to blame for the persecution suffered by abolitionists. Manufacturers who supply the South, merchants who trade with the South, politicians who trade with the South, ministers settled at the South, and editors patronized by the South, are the ones who really promote mobs. Withdraw the aristocratic influence, and I should be perfectly easy to trust the cause to the good feeling of the people. But, you will say, democracies must always be thus acted upon; and here, I grant, is the great stumbling-block. The impediments continually in the way of bringing good principles into their appropriate forms are almost disheartening; and would be quite so, were it not for the belief in One who is brooding over this moral chaos with vivifying and regenerating power. What can be more beautiful than the spirit of love in the Christian religion? Yet where shall we find Moslem or pagan more fierce and unrelenting than Christians toward each other.

TO E. CARPENTER.

WEST BOYLSTON [Mass.], May 9, 1836.

Abolitionism is rapidly growing respectable here, because the abolitionists are becoming more and more numerous. Since truth is thus made to depend on the voice of the majority, what a comfort it is to reflect that all majorities were minorities in the beginning.

I cannot forbear to repeat to you an interview between Miss Martineau and Mrs. ——, formerly a fashionable friend of mine, deeply skilled in the small diplomacy of worldly wisdom. Mrs. —— said some things in disparagement of Maria Chapman, accompanied with the wise remark that women were not capable of understanding political questions. My friend Mrs. ——, wishing Miss M. to take up the cudgel in defence of the rights of women, put her mouth to her ear-trumpet, and said, " Ask Mrs. —— to repeat her remark to you ! " The lady somewhat reluctantly observed, " I was saying, Miss M., that women ought to attend to their little duties, and let public affairs alone." " Believe me, Madam," replied Miss M., " that those who perform their great duties best are most likely to perform their little duties best." " Oh, certainly, of course, " said Mrs. ——, " but Mrs. C. is so enthusiastic. She told me she felt she had a mission to perform on earth. Now, if I felt so, I should think I ought to be sent to Bedlam." " Madam," replied Miss M., " it appears to me that those of us who think we have no mission to perform on earth ought to be sent to Bedlam."

TO THE SAME.

South Natick, September 4, 1836.

I have lately had a most interesting case brought under my observation. When in Boston I was entreated to exert myself concerning a little child, supposed to be a slave, brought from New Orleans, and kept shut up at No. 21 Pinckney Street. The object was to persuade the child's mistress to leave her at the colored asylum, and failing to effect this object, to ascertain beyond doubt whether the child was a slave, whether there was intention to carry her back to New Orleans, and to obtain sight of her in order to be able to prove her identity. . . . . I will not fill this sheet with particulars. Suffice it to say, the way was opened for us. We obtained all the evidence we wanted, carried it to a lawyer, who petitioned for a writ of habeas corpus; the judge granted the petition; and the man who held little Med in custody was brought up for trial. In consequence of the amount of evidence ready to be proved by three witnesses, the pro-slavery lawyers, did not pretend to deny that the intent was to carry the child back into slavery; but they took the new and extraordinary ground that Southern masters had a legal right to hold human beings as slaves while they were visiting here in New England. Judge Wild expressed a wish to consult with the other judges; and our abolition friends, finding the case turn on such a very important point, resolved to retain the services of Webster, for want of a better man. He was willing to serve provided they would wait a few days. Rufus Choate, a man only second to him in abilities, and whose heart is strongly favorable to anti-slavery, was em ployed.[1] The opposite counsel were full of sophistry and eloquence. One of them really wiped his own eyes at the thought that the poor little slave might be separated from its slave mother by mistaken benevolence. His pathos was a little marred by my friend E. G. Loring, who arose and stated that it was distinctly understood that little Med was to be sold on her way back to New Orleans, to pay the expenses of her mistress's journey to the North. The judges decided unanimously in favor of Med and liberty!

The "Commercial Gazette" of the next day says: "This decision, though unquestionably according to law, is much to be regretted; for such cases cannot but injure the custom of our hotels, now so liberally patronized by gentlemen from the South." Verily, Sir Editor, thou art an honest devil; and I thank thee for not being at the pains to conceal thy cloven foot.

TO REV. CONVERS FRANCIS.

BOSTON, October 25, 1836.

I am very glad that you liked "Philothea," and that the dedication pleased you. Among my personal friends the book has proved far more of a favorite than I had supposed it would. I have heard the echo of newspaper praise, but have not in fact seen a single notice of "Philothea." For my own sake, I care far less about literary success than I could easily make people believe; but I am glad if this work adds to my reputation, because it will help to increase my influence in the anti-slavery cause. It will be another mite added to the widow's fund for the treasury

---

[1] The expectations thus excited that Mr. Choate would become an opponent of slavery were doomed to disappointment; during the latter years of his life he was utterly hostile to the anti-slavery movement

of the Lord. Every day that I live, I feel more and more thankful for my deep interest in a cause which carries me out of myself.

TO E. CARPENTER.

NORTHAMPTON [Mass.], September 6, 1838.

When I remember what a remarkable testimony the early Friends bore (a testimony which seems to me more and more miraculous, the more I compare it with the spirit of the age in which they lived), I could almost find it in my heart to weep at the too palpable proofs that little now remains of that which was full of life.[1] I was saying this, last winter, to George Ripley, a Unitarian minister of Boston. He replied beautifully, "Mourn not over their lifelessness. Truly the dead form alone remains; but the *spirit* that emanated from it is not dead, the *word* which they spake has gone out silently into everlasting time. What are these Temperance, and Peace, and Anti-Slavery Conventions, but a resuscitation of their principles? To me it is a beautiful illustration of the doctrine of the resurrection, when I thus see the spirit leaving the dead form and embodying itself anew."

I feel for your trials, for I know by similar experience that at times they *will* press heavily on the overtaxed and discouraged soul. But we know what awaits those " who endure unto the end." I cannot say I pity you; for is it not a glorious privilege thus to struggle with the errors and sins of the time? Be not discouraged because the sphere of action seems

[1] This letter refers to the opposition to active anti-slavery effort manifested by the New York yearly meeting of Friends of what is called the Hicksite division. On the Orthodox side there was the same disposition to discountenance decided abolition labors, although both societies professed to maintain a testimony against slavery.

narrow, and the influence limited; for every word and act that a human being sends forth lives forever. It is a spiritual seed cast into the wide field of opinion. Its results are too infinite for human calculation. It will appear and reappear through all time, always influencing the destiny of the human race for good or for evil. Has not the one idea that rose silently in Elizabeth Heyrick's [1] mind spread, until it has almost become a World's idea? Have not the "stern old Calvinists of Charles's time," despised as they were, given their character to nations? Who can predict the whole effect on habit and opinion in New Rochelle, fifty years hence, of the spiritual warfare now going on in half of a small meeting-house, in that secluded village? To a philosophical mind, nothing that concerns the soul of man can be small or limited. However humble its form, it is linked with infinity. Tell your good father my "prayers" he shall have; but not my "tears." Could *he* have wept for Luther when he stood before principalities and powers, at the Diet of Worms, and calmly declared, "It is neither safe nor prudent to do aught against conscience. Here stand I. I cannot otherwise, God assist me. Amen." It is odd enough that while the plain Quakers of New Rochelle are making such a fuss about colored people sitting on the same floor with them, the King of France makes no objection to having sons in the same school with black boys.

---

[1] To Elizabeth Heyrick, of England, a member of the Society of Friends, belongs the honor of having been the first to promulgate, in a pamphlet published by her in 1825, the doctrine of "Immediate, not Gradual Emancipation." The abolitionists of Great Britain, then struggling for the overthrow of slavery in the West Indies, speedily adopted it as their key-note and cry, and Mr. Garrison, in establishing the *Liberator*, declared it to be the only impregnable position to assume in agitating for the abolition of slavery everywhere.

TO MISS HENRIETTA SARGENT.

SOUTH NATICK, November 13, 1836.

I suppose you heard of me on my way to Doctor Channing's? I found the reverend Doctor walking down Mount Vernon Street, but he insisted so strongly upon going back, that I at last consented. He was very kind and complimentary, in manners and conversation. He soon began to talk of anti-slavery. I could see that he had progressed (as we Yankees say) considerably since I last conversed with him; but he still betrayed his characteristic timidity. Almost every sentence began with, "I am doubtful," or "I am afraid." He was "doubtful" of the policy of sending out seventy agents. He was "afraid" there would be among them some indifferent men. I told him that they gave pretty good evidence they were not indifferent to the cause. He did not mean that, he meant there would be some among them of indifferent intellectual and moral gifts. I urged that their willingness to go was strong presumptive evidence in favor of their moral character; and expressed a reasonable doubt whether the seventy sent out by the apostles were all equally gifted. He replied, "But they went out on a very simple errand." I rejoined, "And the abolitionists go out on a very simple errand. Their principles are a resuscitation of doctrines preached by the apostolic seventy." He admitted that the foundation principles of Christianity and abolition were identical; but still this subject was so intertwisted with politics, prejudice, and interest, and the manner of illustrating it might be so injudicious, that he thought it every way desirable to have agents peculiarly qualified. I answered that we had good reason to suppose the early opposition to Christianity was interwoven with the prejudices and interests of nations. If it were not so, why had the apostles been persecuted even unto death? We, like the apostles, could only choose the willing-hearted, and trust that God would bless their mission. Even if it were desirable to select the "wise and prudent" of this world, there was abundant reason to suppose that now, as then, they would not be in readiness to perform the Lord's mission.

I do not know how much longer we might have "argufied" about the seventy, if we had not been interrupted by Mrs. M., who was soon followed by several other ladies. From courtesy I forebore to renew a subject which might be embarrassing to mine host, in the presence of visitors who doubtless would not so much as touch it with a pair of tongs; but I was much pleased to have the Doctor interrupt some general remarks which I made on literature, with this question: "But, Mrs. Child, I want you to tell me something more about the progress of anti-slavery." I related several anecdotes illustrative of the progressive movement of the public mind, assuring him that all ranks and classes had been moved, in spite of themselves, nay even while many cursed the stream which propelled them. I did not forget to relate how many Southerners in New York, during the past summer, had been into the anti-slavery office to inquire for the best book on emancipation. He seemed much affected by the story of the anonymous fifty dollars sent to the Society, as "the master's mite toward the relief of those in bondage."

TO E. CARPENTER.

March 20, 1838.

I thought of you several times while Angelina was addressing the committee of the Legislature.[1] I knew you would have enjoyed it so much. I think it was a spectacle of the greatest moral sublimity I ever witnessed. The house was full to overflowing. For a moment a sense of the immense responsibility resting on her seemed almost to overwhelm her. She trembled and grew pale. But this passed quickly, and she went on to speak gloriously, strong in utter forgetfulness of herself, and in her own earnest faith in every word she uttered. " Whatsoever comes from the heart goes to the heart." I believe she made a very powerful impression on the audience. Boston, like other cities, is very far behind the country towns on this subject; so much so that it is getting to be Boston *versus* Massachusetts, as the lawyers say. The Boston members of the legislature tried hard to prevent her having a hearing on the second day. Among other things, they said that such a crowd were attracted by curiosity the galleries were in danger of being broken down; though in fact they are constructed with remarkable strength. A member from Salem, perceiving their

[1] Angelina Grimké, a native of South Carolina, and a member of the Society of Friends, addressed a committee of the Massachusetts Legislature on the subject of slavery in the House of Representatives, February 21, 1838, and on two subsequent days. She and her sister Sarah left their home and came to the North to reside because of their abhorrence of slavery, and they were the first women to speak in public against the system. Their testimonies, given from personal knowledge and experience, produced a profound impression, and large audiences gathered to listen to them wherever they went.

drift, wittily proposed that a " committee be appointed to examine the foundations of the State House of Massachusetts, to see whether it will bear another lecture from Miss Grimké."

One sign that her influence is felt is that the "sound part of the community" (as they consider themselves) seek to give vent to their vexation by calling her Devil-ina instead of Angel-ina, and Miss Grimalkin instead of Miss Grimké. Another sign is that we have succeeded in obtaining the Odeon, one of the largest and most central halls, for her to speak in; and it is the first time such a place has been obtained for anti-slavery in this city.

Angelina and Sarah have been spending the winter at the house of Mr. P——, about five miles from here. The family were formerly of the Society of Friends — are now, I believe, a little Swedenborgian, but more Quaker, and swinging loose from any regular society; just as I and so many hundred others are doing at the present day. I should like earnestly and truly to believe with some large sect, because religious sympathy is so delightful; but I now think that if I were to live my life over again I should not outwardly join any society, there is such a tendency to spiritual domination, such an interfering with individual freedom.

Have you read a little pamphlet called "George Fox and his First Disciples"? I was charmed with it. Don't you remember I told you I was sure that the *thou* and *thee* of Friends originated in a principle of Christian equality? This pamphlet confirms my conjecture. In the English language of George Fox's time, and in most European languages now, *thou* was used only to familiars and equals.

Kings say *we*, and nobles are addressed as *you*. The Germans carry this worshipful plurality to an absurd extent. The prince being missed by his companions on a hunting excursion, one of the noblemen asked a peasant, " Hast thou seen the prince pass this way?" "No, my lord," replied the peasant, "but their dog have passed." It was this distinction of language addressed to superiors, and to inferiors or equals, that the early Friends resisted. The custom had life in it then, for it was merely the outward expression or form of a vital principle. What is it now? An inherited formality, of which few stop to inquire the meaning. Thus have all human forms the seed of death within them; but luckily when the body becomes dead, the inward soul or principle seeks a new form and lives again. The Friends as a society may become extinct; but not in vain did they cast forth their great principles into everlasting time. No truth they uttered shall ever die; neither shall any truth that you or I may speak, or express in our lives. Two centuries after William Penn brought indignation upon himself by saying ; "thou" to the Duke of York, the French revolutionists, in order to show that they were friends of equality, wrote in their windows, " In this house we 'thou' it." And this idea, dug up by the Friends from the ashes of early Christianity, has in fact given rise to the doctrine of "spiritual brotherhood," echoed and reëchoed from Priestley to Channing.

TO MRS. ELLIS GRAY LORING.

NORTHAMPTON [Mass.], June 9, 1838.

A month elapsed after I came here before I stepped into the woods which were all around me blooming with wild flowers. I did not go to Mr. Dwight's ordination, nor have I yet been to meeting. He has been to see me, however, and though I left my work in the midst, and sat down with a dirty gown and hands somewhat grimmed, we were high up in the blue in fifteen minutes. I promised to take a flight with him from the wash-tub or dish-kettle any time when he would come along with his balloon. . . .

C. is coming down next week, and I think I shall send a line to some of you by her. Her religious furor is great, just at this time, but of her theological knowledge you can judge when I tell you that when I spoke of old John Calvin, she asked me if he was the same as John the Baptist. . . .

I don't suppose any present was quite so satisfactory as the pretty green watering pot. Father said I was out with it in the rain as well as the sunshine.

TO REV. CONVERS FRANCIS.

NORTHAMPTON, July 12, 1838.

Your kind letter in reply to mine was most welcome. The humility with which you say that you "may have been permitted now and then to suggest things not useless to my genius," sounds oddly enough. Such expressions from a mind so immeasurably superior to mine, in its attainments, would seem to be feigned and excessive, did I not know that you speak sincerely. If I possessed your knowledge, it seems to me as if I could move the whole world. I am often amused and surprised to think how many things I have attempted to do with my scanty stock of learning. I know not how it is, but my natural temperament is such that when I wish to do anything I seem to have an instinctive faith that I can do it;

whether it be cutting and making a garment, or writing a Greek novel. The sort of unconsciousness of danger arising from this is in itself strength. Whence came it? I did not acquire it. But the "whence? how? whither?" of our inward life must always be answered, "From a mystery; in a mystery; to a mystery." I fully admit your modest suggestion that you have " now and then suggested things useful to me;" but I owe more than this occasional assistance (I am laughing in my sleeve at your humility, and therefore emphasize) to " the fortunate circumstance of your having come into the world before me." To your early influence, by conversation, letters, and example, I owe it that my busy energies took a literary direction at all.

TO FRANCIS G. SHAW.

NORTHAMPTON, August 17, 1838.

With regard to intercourse with slave-holders, far from shunning it myself, I seek it diligently. Many and many an hour's argument, maintained with candor and courtesy, have I had with them; and they have generally appeared to like me, though my principles naturally seemed to them stern and uncompromising. I am not so intolerant as to suppose that slave-holders have not many virtues, and many very estimable qualities; but at the same time, let me caution you against believing all their fair professions on the subject of slavery. Men who are true and honorable on all other subjects will twist, and turn, and deceive, and say what they must absolutely know to be false on this subject.

I account for the inconsistency and tergiversation of such men partly upon the supposition that conscience perpetually whispers to them that the system is wrong, but is not sufficiently revered to overcome the temptation of apparent interest. Still more do I attribute it to the fact that, by education and habit, they have so long thought and spoken of the colored man as a mere article of property, that it is almost impossible for them to recognize him as a man, and reason concerning him as a brother, on equal terms with the rest of the human family. If, by great effort, you make them acknowledge the brotherhood of the human race, as a sacred and eternal principle, in ten minutes their arguments, assertions, and proposed schemes all show that they have returned to the old habit of regarding the slave as a "chattel personal."

TO MISS HENRIETTA SARGENT.

NORTHAMPTON, 1838.

Why do you not write? Are you ill? "Are you sorry with me," as the little French girl used to say; or what is the matter? I really hunger and thirst to hear from you. . . .

My husband and I are busy in that most odious of all tasks, that of getting signatures to petitions. We are resolved that the business shall be done in this town more thoroughly than it has been heretofore. But, "Oh Lord, sir!"

I have never been so discouraged about abolition as since we came into this iron-bound Valley of the Connecticut. I have ceased to believe that public opinion will ever be sincerely reformed on the question till long after emancipation has taken place. I mean that for generations to come there will be a very large minority hostile to the claims of colored people; and the majority will be largely composed of individuals who are found on that side from any and every motive rather than hearty sympathy with the down-trodden race. Public events, probably of the most unexpected character, will help along the desired result. The injudicious course of the South has identified the claims of emancipation and free discussion, and thus thousands have already been roused who care little or nothing for the poor slave. The stupidity and recklessness of Stevenson, in his mad encounter with O'Connell, have fairly laid before the gaze of Europe that most disgusting feature of slavery which abolitionists have been obliged to leave partially veiled, for decency's sake. What God is preparing for us along the Indian frontier, in Mexico, Cuba, and Hayti, I know not; but I think I see "coming events cast their shadows before." We certainly have done all we could to secure the deadly hostility of the red man and the black man everywhere. I think God will overrule events to bring about a change, long before the moral sense of this nation demands it as a matter of justice and humanity. What would have become of the Protestant reformation in England (at least for several generations) if the Pope had acknowledged the legitimacy of Queen Elizabeth. She was as ready to be a Catholic as a Protestant, and a very large proportion of the people were favorable to their ancient form of worship, though they did not care enough about it to sacrifice important interests. God so ordered it that the Pope, desirous of supporting Mary Stuart's claim, and little foreseeing the result of his proceedings, denied the legitimacy of Elizabeth. She was obliged to throw herself on the Protestants, and, of course, carried with her the ambitious, the timid, and the time-serving.

TO REV. CONVERS FRANCIS.

NORTHAMPTON, December 22, 1838.

If I were to choose my home, I certainly would not place it in the Valley of the Connecticut. It is true, the river is broad and clear, the hills majestic, and the whole aspect of outward nature most lovely. But oh! the narrowness, the bigotry of man! To think of hearing a whole family vie with each other, in telling of vessels that were wrecked, or shattered, or delayed on their passage, because they sailed on Sunday! To think of people's troubling their heads with the question whether the thief could have been instantaneously converted on the cross, so that the Saviour could promise him an entrance to Paradise! In an age of such stirring inquiry, and of such extended benevolence — in a world which requires all the efforts of the good and wise merely to make it receptive of holy influences, what a pity it is that so much intellect should be wasted upon such theological jargon! No wonder that the intelligent infidel, looking at mere doctrines and forms, should be led to conclude that religion had done more harm in the world than good. The really inward-looking find in these no language by which they can give even a stammering utterance to their thoughts and feelings; yet the incubus of forms, from which the life has departed, oppresses them, though they dare not throw them off. Something is coming toward us (I know not what), with a glory round its head, and its long, luminous rays are even now glancing on the desert and the rock. The Unitarian, busily at work pulling down old structures, suddenly sees it gild some ancient pillar, or shed its soft light on some moss-grown altar; and he stops with a troubled doubt whether *all* is to be destroyed; and if destroyed, wherewith shall he build anew? He looks upward for the coming dawn, and calls it transcendentalism. The Calvinist at work with strong arm and sincere heart at his fiery forge, fashioning the melted metal in time-honored moulds, sees a light, before which his fires grow dim, and the moulded forms seem rigid and uncouth. Perplexed, he asks if the martyred fathers *did* die for a faith that must be thrown aside like a useless stove of last year's patent. His grim iron forms return no answer, for there is not in them that which *can* answer the earnest questionings of the human soul. He too looks upward, sees the light, and calls it Perfectionism.

Having accidentally fallen into this vein of thought brings Emerson to my remembrance. How absurdly the Unitarians are behaving, after all their talk about liberality, the sacredness of individual freedom, free utterance of thought, etc. If Emerson's thoughts are not their thoughts, can they not reverence them, inasmuch as they are formed and spoken in freedom? I believe the whole difficulty is, they are looking outwardly to what the logical opponents will say, not inwardly with calm investigation. I am not at all disturbed by what any man believes, or what he disbelieves; and as for the Unitarian views, they arise from doubts too familiar to my own mind to be intolerant at this period of my life. But I do like to have men utter their thoughts honestly, and not be afraid that it will not do to break down old forms. Of the many who make an outcry about Emerson's scruples concerning the sacrament, what proportion do you suppose really regard that institution as saered? "What can be more unprofitable than to see men struggling with their whole force and industry to stretch out the old formula and phraseology, so that it may cover the new, contradictory, entirely uncoverable thing? Whereby the poor formula does but crack, and one's honesty along with it. This stretching out of formulas till they crack is, especially in time of swift changes, one of the sorrowfullest tasks poor humanity has."

I by no means charge the Unitarians with being the only ones that strive to stretch out old formulas; but it is more observable in them, because so inconsistent with their own free theories.

TO FRANCIS G. SHAW.

NORTHAMPTON, 1840.

I too should like to see "the poetry of motion" in Fanny Elssler. But the only thing (except seeing dear friends) that has attracted me to Boston, was the exhibition of statuary. In particular I have an earnest desire to see the "Infant guided to Heaven by Angels." I am ashamed to say how deeply I am charmed with sculpture; ashamed, because it seems like affectation in one who has had such very limited opportunity to become acquainted with the arts. I have a little plaster figure of a caryatid, which acts upon my spirit like a magician's spell. Sarah (she reproves me when I call her Mrs. S.) did not seem to think much of it; but to me it has an expression of the highest kind. Repose after conflict — not the repose of innocence, but the repose of wisdom. Many a time this hard summer I have laid down dish-cloth or broom and gone to refresh my spirit by gazing on it a few minutes. It speaks to me. It says glorious things. In summer I place flowers before it; and now I have laid a garland of acorns and amaranths at its feet. I do dearly love every little bit of real sculpture.

TO A CHILD.

NORTHAMPTON, August 16, 1840.

DEAREST NONY, — Now I will write to you. I have no kitten to purr aloud; and my great black cat is not sufficiently well-behaved to deserve a written description. But my swallows still keep about the house. Almost every evening one or two of them come in at dark in search of flies; and they go circling round my head, so that I sometimes feel their wings fan my face. Once in a great while they come in now to look at the old nest, and squat down in it for a minute or two; just as children love to go back to the old homestead, to see the place where they were born. But the pleasantest sight of all was when the little ones were learning to fly. *Such* a twittering and bustling! And when the baby birds, in spite of the mother's unwearied efforts, still continued too timid to drop down from the edge of the nest, she brought in eight or ten of her neighbor swallows to instruct and encourage them. She did this three times in succession. The wood-shed seemed full of birds, for a few minutes at a time, flying and perching, and clinging to the beams, in all manner of pretty attitudes. I don't know but you grow tired hearing about my birds; but it seems as if I could watch them forever. Every day I fear it is the last time I shall see them; for they will soon go away to the South, to find a warmer home for winter.

TO FRANCIS G. SHAW.

NORTHAMPTON, 1840.

I did hope mightily to see you, and I wanted to have you hear John Dwight preach. John's is a mild, transparent, amber light, found

> "In einem andern Sonnen lichte,
> In einer glucklichen Natur."

Shame on me for quoting German so pompously, when these are almost the only lines I know.

You have seen the illustrations of John Bunyan, the literary part prepared by Bernard Barton? Oh, it is a lovely book! The memory of it haunts me like a sweet dream. You looked at it in church one day; and I pointed to you the picture of the river of life, where the light was so supernaturally transparent, and soft, and warm; like the sun shining through crystal walls upon golden floors. Well, that picture is like some of John Dwight's sermons. Blessings on him! He has ministered to my soul in seasons of great need. I think that was all he was sent here for, and that the parish are paying for a missionary to me. Who are the rest of the world, that God should send missionaries to them?

TO MISS AUGUSTA KING.

NORTHAMPTON, October 21, 1840.

My heart has written you several epistles in reply, but the hand could not be spared. Oh for some spiritual daguerreotype, by which thoughts might spontaneously write themselves! How should you like that? Would you dare venture upon it for the sake of the convenience?

Oh, but you should have seen Lonetown woods in

the rich beauty of autumnal foliage! Color taking its fond and bright farewell of form, — Like the imagination giving a deeper, richer, warmer glow to old familiar truths, before the winter of rationalism comes, and places trunk and branches in naked outline against the clear cold sky.

I have had a charming letter from Mr. W., a real German effusion, filling matter brimful of life; so that statues beseech, and are sad that we do not understand their language; and flowers dance in troops to wind-music; and the brook goes tumbling to the river, roaring as he falls, and the river smiles that he comes to her unharmed. It is the old instinct that peopled nature with the graceful forms of naiad, dryad, and oread. Thus imperfectly, with all our strivings, do we spell out the "literature of God," as Margaret Fuller eloquently calls creation. . . .

A truce with my "Orphic sayings!" Here am I well nigh thirty-nine years old, and cannot for the life of me talk common sense. What shall I do to place myself in accordance with the received opinions of mankind? if I had been a flower or a bird, Linnæus or Audubon might have put me into some order; if I had been a beaver or an antelope, Buffon might have arranged me. One would think that being a woman were more to the purpose than either; for if to stand between " two infinities and three immensities," as Carlyle says (the two infinities being cooking done and to be done, and the three immensities being making, mending, and washing), if this won't drive poetry out of a mortal, I know not what will.

TO REV. CONVERS FRANCIS.

NORTHAMPTON, October 30, 1840.

Is not the idea of this present age written in the fact that any man can have his likeness taken in a minute by machinery? In "the philosophy of clothes" has it ever occurred to you, that in those Eastern countries, where a belief in fatalism stops the activity of human thought, the fashion of the garments changes not; while in France, where churches and governments are demolished in three days, the fashion of the garments is forever changing? I apprehend the clothing of a nation reveals much to the inhabitants of the aforesaid spiritual daguerreotype region. We borrow our fashions. How is it with our thoughts? By the way, did you hear that excellent joke, that Louis Phillippe had written to Dr. Channing to manufacture a religion for the French people?

My thoughts run on in the wildest way to-day. For the first time these six weeks, I have somebody in the kitchen to do my work; and there is a whole boys' school set loose in my brain, kicking up heels, throwing up caps, hurrahing, chasing butterflies, — everything in short, except drowning kittens. So you must not look for anything like coherence.

To go back to my hobby of twenty years, *i. e.* the forms of ideas. See you not how that old jangling pair, necessity and free-will, are shown in the tendency of all things to decay and reproduction? in mysticism and rationalism? in conservatism and reform? Forever in the universe, and the universe containing man, there is one hand winged, and the other chained. Because of necessity and free-will, the revolving worlds keep their places. The sun is their necessity, centrifugal force their strong free-will. And those two opposing ideas, which regulate the motion of the stars, are constantly taking form in the most trivial actions of my daily life. By my soul, though free-will has a hard battle in these latter times, necessity presses like a patent screw.

TO THE SAME.

NORTHAMPTON, January, 1841.

I marvel that you, who are no stranger to philosophy in its best sense, and who have the highest peaks of your mind at least a little gilded with transcendentalism, suppose that the " deadening drudgery of the world" can " imprison the soul in caverns." It is not merely an eloquent phrase, but a distinct truth, that the outward has no power over us but that which we voluntarily give it. It is not I who drudge, it is merely the case containing me. I defy all the powers of earth and hell to make me scour floors and feed pigs, if I choose meanwhile to be off conversing with the angels. . . . You are right, my dear brother, to attribute such freshness as I have to a vivid religious sentiment, not a theological tenet. If I can in quietude and cheerfulness forego my own pleasure, and relinquish my own tastes, to administer to my father's daily comfort, I seem to those who live in shadows to be cooking food or mixing medicines; but I am in fact making divine works of art, which will reveal to me their fair proportions in the far eternity. If I can smother the rising anger, and melt wrath with love, I have written a glorious piece of music, to be sung in my " Father's house of many mansions." Nay, more, perhaps I am doing somewhat to make a holier music descend to this world, first in purified affections, and ultimately in written notes. In this view of the ever-active agency of spirit, how appalling is the responsibility of a human soul; how glorious its capabilities. Another means of keeping my soul fresh is my intense love of Nature. Another help, perhaps stronger than than either of the two, is domestic love. . . .

A Southern gentleman, some time since, wrote to me from New Orleans, postage double and unpaid, inviting me to that city, promising me a "warm reception, and lodgings in the calaboose, with as much nigger company as you desire."[1] He wrote according to the light that was in him. He did not know that the combined police of the world could not imprison *me*. In spite of bolts and bars, I should have been off, like a witch at midnight holding fair discourse with Orion, and listening to the plaintive song of Pleiades mourning for the earth-dimmed glory of their fallen sister. How did he know, in his moral midnight, that choosing to cast our lot with the lowliest of earth was the very way to enter into companionship with the highest in heaven?

TO JOSEPH CARPENTER.

NORTHAMPTON, February 8, 1841.

The only house on our farm is a sort of shanty with two rooms and a garret, where a smart colored man and his wife (fugitives from injustice) now reside. We expect to whitewash it, build a new woodshed, and live there the next year. I shall keep no help, and there will be room enough for David and

[1] The above extract from the letter written by the Southerner was one of many of the same kind she received, because of her devotion to the cause of abolition.

me. I intend to half bury it in flowers. As for the hyacinth bean, what else could I expect when I trusted a Quaker with anything purely ornamental! I have since obtained some seed; and I valued them only because they grew around my door in Cottage Place, where I spent the happiest years of my life.

TO MRS. E. C. PIERCE.

NEW YORK, May 27, 1841.

Your last letter was all filled with accounts of your outward life. What do I care whether you have one room or six, provided you are happy? I want to know what your spirit is doing? What are you thinking, feeling, and reading? As for feeling, you cannot, I know, reveal to me or any one the world of sweet emotions that are now opening in your heart; but you can give me a glimpse. And see that you do it, instead of telling me how many gowns the baby has, and whether he sleeps in a swing cradle. You need not tell me about working all the time. You shall not do it. There is no sense in burying your soul under butter and cheese, any more than under laces and ruffles. Your husband, be he ever so plain a Friend, must mind me, and observe stated seasons. On every anniversary of your wedding day, he must give you a book. . . .

My task here is irksome to me. Your father will tell you that it was not zeal for the cause, but love for my husband, which brought me hither. But since it was necessary for me to leave home to be earning somewhat, I am thankful that my work is for the anti-slavery cause. I have agreed to stay one year. I hope I shall then be able to return to my husband and rural home, which is humble enough, yet very satisfactory to me. Should the "Standard" be continued, and my editing generally desired, perhaps I could make an arrangement to send articles from Northampton. At all events, I trust this weary separation from my husband is not to last more than a year. If I must be away from him, I could not be more happily situated than in Friend Hopper's family. They treat me the same as a daughter and a sister.

P. S. Only think of it! New York has repealed her nine months' law, and every slave brought here is now immediately free.

TO MR. ELLIS GRAY LORING.

NEW YORK, May 27, 1841.

DEAREST FRIEND, — Blessings on you for your cheering letter. I trust it expresses the general anti-slavery sentiment. I am afraid many will think me not gritty enough. The editing is much more irksome than I supposed. The type is fine, and that large sheet swallows an incredible amount of matter. The cry still is, as C. says, "More! more!" An anti-slavery editor is a sort of black sheep among the fraternity, and I have no courtesies from booksellers. —— assists me by getting books out of club libraries, etc.; but still my range for extracts is very limited. The first familiar face I met here was Mr. B——. He is preaching New Church doctrines with great effect. Is it not strange that I can neither get in nor out of the New Church? Let me go where I will, it keeps an outward hold upon me, more or less weak on one side, while reforms grapple me closely on the other. I feel that they are opposite, nay, discordant. My affections and imagination cling to one with a love that will not be divorced; my reason and conscience keep fast hold of the other, and will not be loosened. Here is the battle of free-will and necessity with a vengeance! What shall I do? The temptation is to quit reforms, but that is of the devil; for there is clearly more work for me to do in that field. I suppose I must go on casting a loving, longing look toward the star-keeping clouds of mysticism, which look down so mysterious and still into my heart, "and make it also great," while with busy hands I row the boat of practical endeavor. I would I were at one with myself. A Quaker, whose brother has joined the New Church, brings a message to me. That very brother is an admonition; for he used to be a warm anti-slavery and peace man, and the church influence has made him abjure both. . . .

You are right in supposing that abolition principles and non-resistance seem to me identical; rather that the former is a mere unit of the latter. I never saw any truth more clearly; insomuch that it seems strange to me that any comprehensive mind can embrace one and not the other.

EXTRACTS FROM LETTERS FROM DR. WILLIAM ELLERY CHANNING TO MRS. CHILD.

December 21, 1841.

Allow me to express the strong interest I take in you and your labors. You have suffered much for a great cause, but you have not suffered without the sympathy and affection of some, I hope not a few, whose feelings have not been expressed. Among those I may number myself. I now regret that when you were so near to me I saw so little of you. I know that you have higher supports and consolations than the sympathy of your fellow creatures, nor do

I offer mine because I attach any great value to it, but it is a relief to my own mind to thank you for what you have done for the oppressed, and to express the pleasure, I hope profit, which I have received from the various efforts of your mind.

I have been delighted to see in your "Letters from New York" such sure marks of a fresh, living, hopeful spirit; to see that the flow of genial noble feeling has been in no degree checked by the outward discouragements of life. The world's frowns can do us little harm if they do not blight our spirits, and we are under obligations to all who teach us, not in words, but in life, that there is an inward power which can withstand all the adverse forces of the world."

March 12, 1842.

MY DEAR FRIEND, — You see I reciprocate your familiar and affectionate phrase, and I do it heartily. There are, indeed, few people whom I address in this way, for I fear to use language stronger than my feelings, and I shrink so much from the appearance of flattering words, that I not seldom smother affections that struggle for utterance. But I grow free as I grow older. Age has no freezing influence, and the inward fountain gushes out more naturally. To you I ought to open my heart after what you have told me of the good a loving, cheering word does you. I confess I had thought of you as raised more than the most of us above the need of sympathy. I had heard so often of your brave endurance of adversity, and was conscious of having suffered so little myself for truth and humanity, that I almost questioned my right to send you encouraging words, and certainly did not expect so affectionate a response. It shows me I can do more than I believed by expressions of esteem and admiration. If I can lift up and strengthen such a spirit, how can I keep silence ? . . .

I understand fully your language when you speak of reform as your work-shop. I fear I understand it too well; that is, I am too prone to shrink from the work. Reform is the resistance of rooted corruptions and evils, and my tendency is to turn away from the contemplation of evils. My mind seeks the good, the perfect, the beautiful. It is a degree of torture to bring vividly to my apprehension what man is suffering from his own crimes, and from the wrongs and cruelty of his brother. No perfection of art expended on purely tragic and horrible subjects can reconcile me to them. It is only from a sense of duty that I read a narrative of guilt or woe in the papers. When the darkness is lighted up by moral greatness or beauty, I can endure and even enjoy it. You see I am made of but poor material for a reformer. But on this very account the work is good for me. I need it not, as many do, to give me excitement, for I find enough, perhaps too much, to excite me in the common experience of life, in meditation, in abstract truth; but to save me from a refined selfishness, to give me force, disinterestedness, true dignity and elevation, to link me by a new faith to God, by a deeper love to my race, and to make me a blessing to the world.

I know not how far I have explained my shrinking from the work of reform, but, be the cause what it may, let us not turn away from us the cross, but willingly, gratefully accept it when God lays it on us, and he does lay it on us whenever he penetrates our hearts with a deep feeling of the degradation, miseries, oppressions, crimes, of our human brethren, and awakens longings for their redemption. In thus calling us, he imposes on us a burden such as the ancient prophets groaned under. We must drink of the cup and be baptized into the baptism of our Master. We must expect persecution in some form or other: but this is a light matter compared with the painful necessity of fixing our eyes and souls on evil, and with the frequent apparent failure of our labor. Here, here is the trial. Could we lift up our fellow-creatures at once to the happiness and excellence which we aspire after, what a joy would reform be! But, alas, if we do remove a few pressing evils, how many remain! What a cloud still hangs over the earth! Sometimes evil seems to grow up under the efforts to repress it. Were it not for our faith, who could persevere? But with this faith what a secret sustaining joy flows into and mingles with sincere labors for humanity! The little we accomplish becomes to us a pledge of something infinitely greater. We know that the brighter futurity which our hearts yearn for is not a dream, that good is to triumph over evil, and to triumph through the sacrifices of the good.

You see I would wed you and myself to reform, and yet we must do something more than reformers. We must give our nature a fair chance. We must not wither it by too narrow modes of action. Let your genius have free play. We are better reformers, because calmer and wiser, because we have more weapons to work with, if we give a wide range to thought, imagination, taste, and the affections. We must be cheerful, too, in our war with evil; for gloom is apt to become sullenness, ill-humor, and bitterness.

REMINISCENCES OF DR. CHANNING BY MRS. CHILD, WRITTEN AFTER HIS DEATH AND PUBLISHED IN HIS MEMOIRS.

I shall always recollect the first time I ever saw Dr. Channing in private. It was immediately after I published my "Appeal in favor of that class of Americans called Africans," in 1833. A publication taking broad anti-slavery ground was then a rarity. Indeed, that was the first book in the United States of that character ; and it naturally produced a sensation disproportioned to its merits. I sent a copy to Dr. Channing, and a few days after he came to see me at Cottage Place, a mile and a half from his residence on Mt. Vernon Street. It was a very bright sunny day ; but he carried his cloak on his arm for fear of changes in temperature, and he seemed fatigued with the long walk. He stayed nearly three hours, during which time we held a most interesting conversation on the general interests of humanity, and on slavery in particular. He told me something of his experience in the West Indies, and said the painful impression made by the sight of 'slavery had never left his mind. He expressed great joy at the publication of the " Appeal," and added, " The reading of it has aroused my conscience to the query whether I ought to remain silent on the subject. He urged me never to desert the cause through evil report or good report. In some respects he thought I went too far. He then entertained the idea, which he afterwards discarded, that slavery existed in a milder form in the United States than elsewhere. I was fresh from the bloody records of our own legislation, and was somewhat vehement in my opposition to this statement, and he sought to moderate my zeal with those calm, wise words which none spoke so well as he.

We afterwards had many interviews. He often sent for me when I was in Boston, and always urged me to come and tell him of every new aspect of the anti-slavery cause. At every interview I could see that he grew bolder and stronger on the subject, while I felt that I grew wiser and more just. At first I thought him timid and even slightly time-serving, but I soon discovered that I formed this estimate merely from ignorance of his character. I learned that it was justice to all, not popularity for himself, which rendered him so cautious. He constantly grew upon my respect, until I came to regard him as the wisest as well as the gentlest apostle of humanity. I owe him thanks for helping to preserve me from the one-sidedness into which zealous reformers are apt to run. He never sought to undervalue the importance of anti-slavery, but he said many things to prevent my looking upon it as the only question interesting to humanity. My mind needed this check, and I never think of his many-sided conversations without deep gratitude. His interest in the subject constantly increased, and I never met him without being struck with the progress he had made in overcoming some difficulty which for a time troubled his sensitive conscience. I can distinctly recollect several such steps. At one time he was doubtful whether it were right to petition Congress on the subject, because such petition exasperated our Southern brethren, and, as he thought, made them more tenacious of their system. He afterward headed a petition himself. In all such cases he was held back by the conscientious fear of violating some other duty, while endeavoring to fulfil his duty to the slave. Some zealous reformers misunderstood this, and construed into a love of popularity what was, in fact, but a fine sense of justice, a more universal love of his species.

TO REV. CONVERS FRANCIS.

NEW YORK, February 17, 1842.

My domestic attachments are so strong, and David is always so full of cheerful tenderness, that this separation is dreary indeed; yet I am supplied, and that too in the most unexpected manner, with just enough of outward aids to keep me strong and hopeful. It has ever been thus, through all the changing scenes of my trying pilgrimage. Ever there is a harp in the sky, and an echo on earth. One of my aids is Friend Hopper's son, who with unwearied love brings me flowers and music, and engravings and pictures and transparencies, and the ever-ready sympathy of a generous heart. Another is a young German, full of that deep philosophy that is born of poetry. Then, ever and anon, there comes some winged word from Maria White, some outpourings. of love from young spirits in Boston or in Salem. Quite unexpectedly there came from Dr. Channing, the other day, words of the truest sympathy and the kindliest cheer. The world calls me unfortunate, but in good truth I often wonder why it is the angels take such good care of me. Bettine is a perpetual refreshment to my soul. Nothing disturbs me so much as to have any Philistine make remarks about her. Not that I think her connection with Goethe beautiful or altogether natural. (I need not have said that; for if it were truly natural, it would be altogether beautiful, let conventionalisms try their worst upon it.) Did I ever tell you how expressively John Dwight said all that is to be said on this subject?

" It is evident that Goethe was to Bettine merely the algebraic X that stands for the unknown quantity."

Mr. Brisbane, the Fourier Association man, told me that he was well acquainted with Bettine in Germany, and that no one who knew her would doubt for a moment that she did all the strange things recorded in her letters. He said she would talk with him by the two hours together, lying all quirled up in a heap on the carpet, and as often as any way with her feet bare; but that this, and other tricks more odd still, were played with such innocent and infantile grace that, withered as she was, he could not help regarding her like a child three years old. Yet, in the midst of her wildest frolics, she would start off suddenly and wing the highest flights of poetic romance, or dive into the deepest vein of spiritual philosophy. The artists were plagued to death with her, for she would go into all their studios just when she chose, seize their clay, tools, or brushes, and model or paint to her heart's content; often leaving her work unfinished and seizing upon fresh clay or canvas to embody some new freak of her brain. Some of these productions, he said, were of exquisite grace and beauty. Altogether, she was the strangest yet, the most captivating mortal he ever met. She had a son twenty years old, a man observable for practical wisdom and business tact. She was then a little withered, odd-looking old woman; but with a fire in her dark eye easily kindled into brilliant beauty.

As for conventional forms, the giant soul should indeed rend them like cobwebs when they cross the pathway of Truth and Freedom. But there is an eternal distinction between right and wrong, Goethe and Bettine to the contrary notwithstanding.

TO MISS AUGUSTA KING.

NEW YORK, September 19, 1843.

A day or two after Parker left, A. and L. called to see me. I asked, "What brings you to New York?" "I don't know," said Mr. A.; "it seems a miracle that we are here." But whatever the miracle might be, I believe it restored no blind to sight. Mr. C. and J. H. went to hear a discussion between them and W. H. C. It was held in a very small room, the air was stifling, and both came home with a headache. I asked Mr. C. what they talked about? "I don't know." "But can't you tell anything they said?" For some time he insisted that he could not, but being unmercifully urged, he at last said, "L. divided man into three states; the disconscious, the conscious, and the unconscious. The disconscious is the state of a pig; the conscious is the baptism by water; and the unconscious is the baptism by fire." I laughed, and said, "Well, how did the whole discussion affect your mind?" "Why, after I had heard them talk a few minutes," replied he, "I'll be cursed if I knew whether I had any mind at all!"

J. stayed rather longer, though he left in the midst. "How have you been pleased?" said I. "They've put my mind and body in a devil of a muss," replied he; "and I wish they had stayed at home." "What did they talk about?" "They didn't know themselves — how then should I?" Being mischievous, I insisted that he should give some account. Being thus urged, he said they talked about mind and body. "What did they say?" "Why, W. H. C. seemed to think there was some connection between mind and body; but those Boston folks, so far as I could understand 'em, seemed to think the body was all a d——d sham."

This swearing, I would have you to understand, is not habitual, but was merely assumed for the moment, for fun and as a safety valve to a vexed spirit. I write it to you, thinking it may excite a smile.

TO MISS ANNA LORING.

NEW YORK, December 26, 1843.

I had a very happy Christmas, and I will tell you how it happened. The watchmen picked up a little vagabond in the street, who said he had neither father nor mother, and had lost his way. He said his mother used to get drunk and sleep in the streets, but that he had not seen her for five years. They put him in the Tombs, not because he had committed any crime, but because he had nowhere to go. He was about ten years old. I applied to the orphan asylum, but he was older than their rules allowed them to admit. The poor child worried my mind greatly. On Christmas morning the asylum ladies sent me five dollars and a pair of nice boots for him. Mr. Child went to the Tombs for him, and after a good deal of difficulty found him and brought him home. He was in a situation too dirty and disgusting to describe. I cut off his hair, put him in a tub of water, scrubbed him from head to foot, bought a suit of clothes, and dressed him up. You never saw any little fellow so changed, and so happy in the change! But above all things his boots delighted him. I could hardly keep his eyes off them long enough to wash his face. "Are them boots for me?" he asked; and when I told him yes, it seemed as if the sun had shone out all over his face. "I never expected to have such a boot to my foot," said he. I shall remember this Christmas the longest day I live. As he sits before me now, making pictures on his slate, he every now and then thrusts out his foot, and examines the boots from toe to heel. He is nearly white, quite good-looking, remarkably bright, and very docile and affectionate. I do not yet know what I shall do with him, but I hope to get him a good place in the country. When I asked what he used to do, "I don't know exactly," said he; "sometimes I sat down on a stone, let the sun shine on me, and cried." Poor little fellow! His joy and gratitude have given me a happy Christmas.

Two years later: —

My Christmas boy, of whom I wrote you an account two years ago, has at last obtained a good place in the country. I suppose I have written half a hundred letters about him, trying to get a situation for him; for my heart bled for the poor little friendless orphan.

TO MISS HENRIETTA SARGENT.

NEW YORK, June 23, 1844.

None of us here think much of the Delphic sayings of your "charmed lady." She seems to have hit very wide of the mark. David is particularly dissatisfied with it; for he thinks I am preëminently distinguished for the supremacy of heart over head; that I am almost ridiculously a woman in my affections. For myself, knowing the extreme superficiality of my learning, I could not help smiling at the assertion that my head was "heavy with intellectual knowledge." She had better have said, full of rainbows and buttercups. I imagine that placing the mere name in the hand of the somnambulist is no criterion at all. It ought to be some MS. bearing an impress of the author's sentiments and thoughts.

I will copy for you what the Rev. Mr. Kent said when some fragmentary portions of one of my letters to the "Courier," in manuscript, were given to him in a sealed and blank envelope, without the person who gave it knowing who was the writer. It was a portion of my last letter, about the circulation of the blood of the human frame. On touching it, Mr. K. (whose state is said to be similar to ――'s) said : " The impression of this letter is pleasant — exceedingly so. Yet it seems somewhat disconnected. (It was in fragments.) The writer is of a very happy disposition ; purely and truly religious, without being sad or sombre ; full of benevolence and philanthropy ; very enthusiastic and poetical ; has written poetry ; mind quite philosophical, more so than one so poetic and romantic would be supposed to be ; great delicacy and depth of feeling. My impression is that the letter was written by a woman, but there is so much strength of intellect in it, that it may have been written by a man. Would not like to say certainly that it was written by a woman, but my feeling is strong that it was so. The mind is good, very good ; perhaps not first-rate, that is, not a giant, but very good, and very far above mediocrity. The person could not be guilty of a base action. Strong in her own integrity, very social, very lively, and fond of the approval of friends. A phrenologist would say that love of approbation was quite prominent. Very industrious and persevering ; charitable, and very kind-hearted. A reflecting mind ; reflects much and profoundly ; is inclined to transcendentalism. The German philosophy would suit it best. The letter was written on some subject of much interest to the writer, and under a rather agreeable state of feeling. The first impression conveyed, on touching this letter, was that of goodness, purity, and intelligence of the highest order."

I send it to you as it was sent to me by the agent of the "Courier." As you seemed to be curious on this subject of neurology, I thought it would gratify your curiosity to see it.

Dr. Palfrey called on me, on his way to New Orleans. I agreed to find places for five of his slaves, and have done so. He behaved nobly. His brothers offered to let him take his share in real estate; and that would have satisfied the conscience of most people; but he at once answered that he should consider such an arrangement equivalent to selling the slaves; and begged that as many slaves as possible might be put into his share. He told me that he had some fears as to how Mrs. P. would approve of his resolution, since it would alienate considerable property from her children, when his own pecuniary affairs were considerably embarrassed; but, to his surprise and delight, she promptly replied, " I want no child of mine to inherit a dollar from the sale of slaves." We have not labored in vain — have we, dear Henrietta?

TO MISS AUGUSTA KING.

NEW YORK, October 30, 1844.

Emerson has sent me his new volume.[1] As usual, it is full of deep and original sayings, and touches of exceeding beauty. But, as usual, it takes away my strength. . . . What is the use of telling us that everything is " scene-painting and counterfeit," that

[1] *Essays.* Second Series.

nothing is real, that everything eludes us? That no single thing in life keeps the promise it makes? Or, if any keeps it, keeps it like the witches to Macbeth? Enough of this conviction is forced upon us by experience, without having it echoed in literature. My being is so alive and earnest that it resists and abhors these ghastly, eluding spectres. It abhors them and says: " Be ye ghosts, and dwell among ghosts. But though all the world be dead, and resolved into vapory elements, *I* will live?" Emerson would smile at this; because it shows how deeply I feel the fact I quarrel with. But after all, if we extend our vision into the regions of faith, all this mocking and unreality vanishes; and in the highest sense all things keep the promises they make. Love, marriage, ambition, sorrow, nay even strong religious impressions, may and will fall short of the early promise they made, if we look at this life only. But they are all means, not ends. In that higher life we shall find that no deep feeling, no true experience, has slid over the surface of our being, and left no impression.

What have you seen and heard of Theodore Parker since his return? A friend requested him to buy a few engravings in Italy, and I think he chose admirably. One of them was intended for me, and if my spirit had been with him (as perhaps it was) he could not have chosen to my more complete satisfaction. It is the Cumæan Sibyl, by Domenichino. She holds a scroll of music in her hand, and seems listening intently to the voices of the universe. It is the likeness of my soul in some of its moods. Oh, how I have listened!

It is curious, but, standing as I am on the verge of declining life, my senses are all growing more acute and clear; so acute that my sources of pain and pleasure are increased tenfold. I am a great deal more alive than I used to be.

I live in the same quiet, secluded way. I am never seen in public, and the question is sometimes asked, "Where on earth does she pick up all she tells of New York in her letters to the 'Courier?' for nobody ever sees her." Willis saw my "cap," though, on one occasion. A bit of lace outside of my head was as much as I should expect him to see of me. I suppose you have seen his announcement to the public in what box I sat at Niblo's; a fact doubtless of great importance to the public, fashionable and literary. If you have seen the paragraph in his paper, you will know what I mean by the "cap."

TO PROF. CONVERS FRANCIS.

NEW YORK, December 6, 1846.

About once a fortnight I go to a concert, music being the only outward thing in which I do take much pleasure. Friend Hopper bears a testimony against it, because he says it is spiritual brandy which only serves to intoxicate people.

We had quite a flare-up here about a fugitive slave, and I wrote the "Courier" an account of it. I have been much amused at the attacks it has brought on me from the papers. The pious prints are exceedingly shocked because I called him "a living gospel of freedom, bound in black." It is so blasphemous to call a man a gospel! The Democratic papers accused me of trying to influence the state election then pending. The fun of it is, that I did not know there was an election. I could not possibly have told whether that event takes place in spring or fall. I have never known anything about it since I was a little girl on the lookout for election cake. I know much better who leads the orchestras than who governs the State.

TO MRS. NATHANIEL SILSBEE.

NEW YORK, February 12, 1847.

DEAR UNKNOWN, — I have a question of morality and good manners to propound to thee. Dost thou think it quite proper to address anonymous letters to people in a hand cramped on purpose to disguise it? Ah, thou rogue! Now look me right in the eye and say dost thou know of anybody who has played such a trick, and didst thou think to blind a weasel in that fashion?

Yesterday was my birthday, and on that day many pleasant things occurred. Imprimis, Harnden's Express car stopped at the door, and a package was brought up to me. I opened it and found a very beautiful edition of Mrs Jameson's "Characteristics of Women," purporting to come "from a woman who had benefited much from Mrs. Child's characteristics." "Ahem!" said I, "this evidently comes from a woman who knows how to shed the graces over life."

The next pleasant thing was that my lovely S. L. came in with a large bouquet of violets, the fragrance of which filled the room. "Oh, dear Maria, though you were so silent about your birthday, I did not forget it," said she; and she played a rondeau and an old Norwegian peasant melody which Ole used to play. They all know the road to my heart, the rogues!

The third pleasant incident was that the flower merchant in Broadway, who sold the violets, would not take a cent for them, because S. happened to say they were for Mrs. Child's birthday and he overheard her. "I cannot take pay for flowers intended for her," said he. "She is a stranger to me, but she has given my wife and children so many flowers in her writings, that I will never take money of her." It brought the tears to my eyes. I wish I was good. I ought to be, everybody is so kind to me.

The fourth pleasant incident was the entrance of J. L., the cantatrice, and a very sweet warbler she is. "I did not forget your birthday," she said, and she placed on my head a crimson wreath and sang and played for me Ole's favorite melody: "Near the lake where droops the willow," which he has introduced beautifully in his "Niagara," swelling upon the wind instruments as if borne on the wings of angels.

Meeting with so much unexpected kindness filled me with universal benevolence. I ran right off and gave a large portion of my violets to my friend, Mrs. F. G. S., who is here under Dr. Elliott's care and blind for the present, and the fragrance refreshed her though she could not see the beautiful tint. Then I ran in another direction and carried my little music-box, and another portion of my violets, to a poor man who is dying slowly. I wanted to give something and do something for the whole world. . . . But I must take care, for my own private theories on this subject touch the verge of radicalism.

I have a confession to make to you. I intended to send you some little "rattletrap" on your birthday. But I said to myself, "that will seem like reminding her of my birthday.[1] She is rich and I am poor. If I send her plaster she will perhaps send me marble; it will be more delicate not to do it." I am ashamed,

---

[1] Their birthdays came in the same month.

thoroughly ashamed, of those mean ideas, for the thought "I am poor and thou art rich" ought never to enter to interrupt the free flowing of human souls toward each other. Nevertheless I did it as I have done many other things that I regret and am ashamed of.

Good-by, invisible fairy princess, dropping anonymous gifts from thy golden car in the clouds.

I am ever thy affectionate and grateful subject.

TO MISS LUCY OSGOOD.

NEW YORK, March 26, 1847.

I believe the Quakers are right in supposing that a salaried priesthood are positive obstacles in the way of human progress. I think, too, that the vocation impedes individual growth. Great, good, and progressive souls there doubtless are among the clergy; but I do not think they are as large, as free, as expansive as the same natures would have been if removed from the social pressure to which all clergymen are obliged to submit. The most mettlesome horse loses his elasticity and bounding grace after plodding a while round the mill-wheel circle. You see how far apart we are! You always at home among clericals, I at home only among poets and artists! You reading Italian sermons of past centuries, I bothering my brain to prove to myself (I have done wishing to prove anything to anybody except myself) Goethe's theory of Colors, by a similar theory of Tones!

You know I always wondered why on earth you were interested in such a butterfly as I am. That I love you very sincerely is a positive fact, and not as unaccountable as your regard for me. Our friendship

always seems to me like a companionship between
Minerva and Fenella. I am sure all your wisdom
will not enable you to tell what extraordinary leaps
and somersets I may yet make, or whether the next
rope I dance on will be tight or slack.

TO FRANCIS G. SHAW.

NEW YORK, 1847.

I have read "The Countess of Rudolstaat." It
seems to me an excellent translation; but I think, as
I thought of it in French, that it is less attractive
than "Consuelo." I doubt whether even its being a
continuation of that story will make it sell so well.
It is replete with beautiful thought and high aspirations; but even to me, who sympathize with the aspirations, it is tedious. I am sorry that I am so
wicked, but Albert, with his Hussites and Invisibles,
is a bore to me, from beginning to end. I don't
know what is the matter with me, but all that German part of the story has something about it cold and
blue and cloudy. It chills me like walking in caverns. I long for the sunny sky of Italy again. However, I am glad the story leaves them tramping
through the free forests to the sound of guitar and
violin. There is something pleasant in that. I would
not mind having it for my heaven, with rosy children
and the man I loved, provided he was not a Hussite;
which, by the way, he would not be likely to be, if I
loved him. I suppose the trouble is that I am now
wholly in the dispensation of art, and therefore theo-
logians and reformers jar upon me. Even in music
I love better the production of Catholic composers.
In Protestant music thought predominates over feeling too much.

LETTERS.

TO PROF. CONVERS FRANCIS.

NEW ROCHELLE, January 20, 1848.

Here I am in my little out-of-the-way den, as comfortable " as a grub in a nut."
I have found it to hold good, as a general rule, that a person who will ask for a letter of introduction is sure to be a bore. If I were going to Europe, and letters of introduction to Wordsworth, Dickens, etc., were offered me, I would never present them, unless I happened by some accident to receive indications of a wish to be introduced, on the part of the men themselves. What right have I to intrude upon their time, and satisfy my impertinent curiosity by an inventory of their furniture and surroundings? Dignify it as they may, by talk about reverence for genius, loving a man for his writings, etc., I have always believed it a game of vanity, both with those who offer it, and those who are pleased with it. However, it is no matter whether I am wrong, or the customs of society are wrong. I am snugly out of the way of them here. Never was such a lonely place! As I trudged from the depot to honest Joseph's, about four miles, I met no living thing except one pig and four geese. But my low-walled room, over the old Dutch stoop, faces the south, and when I open my eyes in the morning they are greeted by beautiful " golden water " on the wall, the reflection of the rising sun through the lattice bars of my willow window curtains. I eat well, sleep well, dream pleasantly, read agreeable books, and am serenely contented with existence. I can go to the city whenever I choose, and am always sure of a cordial welcome at Friend Hopper's, where I hire a little bit of an upper bed-room

for my especial convenience. So you see I am quite like a lady "of property and standing," with both country and city residence.

TO THE SAME.

NEW ROCHELLE, January 14, 1849.

As for amusements, music is the only thing that excites me, and the excitement that affords is most frequently tinged with sadness, though sometimes it goes tingling through my whole soul, like spiritual electricity. Your eloquent extract is rather " obscura." However, I feel that music is " the song of creative origination," though I cannot explain it. When I try to put it into thought, I say that all colors, all perfumes, all chemical affinities, rose into being and arranged themselves according to the keys of music, and the modulation of music. Bettina had the same idea. When writing on music, she said " the secret of creation seems to lie on my tongue." My friends, the ancient Hindoos, say the seven notes of music were the first thing created by the wife of Brama, even before they made the mundane egg. But enough of this. I have a chronic insanity with regard to music. It is the only Pegasus which now carries me far up into the blue. Thank God for this great blessing of mine! However, if I am to sing through eternity I hope it won't be with all " elders," as Revelation has it. You perceive I am in a wicked mood to-day. In all moods, I love you truly, and am ever your grateful and affectionate sister.

TO THE SAME.

NEW YORK, July 14, 1848.

My book [1] gets slowly on. I am not sustained by the least hope that my mode of treating the subject will prove acceptable to any class of persons. No matter! I am going to tell the plain unvarnished truth, as clearly as I can understand it, and let Christians and Infidels, Orthodox and Unitarians, Catholics and Protestants and Swedenborgians, growl as they like. They all will growl if they notice the book at all; for each one will want to have his own theory favored, and the only thing I have conscientiously aimed at is not to favor any theory. . . . How queer it seems to me to read long arguments to prove that Philo must have had some idea of the Christian Trinity! Because Plato stands behind Christ, they cannot see him, though his head and shoulders are so plainly visible. One thing I have learned, in the course of my labors. It is of no use to ask questions of others, or seek assistance from them, unless it be concerning the titles of books which contain the most trustworthy information. More and more I feel that every sort of salvation we do attain to in this life must be worked out by ourselves.

TO ELLIS GRAY LORING.

NEW YORK, November 7, 1849.

I spent most of last Sunday with Fredrika Bremer; four or five hours entirely alone with her. Mrs. S. very kindly invited me to meet her there. What a refreshment it was! She is so artless and

---

[1] *The Progress of Religious Ideas through Successive Ages.* By L. Maria Child. In three volumes. New York, 1855.

unaffected, such a reality! I took a wonderful liking to her, though she is very plain in her person, and I am a fool about beauty. We talked about Swedenborg, and Thorwaldsen, and Jenny Lind, and Andersen. She had many pleasant anecdotes to tell of Jenny, with whom she is intimately acquainted. Among other things, she mentioned having once seen her called out in Stockholm, after having successfully performed in a favorite opera. She was greeted not only with thundering claps, but with vociferous hurrahs. In the midst of the din she began to warble merely the notes of an air in which she was very popular. The ritournelle was, " How shall I describe what my heart is feeling ? " She uttered no words, she merely warbled the notes, clear as a lark, strong as an organ. Every other sound was instantly hushed. Graceful — was it not? Fredrika plays the piano with a light and delicate touch, and in a style indicative of musical feeling. She played to me a charming quaint old Swedish melody, the Song of Necken, the ancient Spirit of the Rivers, as he sat on the waters, singing to the accompaniment of his harp. She sketches admirable likenesses with colored crayons. She showed me one she had made of Andersen, a whole gallery of celebrated Danes, and a few Americans whom she has sketched since her arrival. I particularly liked her for one thing; she did not attempt to compliment me, either directly or indirectly. She never heard of J. R. Lowell till she came here. His poetry has inspired her with strong enthusiasm. She said to me, " He is the poet prophet of America." Emerson seems to have made on her the same vivid impression that he makes on all original and thinking minds. What a fuss they will make with Fredrika in Boston! She will have no peace of her life. I hope they will not be ambitious of burying her by the side of Dr. Spurzheim.

TO MRS. NATHANIEL SILSBEE.

WEST NEWTON [Mass.], September 14, 1850.

The morning after you left, when I opened the front door I found a box against it which proved to be *the* box. My dear lady, you are too overpowering in your goodness! It made me cry to see how you loaded me with benefits. But I pray you curb your generosity a little. I love you for your own sake, and if in some unlucky hour my conscience whispers to my heart that I ought to love you because you are so good to me, then it will be hot work, for my savage love of freedom will resist the claim like a tiger. So pray don't bring me into such a dilemma. The pitcher is a superb affair. Antique and classical to my heart's content. I seem to be very anti-temperance in my surroundings. The pitcher is tipsy, my beautiful young Cupidon has his heart merry with wine, the head of my sacrificial bull is crowned with grapes, and my candlesticks are interwoven grape-vines. Luckily, I have no weakness of that sort. If myrtle wreaths abounded everywhere, I might feel a little conscious. You say the candlesticks are associated with pleasant times in New York, which we shall never have again. How do you know that, lady fair? I have been saddened by such a thought sometimes, but there gleamed across the shadow a bright idea that perhaps some day you and I would set off to New York a-pleasuring, afoot and alone. I could stay quietly at Friend Hopper's while you flirted among the fashionables, and when you had leisure, we could go and sit together on carpet bales, or eat ginger-snaps on a door-step in Staten Island. What does the Lady Mayoress of Salem think of that dignified suggestion?

TO JOSEPH CARPENTER.

WEST NEWTON, August 24, 1851.

There seems to be a lull just now in fugitive slave matters. What experiment our masters will try next, remains to be shown. The commercial and moneyed portion of the community will doubtless obey their orders to any extent. But in the heart of the people I think a better and braver sentiment is gradually being formed. A friend of mine in Medford sheltered a fugitive a short time ago. When the firemen of the town heard of it, they sent for the man chattel, elected him a member of their company, and promised, at a given signal, to rally for his defence in case he was pursued, and to stand by him to the death, one and all.

TO MRS. S. B. SHAW.

WEST NEWTON, 1852.

Do you know that Harriet Hosmer, daughter of a physician in Watertown, has produced a remarkably good piece of statuary? It is a bust of Vesper, the Evening Star. I never saw a tender, happy drowsiness so well expressed. A star shining on her forehead, and beneath her breast lies the crescent moon. Her graceful hair is intertwined with capsules of the poppy. It is cut with great delicacy and precision, and the flesh seems to me very flesh-like. The poetic conception is her own, and the workmanship is all her own. A man worked upon it a day and a half, to chip off large bits of marble; but she did not venture to have him go within several inches of the surface she intended to work. Miss Hosmer is going to Rome in October, accompanied by her father, a plain, sensible man, of competent property. She expects to remain in Italy three years, with the view of becoming a sculptor by profession. . . .

Mrs. Stowe's truly great work, "Uncle Tom's Cabin," has also done much to command respect for the faculties of woman. Whittier has poured forth verses upon it; Horace Mann has eulogized it in Congress; Lord Morpeth is carried away with it; the music stores are full of pieces of music suggested by its different scenes; somebody is going to dramatize it; and 100,000 copies sold in little more than six months! Never did any American work have such success! The passage of the Fugitive Slave Law roused her up to write it. Behold how "God makes the wrath of man to praise Him!" Charles Sumner has made a magnificent speech in Congress against the Fugitive Slave Law. How thankful I was for it! God bless him! The Republican party don't know how to appreciate his honesty and moral courage. They think he makes a mistake in speaking the truth, and does it because he don't know any better. They do not perceive how immeasurably superior his straightforwardness is to their crookedness. History will do him justice.

It is really droll to see in what different states of mind people read "Uncle Tom." Mr. Pierce, Senator from Maryland, read it lately, and when he came to the sale of "Uncle Tom," he exclaimed with great emotion, "Here's a writer that knows how to sympathize with the South! I could fall down at the feet of that woman! She knows how to feel for a man when he is obliged to sell a good honest slave!" In his view the book was intended as a balsam for bereaved slave-holders.

TO FRANCIS G. SHAW.

WAYLAND, January 22, 1854.

Did you ever see, among a series of frescoes by Correggio, somewhere in Italy, Diana with a crescent on her brow, guiding her chariot through the clouds? The engraving of it by Toschi is, to me, the most graceful, beautiful, altogether perfect thing I ever did see. It is a glorious woman, and yet, in expression, the real full moon, guiding her bright chariot through the heavens. If I lived where it was I should make a little golden altar, and burn incense before it. You see there is no washing my Greek heathenism out of me. What is the reason that a region so totally unlike my homely environment in the outward world has always seemed to me so like a remembered home? . . .

Things are going on at a terrible rate on the slavery question. They are trying in Congress to vote payment to the piratical claimants of the Amistad, and to abolish the obligation of Southerners in the Missouri compromise. Think of that! Gerrit Smith is in Congress now, and has made a noble speech. He was interrupted by a member from Maryland, who tried to put him down at the outset by saying, "It appears that the gentleman from New York intends to give us an anti-slavery speech." With dignified courtesy, Mr. Smith replied, "I do intend to make an anti-slavery speech; and if the gentleman from Maryland wishes to make a pro-slavery speech,

I shall listen to him with all courtesy." He is the first one that has stood up like a man, and boldly professed to be an abolitionist. The Southerners respected him, in spite of themselves; for honesty and boldness will be respected. It is reported that one said to another, " We have not only got an honest man among us, but the best debater of us all." The honest man was a rarity!

Dear Sarah's beautiful articles found a ready sale at the anti-slavery fair. Was it not a touching incident that a poor German peasant, who had read " Uncle Tom," should have taken down two engravings from the walls of his cabin and sent them to the fair in Boston? I would have expended my last dollar for them, but unfortunately they were lost by shipwreck. Such things make us forget a thousand disappointments in human nature. . . .

Sarah writes that you were disappointed in the Sphinx. The description of travellers has not led me to suppose there was anything attractive in the Sphinx itself. But Gliddon's " Panorama of the Nile," where the Sphinx appears just as evening closes her curtains and " pins them with a star," made a deep impression on my imagination. The huge, dark, almost shapeless mass, strange, silent relic of such a remote past, so dim and solemn in the desert stillness, seemed to me invested with awful grandeur. I don't wonder your brother was afraid to stay alone with those colossal statues of Egypt. A mysterious, disturbing influence comes over the soul when the Past looks us in the face, so like the eternal eye of God.

With regard to the present, here in our own country, my dear friend, it is gloomy enough. . . . Of all our servile Senates, none have been so completely servile to the slave interest as the present one. They have passed the Nebraska Bill in open defiance of the people.... These measures have been followed up by the most outrageous insults and aggressions upon the North. Only three days ago another poor slave was hunted in Boston, and though a pretty general indignation was excited, he was given up by the Boston magistrates and triumphantly carried back to bondage, guarded by a strong escort of United States troops.[1] The court-house was nearly filled with troops and hired ruffians, armed with cutlasses and bowie-knives. No citizen was allowed to enter without a pass, as is the custom with slaves; and these passes were obtained with great difficulty, none being given to any one suspected of being friendly to the slave. The Rev. Samuel May had his pass taken from him, and he was thrust out rudely by the soldiers. Men were even arrested and imprisoned for merely making observations to each other which the ruling powers considered dangerous. My dear friend, my very soul is sick in view of these things. They tell me "The Lord will surely arise for the sighing of the poor and the needy," as he has promised. I think to myself, "Oh yes, that promise was made some three thousand years ago, and the fulfilment seems as far off as ever." But I suppress the impatient blasphemy, and only say, as poor Aunt Chloe does in "Uncle Tom," "Yes, missis, but the Lord lets dreadful things happen."

Whether there is any limit to the servile submission of the North, I know not. The South seems resolved to try to the utmost how much kicking and cuffing she will bear. The "Richmond Enquirer" compares the connection between North and South

[1] The rendition of Anthony Burns.

to the relation between Greece and her Roman masters. "The dignity and energy of the Roman character, conspicuous in war and politics, were not easily tamed and adjusted to the arts of industry and literature. The degenerate and pliant Greeks, on the contrary, obsequious, dexterous, and ready, monopolized the business of teaching and manufacturing in the Roman Empire, allowing their masters ample leisure for the service of the state, in the Senate or the field. We learn from Juvenal that they were the most useful and capable servants, whether as pimps or professors of rhetoric." Now do you know that my inmost soul rejoices in all these manifestations of contempt? The North richly deserves them, and I have a faint hope that they may be heaped on till some of the old spirit is roused. There was a large meeting at Faneuil Hall when the slave was arrested. Mr. Russell presided, and the speeches and resolutions were uncommonly spirited and eloquent. But they talked boldly of a rescue the next morning, and so did more harm than good by forewarning the Southerners, and giving them time to summon a great array of United States troops. If they had only struck when the iron was hot, and used very slight precautions, I think the poor slave might have been rescued without shedding blood. But it was not done, and "order reigns in Warsaw," as the Russian officials declared after the knout had driven all the Polish heroes into Siberia. My soul is just now in a stormy state, and it curses "law and order," seeing them all arrayed on the wrong side. This fierce mood will soon give place to a milder one. But oh, my friend, these continually baffled efforts for human freedom, they are agonizing to the sympathizing soul.

TO ELLIS GRAY LORING.

WAYLAND, February 24, 1856.

David has signed my will and I have sealed it up and put it away. It excited my towering indignation to think it was necessary for him to sign it, and if you had been by, you would have made the matter worse by repeating your old manly "fling and twit" about married women being dead in the law. I was not indignant on my own account, for David respects the freedom of all women upon principle, and mine in particular by reason of affection superadded. But I was indignant for womankind made chattels personal from the beginning of time, perpetually insulted by literature, law, and custom. The very phrases used with regard to us are abominable. "Dead in the law," "Femme couverte." How I detest such language! I must come out with a broadside on that subject before I die. If I don't, I shall walk and rap afterward.

TO PROF. CONVERS FRANCIS.

WAYLAND, February 27, 1856.

Concerning theology, I still have a difficulty in seeing eye to eye with you. If there is such a science, I should define it as treating of man's relations with God; while ethics treat of his relations with fellow-men. Is there any basis for a science concerning the nature of the Divine Being, and the relations of human souls with him? What have we for guides into the infinite, except faith and aspiration? And must not faith and aspiration necessarily differ in individuals, according to temperament, education, and other external influences?

I am passing through strange spiritual experiences

not at all of my own seeking or willing. Ideas which formerly seemed to me a foundation firm as the everlasting hills, are rolling away from under my feet, leaving me on a ladder poised on the clouds. Still the ladder stays fixed, like Jupiter and the Virgin Mary seated on clouds in pictures. I have ceased to believe that any revelation written for one age or in one age can be adapted to all ages. I once thought that an inner spiritual meaning invested the Christian sacred books with a character infinite and eternal. I tried Swedenborg's key of correspondences, but it unlocked nothing. Wander where I would, I found nothing inscribed on the walls, but that everlasting duality of "Love and Wisdom." Every mineral said it, every flower said it, and the archangel said no more.

TO MRS. S. B. SHAW

WAYLAND, March 23, 1856.

This winter has been the loneliest of my life. If you could know my situation you would pronounce it unendurable. I should have thought it so myself if I had had a foreshadowing of it a few years ago. But the human mind can get acclimated to anything. What with constant occupation and the happy consciousness of sustaining and cheering my poor old father in his descent into the grave, I am almost always in a state of serene contentment. In summer, my once extravagant love of beauty satisfies itself with watching the birds, the insects, and the flowers in my little patch of a garden. I have no room in which to put the vases and engravings and transparencies that friends have given me from time to time. But I keep them safely in a large chest, and when birds and flowers are gone I sometimes take them out, as a child does its playthings, and sit down in the sunshine with them, dreaming how life would seem in such places, and how poets and artists came to imagine such images. This process sometimes gives rise to thoughts which float through the universe, though they began in a simple craving to look at something beautiful. A photograph of Raphael's Sibyls, given to me by Mrs. S., remarkably has this effect upon me. I don't know what it is that draws me so toward those ancient Grecians! I suppose this same attraction toward Grecian forms of art is what made me in love with Mendelssohn's music; because I felt (without understanding) its harmonious proportions, its Doric simplicity, its finished beauty. I recognize the superior originality and power of Beethoven; but he does not minister to my soul as he does to yours. He overpowers me, — fills me with awe. His music makes me feel as if I were among huge black mountains, looking at a narrow strip of brilliant stars, seen through narrow clefts in the frowning rocks, in the far-off heaven. I love best to hear the "Pastoral Symphony," which is the least Beethovenish of all. The fact is, my nature has less affinity for grandeur and sublimity, than it has for grace and beauty. I never looked twice at engravings from Michael Angelo; while I dream away hours and hours over copies from Raphael.

TO MISS LUCY OSGOOD.

WAYLAND, May 11, 1856.

Since you will think of me as an "author," I am glad that you think of me as "an alive author;" for so long as I write at all, I desire to be very much alive.

This is the second time I have walked out in stormy weather without a cloak. My " Appeal " in favor of anti-slavery, and attacking colonization, marched into the enemy's camp alone. It brought Dr. Channing to see me, for the first time ; and he told me it had stirred up his mind to the conviction that he ought not to remain silent on the subject. Then came Dr. Palfrey, who, years afterward, said that the emancipation of his slaves might be traced to the impulse that book had given him. Charles Sumner writes me that the influence of my anti-slavery writings years ago has had an important effect on his course in Congress. . . . Who can tell how many young minds may be so influenced by the " Progress of Religious Ideas " as to materially change their career? I trust I have never impelled any one in the wrong direction. In the simplest things I write, whether for children or grown people, I always try to sow some seeds for freedom, truth, and humanity. S. J. May writes to me very warmly about the big book. He says he has commended it from his pulpit, as " the most valuable contribution to an enlarged, charitable, and true theology that has been made by any one in our country." Of course, you will not understand him as meaning to compare me with such minds as Theodore Parker ; but he considers my book more valuable than those written by many abler pens, because it is not written in the spirit of an opponent to prevailing false theologies.

You are right in supposing that while engaged on that work I " felt like an inhabitant of the second and third centuries." Everything around me seemed foreign,-as it did when I came out of Athens into Boston, after writing " Philothea." That was a pleasant ramble into classic lands; but this "Progress of Religious Ideas" was a real pilgrimage of penance, with peas in my shoes, walking over rubble-stones most of the way. You have no idea of the labor! It was greatly increased by my distance from libraries, nearly all the time, which rendered copious extracts necessary. How absurdly the Old Testament is treated by Christians! used for all convenient purposes, neglected whenever it is inconvenient! Moses is good authority for holding slaves, but not for the healthy practice of abstaining from the use of pork. . . . Most devoutly do I believe in the pervasive and ever-guiding Spirit of God; but I do not believe it was ever shut up within the covers of any book, or that it ever can be. Portions of it, or rather breathings of it, are in many books. The words of Christ seem to me full of it, as no other words are. But if we want truth, we must listen to the voice of God in the silence of our own souls as he did.

TO MRS. S. B. SHAW.

WAYLAND, 1856.

The outrage upon Charles Sumner made me literally ill for several days. It brought on nervous headache and painful suffocations about the heart. If I could only have done something, it would have loosened that tight ligature that seemed to stop the flowing of my blood. But I never was one who knew how to serve the Lord by standing and waiting; and to stand and wait then! It almost drove me mad. And that miserable Faneuil Hall meeting! The timeserving Mr. —— talking about his "friend" Sumner's being a man that "hit hard!" making the people laugh at his own witticisms, when a volcano was seething beneath their feet! poisoning the wellspring of popular indignation, which was rising in its might! Mr. A., on the eve of departing for Europe, wrote to me, " The North will not really do anything to maintain their own dignity. See if they do! I am willing to go abroad, to find some relief from the mental pain that the course of public affairs in this country has for many years caused me." But I am more hopeful. Such a man as Charles Sumner will not bleed and suffer in vain. Those noble martyrs of liberty in Kansas will prove missionary ghosts, walking through the land, rousing the nation from its guilty slumbers. Our hopes, like yours, rest on Fremont. I would almost lay down my life to have him elected. There never has been such a crisis since we were a nation. If the slave-power is checked now, it will never regain its strength. If it is not checked, civil war is inevitable; and, with all my horror of bloodshed, I could be better resigned to that great calamity than to endure the tyranny that has so long trampled on us. I do believe the North will not, this time, fall asleep again, after shaking her mane and growling a little.

I saw by the papers that Mr. Curtis was in the field, and I rejoiced to know he was devoting his brilliant talents and generous sympathies to so noble a purpose. I envy him; I want to mount the rostrum myself. I have such a fire burning in my soul, that it seems to me I could pour forth a stream of lava that would bury all the respectable servilities, and all the mob servilities, as deep as Pompeii; so that it would be an enormous labor ever to dig up the skeletons of their memories.

We also talk of little else but Kansas and Fremont.

What a shame the women can't vote! We'd carry our "Jessie" into the White House on our shoulders; wouldn't we? Never mind! Wait a while! Woman stock is rising in the market. I shall not live to see women vote; but I'll come and rap at the ballot-box. Won't you? I never was bitten by politics before; but such mighty issues are depending on this election that I cannot be indifferent.

TO MISS LUCY OSGOOD.

WAYLAND, July 9, 1856.

I did not intend to leave your New York letter so long unanswered, but the fact is, recent events have made me heart-sick. My anxiety about Charles Sumner and about the sufferers in Kansas has thrown a pall over everything. The fire of indignation is the only thing that has lighted up my gloom. At times my peace principles have shivered in the wind; and nothing could satisfy my mood but Jeanne d'Arc's floating banner and consecrated sword. And when this state of mind was rebuked by the remembrance of him who taught us to overcome evil only with good, I could do nothing better than groan out, in a tone of despairing reproach, "How long, O Lord! how long?" Certainly there are gleams of light amid the darkness. There has been more spirit roused in the North than I thought was in her. I begin to hope that either the slave power must yield to argument and the majesty of public sentiment or else that we shall see an army in the field, stout and unyielding as Cromwell's band. . . .

I thank you very heartily for Mr. Wasson's sermon, "The Universe No Failure." It is the most remarkable discourse I ever read. He puts the lever down deep enough to upheave the foundations of error. He builds his battery high enough to command the most towering fortifications of superstition. That is what we need. Unless the root is dug up, the branches will always be sprouting into new fantastic forms, however they may be lopped and pruned. I exclaimed "Bravo!" to his first sermon; but over this, I shouted "Bravissimo!" I see that he attended the meeting of Progressive Friends.[1] I take considerable interest in that movement. I have hopes that it will prove the nucleus of such a form of worship as I have dreamed of for years.

TO THE SAME.

WAYLAND, July 20, 1856.

I am extremely obliged to you for the loan of Mr. Furness's letter, which was very interesting to me on various accounts. If I had a head easily turned, I might be in danger of the lunatic asylum from the effects of that portion relating to myself. To have a man like Mr. Furness pronounce a letter of mine worth Mr. Sumner's having his head broken for, though the phrase be used only in the way of playful hyperbole, is a gust of eulogy enough to upset a light boat. Luckily, the vessel I sail in is old and heavy, and of late years carries much more ballast than sail. Still, I confess I was much gratified to know that Mr. Furness liked the letter. To my own mind, it seemed so altogether inadequate to express the admiration, respect, and gratitude I feel for Mr. Sumner, that I was in great doubt about sending it. Mr. Child assured me that I need have no fears; that Mr. Sumner would undoubtedly be gratified by it, etc.;

---

[1] A reformatory gathering held yearly in Chester County, Pennsylvania.

but my good husband is so apt to like whatever I do, that I did not consider him a very impartial witness. It is heart-cheering to see a man ready to lay his beautiful gifts so unreservedly on the altar of freedom and humanity as W. H. Furness has done. On various occasions I have felt deeply grateful to him for the brave, true words he has spoken, and what he said on the Kansas question was worthy of himself and the cause.

TO MRS. ELLIS GRAY LORING.

WAYLAND, October 26, 1856.

I intended to have written to you immediately after I received your very kind and pressing invitation to come to Beverly. . . . Oh, what misery it is, to feel such a fever heat of anxiety as I do, and yet be shut up in a pen-fold, where I cannot act! It seems to me sometimes as if I could tear up a mountain, and throw it so that all false Democrats and stiff old fogies would be buried under it forever. All the fire there is in me is burning: and Nature gave me a fearful amount of it. You see, dear, I should be a very dangerous and explosive guest, just at this time; especially if you happened to have any amiable apologizers about.

TO DAVID LEE CHILD.

WAYLAND, October 27, 1856.

I have thought enough about my dear absent mate, but I have found it nearly impossible to get an hour's time to tell him so. In the first place, there was the press waiting for that Kansas story. . . . Then I felt bound to stir up the women here to do something for Kansas; and, in order to set the example, I wrote to Mr. Hovey begging for a piece of cheap calico and of unbleached factory cotton. He sent them, but said he did it out of courtesy to me; he himself deeming that money and energy had better be expended on the immediate abolition of slavery, and dissolution of the Union if that could not be soon brought about. I did not think it best to wait for either of these events before I made up the cloth. Cold weather was coming on, the emigrants would be down with fever and ague, and the roads would soon be in a bad state for baggage wagons. So I hurried night and day, sitting up here all alone till eleven at night, stitching as fast as my fingers could go. It was a heavy job to cut and make more than sixty yards of cloth into garments, but with help from Mrs. R. and the children I completed it in eight days. The women in town, both Orthodox and Unitarian, came up to the work cordially, and sent about sixty dollars' worth of clothing.

I think you will gather from this account that I have had little leisure since you left. Oh dear! how I have missed you. My nest seems so dreary without my kind mate. I have nobody to plague, nobody to scold at, nobody to talk loving nonsense to. I do long to have you get back. Voting day will bring you, of course. If you don't come, I shall put on your old hat and coat, and vote for you.

Alas, I am afraid it is no matter what New England does, since Pennsylvania and Illinois seem likely to go so wrong. My anxiety on the subject has been intense. It seemed as if my heart would burst if I could not do something to help on the election. But all I could do was to write a song for the Free Soil men. If you had been here I should have had somebody to admire my effort, but as it is I don't know whether anybody likes it or not. I have been told that the "Boston Post" was down upon me for the verse about President Pierce. I could n't help it. His name would not rhyme to anything but curse! . . .

The scenery up in that hilly region must indeed be beautiful this sunny autumn. I should mightily enjoy rambling about with you, but then I think the pleasure would be more than balanced by the liability of being called upon by such highly respectable people. I should demur about heaven itself on such terms.

TO MISS LUCY OSGOOD.

WAYLAND, October 28, 1856.

Did you take note of T. W. Higginson's sermon to the people of Lawrence, in Kansas? His text was from the Prophet Nehemiah, commanding the people "to fight for their wives, their children, and their homes." What a convenient book that Old Testament is, whenever there is any fighting to be done. Many people seem to be greatly shocked by Higginson's course; but if they admit that war is ever justifiable, I think they are inconsistent to blame him. If the heroes of '76 were praiseworthy, the heroes of Kansas will be more praiseworthy for maintaining their rights, even unto death. But, "It is treason; it is revolution," they exclaim. They seem to forget that the war of '76 was precisely that. It was a contest with our own government, not with a foreign foe; and the wrongs to be redressed were not worthy of a thought in comparison with the accumulation of outrages upon the free settlers in Kansas. This battle with the overgrown slave power is verily the great battle of Armageddon. I suppose you know that the Supreme Court of the United States has settled everything according to the requisitions of the

South? It has decided that slaves may be brought into the free States, like any other property. Such a decision is in direct opposition to the decision of the Supreme Court of Massachusetts. If the old Commonwealth don't rise in her moral strength at this attempt to lay the yoke on her, why, then, indeed, the spirit of the Puritans and of '76 has died out; and we must all drift together toward a military despotism, with slave-holders for officers and foreigners for soldiers.

TO MRS. S. B. SHAW.

WAYLAND, October 27, 1856.

Your letter accompanying Mr. Curtis's oration came safely to hand. The oration is eloquent, brilliant, manly, and every way admirable. Among the many good things which this crisis has brought forth, I am inclined to pronounce it the best. How glad I am to see Mr. Curtis looming up to such a lofty stature of manliness. This I attribute in part to the crisis, so well adapted to call out all the manhood there is in souls. I smiled to read that he had warmed up N. P. W. to such a degree that he announced his intention to deposit his "virgin vote" for Fremont. It was pleasant to learn that he had anything "virgin" left to swear by. What a Rip! to lie sleeping fifty years, dreaming of kid gloves, embroidered vests, and perfumed handkerchiefs, taking it for granted that his country was all the while going forward in a righteous and glorious career. Isn't it too bad that such parasol-holders should have the right to vote, while earnest souls like you and me must await the result in agonizing inaction? Things look squally; don't they, dear? But while there is life, there is hope. A bright little girl, about five years old, lives near by. She has heard enough of my talk to know that I have Fremont's election deeply at heart, and so she feels bound to keep me booked up during Mr. Child's absence. When she heard her father read that the western counties of Pennsylvania had given a majority for him, she came flying over, and called out, under my window, "*Miss Child!* Pennsylvany's all right," and away she ran. . . . I have been writing for various papers about Kansas. I have been stirring up the women here to make garments for Kansas. . . . Oh, S., you don't realize what a blessing you enjoy in having money enough to obey your generous impulses! The most pinching part of poverty is that which nips such impulses in the bud. But there is compensation in all things. I dare say I took more satisfaction in stitching away at midnight than our friend does in saying to her husband, "My dear, I want one hundred dollars to pay a seamstress for sewing for Kansas."

TO DAVID LEE CHILD

WAYLAND, November 19, 1856.

MY DEAR GOOD DAVID, — Things remain much as when you left. . . . Brother Convers asked me to thank you for your speech. He said he thought it excellent, and remarked that it contained several important facts that were new to him. . . .

How melancholy I felt when you went off in the morning darkness. It seemed as if everything about me was tumbling down; as if I never were to have a nest and a mate any more. Good, kind, generous, magnanimous soul! How I love you. How I long to say over the old prayer again every night. It al most made me cry to see how carefully you had arranged everything for my comfort before you went, — so much kindling stuff split up and the bricks piled up to protect my flowers.

TO MRS. S. B. SHAW.

WAYLAND, December 8, 1856.

Yes, my beloved friend, the old man has gone home;[1] and unless you had had such a charge for three years, you could not imagine how lonely and desolate I feel. Night and day he was on my mind, and now the occupation of my life seems gone. I have much work to do, both mental and manual; but as yet I cannot settle down to work. Always that dreary void! I went to Boston and spent four days; but the dreariness went with me. The old man loved me; and you know how foolishly my nature craves love. . . . Always when I came back from Boston there was a bright fire-light in his room for me, and his hand was eagerly stretched out, and the old face lighted up, as he said, "You're welcome back, Maria." This time, when I came home, it was all dark and silent. I almost cried myself blind, and thought I would willingly be fettered to his bedside for years, if I could only hear that voice again. This is weakness, I know. My spirits will doubtless rebound from the pressure as soon as I can fairly get to work. Work! work! that is my unfailing cure for all troubles. . . .

I am greatly delighted with Mrs. Browning's "Aurora Leigh." It is full of strong things, and brilliant things, and beautiful things. And how glad I am to see modern literature tending so much toward the breaking down of social distinctions!

[1] Death of her father.

TO DAVID LEE CHILD.

WAYLAND, January 7, 1857.

When will my dear good David come? I stayed nine days in Boston, Medford, and Cambridge, and returned here New Year's Day. I had a variety of experiences, nearly all of them pleasant; but they are better to tell than to write. I shall have a great budget to open when you come. I received a letter and a Berkshire paper from you.

Charles Sumner called to see me and brought me his photograph. We talked together two hours, and I never received such an impression of holiness from mortal man. Not an ungentle word did he utter concerning Brooks or any of the political enemies who have been slandering and insulting him for years. He only regretted the existence of a vicious institution which inevitably barbarized those who grew up under its influence.

Henry Wilson came into the anti-slavery fair, and I talked with him an hour or so. He told me I could form no idea of the state of things in Washington. As he passes through the streets in the evening, he says the air is filled with yells and curses from the oyster shops and gambling saloons, the burden of which is all manner of threatened violence to Seward and Sumner and Wilson and Burlingame. While he was making his last speech, the Southern members tried to insult him in every way. One of them actually brandished his cane as if about to strike him, but he ignored the presence of him and his cane, and went on with his speech. He says he never leaves his room to go into the Senate without thinking whether he has left everything arranged as he should wish if he were never to return to it alive.

What do you think Edmund Benson sent me for a Christmas present? An order for one hundred dollars, to be used for Kansas!

TO PROF. CONVERS FRANCIS.

WAYLAND, January 9, 1857.

As for the rank which the world assigns to one avocation over another, I can hardly find words significant enough to express the low estimate I put upon it. The lawyer who feels above the bookseller seems to me just as ridiculous as the orange-woman who objected to selling Hannah More's tracts. "I sell *ballads!*" she exclaimed. "Why, I don't even sell apples!" How absurdly we poor blundering mortals lose sight of the reality of things, under the veil of appearances! In choosing an employment, it seems to me the only question to be asked is, What are we best fitted for? and What do we most enjoy doing?

TO MISS LUCY OSGOOD.

WAYLAND, 1857.

I have lately been much interested about the young Kentucky lady [1] who emancipated all her slaves, in consequence of reading Charles Sumner's speeches. She and I correspond, as mother and daughter, and I should infer from her letters, even if I knew nothing else about her, that she was endowed with a noble, generous, sincere, and enthusiastic nature. It is no slight sacrifice, at nineteen years old, to give up all one's property, and go forth into the world to earn her own living, penniless and friendless; "but I shall earn my living with a light heart, because I shall have a clean conscience." I quote her own words,

[1] Miss Mattie Griffith.

which she wrote in an hour of sadness, in consequence of being cut by friends, reproached by relations, and deluged with insulting letters from every part of the South. Her relatives resort to both coaxing and threatening, to induce her publicly to deny tha she wrote the " Autobiography of a Female Slave." The truthfulness of her nature fires up at this. In one of her letters to me she says, " What a mean thing they would make of me! I'll die first." She is true metal, and rings clear under their blows. Yet she has a loving, womanly heart, made desolate and sad by separation from early friends. We abolitionists ought to rally round the noble young martyr. I wish you had a chance to get acquainted with her. She struck me as quite a remarkable young person.

More and more I become convinced that there is a natural difference in the organization of people. There is Mattie, brought up in a slave-holding community, and under the influence of an intensely aristocratic family, yet, from her earliest years, spontaneously giving all her sympathies to the poor. When she went to school, she was a great pet with a wealthy lady, a friend of her grandfather's. The lady hired a slave of the grandfather, and caused her to be whipped for some offence. Mattie heard of it, on her way from school, and rushed into the lady's house to pour forth her boiling indignation. She called her a " cruel monster," and told her that "the blue flames of hell were preparing for those who treated poor people so!" The lady tried to pacify her, and asked her to sit down and have some cake. " I don't want to sit down in your house!" she exclaimed; and off she went. The grandfather tried to make her apologize to the lady for her rudeness. Finding persuasion useless, he kept her in the garret three days on bread and water. It was of no use, the child always had the same answer. "She is a cruel monster. It is the truth. I am not sorry I said it, and I can't say I am sorry." The grandfather's will gave up to the firmness of her conscientious convictions. M. never apologized. That early incident shows that she is of the stuff martyrs are made of. . . .

I suppose you have heard what a glorious time Mattie had when she emancipated her slaves. They danced and sang and sobbed, and would have kissed her feet, had she permitted. Then they began to think of her, and insisted upon continuing to send their wages to her, because she was not strong enough to work. When she refused, they pleaded hard to send her half their earnings. She wrote to me about it, and added, "I assure you, dear Mrs. Child, there are very few people who know the real beauty of the African character." I believe it.

TO THE SAME.

WAYLAND, 1857.

I have seldom had such a day as the delightful one passed with you and David Wasson. I have marked it in my pilgrimage by a golden pillar, hung with amaranth garlands. I said he was poet, philosopher, and priest. During the evening that I subsequently spent with him I found he was also full of fun. I might have known it, indeed, by those eyes of his, that look out so smiling upon the world. It is many a day since I have met with such a real child of God and Nature. He will not be popular, of course; for

"Souls are dangerous things to carry straight
Through all the spilt saltpetre of this world."

As for "come-outerism," I assure you that if I could only find a church, I would nestle into it as gladly as a bird ever nestled into her covert in a storm. I have stayed away from meeting, because one offered me petrifactions, and another gas, when I was hungry for bread. I have an unfortunate sincerity, which demands living realities, and will not be put off with respectable shams. I sometimes wish it were otherwise; there is such a plenty of respectable shams to be had without the seeking. Another thing that I really feel the want of is one or two sympathizing friends with a sufficient degree of culture to make intercourse easy and mutually agreeable. I am well aware that it is not good to live so much alone as I do; but I see no help for it. Better to be forever alone than to have an indiscriminate inrush of the world into one's sanctum. I find the problem of useful and agreeable social intercourse a very hard one to solve. If our minister, Mr. Sears, were near by, I should scarcely feel the need of any other society; for his mind and heart are full to overflowing. But unfortunately he lives two miles off, on an out-of-the-way road, and it is a job to get to him. He has lately been preaching a series of beautiful sermons on the immortality of the soul. The one last Sunday was on entering upon immortality through the long pathway of old age. It was excellent in itself, and interested me so much by its association with my good old father that I borrowed it, and made copious extracts. To me there is a peculiar charm in Mr. Sears' preaching; for a kind of lunar-halo of Swedenborgianism surrounds it. My first and deepest religious experience came to me through that medium and such an experience is never entirely forgotten by the soul. The angel of my youth calls to me through Mr. Sears' preaching. Ah, would to God he could give me back the undoubting faith, the poetic rapture of spiritual insight, which I then enjoyed! But it cannot be. That was a state of childhood; and childhood will pass away. The intellect will call aloud to the Infinite, and it receives no answer but the echo of its own voice. If the problem of our existence is not solved elsewhere, how cruel must be the Being that placed us here! Meanwhile, nothing surprises me more than that men should judge so harshly of each other for believing, or not believing, since it is a thing obviously beyond our control. The man educated at Seville cannot see spiritual things in the same light that they are seen by the man educated in Boston. At fifty years of age, it is out of our power to believe many things that we believed at twenty. Our states have changed by slow degrees, as the delicate blossom changes to the dry seed-vessel. We may weep for the lost blossom, but it avails not. "Violets dead the sweetest showers will ne'er make grow again." But, thanks to the Heavenly Father, in the dry seed-vessel lies the embryo of future flowers!

TO MRS. S. B. SHAW.

WAYLAND, 1857.

It is a dark, drizzling day, and I am going to make sunshine for myself by sitting down before the old fire-place and having a cosy chat with you. Did you see Mr. H——'s sermon, preached soon after his return from Palestine? He thinks the truth of the Bible is proved by the fact that Jordan is still flowing and the Mount of Olives still standing. He says his faith was greatly strengthened by a sight of them

By the same token he ought to consider Grecian mythology proved, because Olympus and Parnassus are still standing; and a sight of them ought to strengthen his faith in Jupiter and the Muses. What a fuss they have made about finding the name of Jonah among the inscriptions at Nineveh! Does that prove that the whale swallowed him, and that he did not "set easy" on the whale's stomach? I can never get over wondering at the external tendency of a large class of minds.

TO MISS ANNA LORING.

WAYLAND, December 10, 1857.

I wanted very much to introduce to you a baby I met in the cars. She was a fat little thing, not two years old, but as quick as a steel-trap. She was on the opposite side of the cars, but insisted upon trying to stretch her short fat arm across to me, with her hand open, repeating, "How do?" "I am pretty well," said I. "How do you do?" "Mart" (smart), was her quick reply. And this scene she wanted to enact every five minutes, to the great amusement of those around her. At last a little boy came in, about a year older than herself, and was placed on the seat behind her. Feeling the necessity of keeping up the character of her sex for propriety, she took a good deal of trouble to get at him, and push him, saying, "You do 'way! you do 'way!" The boy, who seemed to be as timid as she was "mart," shrunk himself up as close as possible, probably having a prophetic sense of the position it becomes his sex to assume, if they regard their own safety, in these days when women are getting to be so "mart." At last he climbed the seat and turned his back to her. . .

She could not stand being taken no notice of. So she swung her little fat person over the back of her seat, to the imminent peril of falling, and began to poke at him, calling out, "Boy! boy!" He completely withdrew her attention from me. But I could n't help watching her, she was such a funny little impersonation of human nature. I fell to moralizing, thinking to myself what a cheerful world it would be if we all ignored ranks and sexes and sects and barriers of all sorts, and went about with open palm outstretched to everybody, saying, "How do?" If we could only do that, the world's answer would always be, "Mart."

TO MISS LUCY OSGOOD.

WAYLAND, 1858.

I was just about answering your welcome letter, when that overwhelming blow[1] came suddenly, and for a time seemed to crush all life and hope out of me. Nothing but the death of my kind husband could have caused me such bitter grief. Then came your precious letter of sympathy and condolence. I thanked you for it, from the depths of my suffering heart; but I did not feel as if I could summon energy to write to any but the bereaved ones of his own household. You know that he was a valuable friend to me, but no one but myself could know how valuable. For thirty years he has been my chief reliance. In moral perplexities I always went to him for counsel, and he never failed to clear away every cloud. In all worldly troubles I went to him, and always found a judicious adviser, a sympathizing friend, a generous helper. He was only two months

[1] Death of Ellis Gray Loring.

younger than myself, but I had so long been accustomed to lean upon him, that the thought never occurred to me that it was possible that I might be left in the world without him. All my plans for old age were based upon him; all my little property was in his hands; and if I had ever so small a sum, even ten dollars, for which I had no immediate use, he put it on interest, though it were but for a single month. But the loss in this point of view seems trifling compared to the desolation his death has made in my affections. If I could only hear his gentle voice again, I would be willing to throw all the dollars into the sea. Oh, this dreadful silence! How heavily the dark veil drops down between us and that unknown world! Whether it be the vividness of memory, or whether he is actually near me, I know not, — but I have the impression of the perpetual presence of his spirit with singular distinctness. The presence, be it real or imaginary, has the same influence over me that he always had while on earth. It soothes me, makes me feel calm and strong. I think your friend Samuel Johnson wrote the best hymn for the occasion I ever read. I mean the one he wrote for Mr. Longfellow. Blessings be with you.

TO DAVID LEE CHILD.

WAYLAND, June 20, 1858.

I was thankful to receive your kind letter. You say you hope we had some drops of rain here. Such a storm as we had I have seldom witnessed. The day after you went away, there came one of those dreadful hurricanes of wind, smashing my flowers and tearing everything, right and left. I was in hopes it would go down with the sun, but it did not.

Whenever I woke in the night I heard everything rocking and reeling. In the morning I went to look after the poor little sparrow in the rose-bush, whom I had seen the day before, shutting her eyes hard and sticking tight to her nest, which was tossed about like a ship in a heavy gale. I wanted much to help her, but could not. Next morning I found the nest nearly wrenched from the bush and two of the eggs on the ground. They were still warm, so I replaced them, righted the nest and fastened it to the twigs with strings. To my great surprise she returned to her patient labor of incubation. . . .

Mrs. S. returned on Friday, and I went as far as Boston with her. The day was so intensely hot that I regretted having put my head into the city. But as I was toiling along I heard a voice behind me exclaim, "Maria Child!" I turned and recognized John G. Whittier. He said he had missed the cars by some mistake, but now he felt the disappointment was providential; he had for a long time so wanted to see me. I could not bear to go into the office where I had been accustomed to take my friends. I knew the empty chair of that dear lost friend[1] would be too much for me. So I asked him into H.'s office, and there we chatted an hour. Mrs. S. regretted your absence, left kind remembrances for you, and told me I was " a happy woman to have a husband that wrote me such charming love letters." I told her I thought so too.

[1] Ellis Gray Loring.

TO PROF. CONVERS FRANCIS.

WAYLAND, August 8, 1858.

I think you have done a vast amount of good in many ways. Your conversation always tends to enlarge and liberalize the minds with which you come in contact; more than a dozen times I have heard people speak of the good your sympathizing words have done them in times of affliction; and for myself, I can say most truly before God that I consider such intellectual culture as I have mainly attributable to your influence; and most sincerely can I say, moreover, that up to this present hour I prize a chance for communion with your mind more than I do with any other person I know. . . . In a literary point of view, I know that I have only a local reputation, "done in water-colors." . . . I am not what I aspired to be in my days of young ambition; but I have become humble enough to be satisfied with the conviction that what I have written has always been written conscientiously; that I have always spoken with sincerity, if not with power.' In every direction I see young giants rushing past me, at times pushing me somewhat rudely in their speed, but I am glad to see such strong laborers to plough the land and sow the seed for coming years.

TO MRS. S. B. SHAW.

WAYLAND, 1858.

There is compensation in all things. My ignorance and my poverty both have their advantages. You can never take such child-like delight in a little picture, engraving, or statuette, as I do. Now, while I write, Beauty keeps drawing me away from my letter. I stop with my pen poised in air, to contemplate my Galatea, my St. Cecilia, my Flying Hour of the Night, my palace in Venice, my young Bacchus, my glowing nasturtium, and my vase of tremulous grass. Decidedly, there are many compensations for those who are poor, and have never seen the world.

The landscape in front of the window is lovely. No sharp frost has come to blight the foliage, and the scenery is like a handsome woman of fifty, whom Time has touched so lightly that her girlish delicacy of beauty is merely deepened and warmed with a few autumnal tints. Thus gently may you glide into the frosted silver of a bright old age! It must be so, dearest, because so many are cheered by your heart warmth.

TO MRS. LUCY OSGOOD.

WAYLAND, January 16, 1859.

I have buckled to Buckle's "History of Civilization," though I said I would not read it because I dreaded being made uncomfortable by the point of view from which he looks at things. This making moral progress depend entirely on intellectual progress seems to turn things so inside out that it twists my poor brain. I care more that the world should grow better, than it should grow wiser. The external must be developed from the internal. It makes my head ache to look at human growth from any other point of view. That is the great mistake of Fourier. He is wise and great, and often prophetic, but he thinks to produce perfect men by surrounding them with perfect circumstances; whereas the perfect circumstances must be the result of perfect men. How can the marriage relation, for instance, be well ordered, until men and women are more pure? I have no sympathy with the doctrine that

> "The body, not the soul,
> Governs the unfettered whole."

Then I am tempted full strongly enough to believe Emerson's axiom, "We only row, we 're steered by Fate," without having Buckle write a bulky volume to convince me; for when I think I am steered, I immediately become tired of rowing. But there is no help for it. I must read every word of Buckle. It seems to me the most remarkable book of the age; bold, clear, strong, comprehensive, candid, and, above all, free. He pulls out all the linch-pins from the wheels of Juggernaut without any sign of hesitation. "Some think it will spoil the old cart; and they pretend to say there are valuable things in it which may get hurt. Hope not — hope not." The fact is, I shall never be easy till you read it, and write me your opinion of it. It delights me, with none of the modern affectations of style; no resuscitated words, whose only merit is their obsoleteness; no inverted sentences; no parentheses within parentheses; no clouds of language between the reader and the subject; no vague Orphic sayings, which may mean one thing, or another thing, or no thing. "Which things I hate," as saith the apostle. I get so vexed with writers that send me to the dictionary a dozen times an hour to decipher my own language! It 's the fashion nowadays. I suppose it was in ancient times also, for doth not Aristophanes say, "I hate their peacock trains, their six-foot words, and swell of ostentation"? None of this in Buckle. He is a full, deep river, showing clearly every pebble over which it flows. But I don't agree with all his statements. He says that moral truths were exactly the same as they are now ages ago; that intellect is the sole cause of progress. Now I have considerable to say on that subject; but I want to hear what you have to say. Perhaps the term he uses is more at fault than the idea he intends to convey.

LINES WRITTEN BY MRS. CHILD ON THE ANNIVERSARY OF THE DEATH OF ELLIS GRAY LORING.[1]

May 24, 1859.

Again the trees are clothed in vernal green;
Again the waters flow in silvery sheen;
But all this beauty through a mist I see,
For earth bloomed thus when thou wert lost to me.

The flowers come back, the tuneful birds return,
But thou for whom my spirit still doth yearn
Art gone from me to spheres so bright and far,
Thou seem'st the spirit of some distant star.

O for some telegram from thee, my friend!
Some whispered answer to the love I send!
Or one brief glance from those dear guileless eyes,
That smiled to me so sweetly thy replies.

My heart is hungry for thy gentle ways,
Thy friendly counsels, and thy precious praise;
I seem to travel through the dark alone,
Since thou, my wisest, truest guide art gone.

And yet at times so near thou art to me
That each good thought seems still inspired by thee:
I almost hear thee say, "Fear not, my friend,
That friendship pure and loyal e'er can end."

[1] These verses of Mrs. Child, though written on the first anniversary of Mr. Loring's death, were not published till some years after, which accounts for the allusions to the extinction of slavery in Mr. Whittier's response.

O keep me ever near thy holy sphere,
O guide and help me as thou didst while here,
For still I lean on thy pure, faithful heart,
Angel or seraph, wheresoe'er thou art.

LINES TO L. M. CHILD, IN RESPONSE TO HER VERSES ON THE DEATH OF ELLIS GRAY LORING.

BY JOHN G. WHITTIER.

The sweet spring day is glad with music,
    But through it sounds a sadder strain,
The worthiest of our narrowing circle
    Sings Loring's dirges o'er again.

O woman greatly loved! I join thee
    In tender memories of our friend;
With thee across the awful spaces,
    The greeting of a soul I send.

What cheer hath he? How is it with him?
    Where lingers he this weary while?
Over what pleasant fields of heaven
    Dawns the sweet sunshine of his smile?

Does he not know our feet are treading
    The earth hard down on Slavery's grave?
That in our crowning exultations
    We miss the charm his presence gave?

Why on this spring air comes no whisper
    From him to tell us all is well?
Why to our flower time comes no token
    Of lily and of asphodel?

I feel the unutterable longing,
    Thy hunger of the heart is mine;
I reach and grasp for hands in darkness,
    My ear grows sharp for voice or sign.

Still on the lips of all we question,
　The finger of God's silence lies;
Will the lost hands in ours be folded?
　Will the shut eyelids ever rise?

O friend, no proof beyond this yearning,
　This outreach of our hearts, we need;
God will not mock the hope he giveth,
　No love he prompts shall vainly plead.

Then let us stretch our hands in darkness,
　And call our loved ones o'er and o'er;
Some day their arms shall close about us,
　And the old voices speak once more.

No dreary splendors wait our coming
　Where rapt ghost sits from ghost apart;
Homeward we go to Heaven's thanksgiving,
　The harvest gathering of the heart.

CORRESPONDENCE BETWEEN MRS. CHILD, JOHN BROWN, AND GOVERNOR WISE AND MRS. MASON OF VIRGINIA.

TO GOVERNOR HENRY A. WISE.

WAYLAND, Mass., October 26, 1859.

GOVERNOR WISE, — I have heard that you were a man of chivalrous sentiments, and I know you were opposed to the iniquitous attempt to force upon Kansas a Constitution abhorrent to the moral sense of her people. Relying upon these indications of honor and justice in your character, I venture to ask a favor of you. Inclosed is a letter to Captain John Brown.

Will you have the kindness, after reading it yourself, to transmit it to the prisoner?

I and all my large circle of abolition acquaintances were taken by surprise when news came of Captain Brown's recent attempt; nor do I know of a single person who would have approved of it, had they been apprised of his intention. But I and thousands of others feel a natural impulse of sympathy for the brave and suffering man. Perhaps God, who sees the inmost of our souls, perceives some such sentiment in your heart also. He needs a mother or sister to dress his wounds, and speak soothingly to him. Will you allow me to perform that mission of humanity? If you will, may God bless you for the generous deed!

I have been for years an uncompromising abolitionist, and I should scorn to deny it or apologize for it as much as John Brown himself would do. Believing in peace principles, I deeply regret the step that the old veteran has taken, while I honor his humanity towards those who became his prisoners. But because it is my habit to be as open as the daylight, I will also say, that if I believed our religion justified men in fighting for freedom, I should consider the enslaved everywhere as best entitled to that right. Such an avowal is a simple, frank expression of my sense of natural justice.

But I should despise myself utterly if any circumstances could tempt me to seek to advance these opinions in any way, directly or indirectly, after your permission to visit Virginia has been obtained on the plea of sisterly sympathy with a brave and suffering man. I give you my word of honor, which was never broken, that I would use such permission solely and singly for the purpose of nursing your prisoner, and for no other purpose whatsoever.

Yours respectfully,

L. MARIA CHILD.

REPLY OF GOVERNOR WISE.

RICHMOND, Va., October 29, 1859.

MADAM, — Yours of the 26th was received by me yesterday, and at my earliest leisure I respectfully reply to it, that I will forward the letter for John Brown, a prisoner under our laws, arraigned at the Circuit Court for the county of Jefferson, at Charlestown, Va., for the crimes of murder, robbery, and treason, which you ask me to transmit to him. I will comply with your request in the only way which seems to me proper, by inclosing it to the Commonwealth's attorney, with the request that he will ask the permission of the court to hand it to the prisoner. Brown, the prisoner, is now in the hands of the judiciary, not of the executive, of this Commonwealth.

You ask me, further, to allow you to perform the mission "of mother or sister, to dress his wounds, and speak soothingly to him." By this, of course, you mean to be allowed to visit him in his cell, and to minister to him in the offices of humanity. Why should you not be so allowed, Madam? Virginia and Massachusetts are involved in no civil war, and the Constitution which unites them in one confederacy guaranties to you the privileges and immunities of a citizen of the United States in the State of Virginia. That Constitution I am sworn to support, and am, therefore, bound to protect your privileges and immunities as a citizen of Massachusetts coming into Virginia for any lawful and peaceful purpose.

Coming, as you propose, to minister to the captive in prison, you will be met, doubtless, by all our people, not only in a chivalrous, but in a Christian spirit. You have the right to visit Charlestown, Va., Madam; and your mission, being merciful and humane, will not only be allowed, but respected, if not welcomed. A few unenlightened and inconsiderate persons, fanatical in their modes of thought and action to maintain justice and right, might molest you, or be disposed to do so; and this might suggest the imprudence of risking any experiment upon the peace of a society very much excited by the crimes with whose chief author you seem to sympathize so much. But still, I repeat, your motives and avowed purpose are lawful and peaceful, and I will, as far as I am concerned, do my duty in protecting your rights in our limits. Virginia and her authorities would be weak indeed — weak in point of folly, and weak in point of power — if her State faith and constitutional obligations cannot be redeemed in her own limits to the letter of morality as well as of law; and if her chivalry cannot courteously receive a lady's visit to a prisoner, every arm which guards Brown from rescue on the one hand, and from lynch law on the other, will be ready to guard your person in Virginia.

I could not permit an insult even to woman in her walk of charity among us, though it be to one who whetted knives of butchery for our mothers, sisters, daughters, and babes. We have no sympathy with your sentiments of sympathy with Brown, and are surprised that you were "taken by surprise when news came of Captain Brown's recent attempt." His attempt was a natural consequence of your sympathy, and the errors of that sympathy ought to make you doubt its virtue from the effect on his conduct. But it is not of this I should speak. When you arrive at Charlestown, if you go there, it will be for the court and its officers, the Commonwealth's attorney, sheriff and jailer, to say whether you may see and wait on the prisoner. But, whether you are thus permitted or not (and you will be, if my advice can prevail), you may rest assured that he will be humanely, lawfully, and mercifully dealt by in prison and on trial.

Respectfully, HENRY A. WISE.

MRS. CHILD TO GOVERNOR WISE.

In your civil but very diplomatic reply to my letter, you inform me that I have a constitutional right to visit Virginia, for peaceful purposes, in common with every citizen of the United States. I was perfectly well aware that such was the *theory* of constitutional obligation in the slave States; but I was also aware of what you omit to mention, viz.: that the Constitution has, in reality, been completely and systematically nullified, whenever it suited the convenience or the policy of the slave power. Your constitutional obligation, for which you profess so much respect, has never proved any protection to citizens of the free States who happened to have a black, brown, or yellow complexion; nor to any white citizen whom you even suspected of entertaining opinions opposite to your own, on a question of vast importance to the temporal welfare and moral example of our common country. This total disregard of constitutional obligation has been manifested not merely by the lynch law of mobs in the slave States, but by the deliberate action of magistrates and legislators. What regard was paid to constitutional obligation in South Carolina, when Massachusetts sent the Hon. Mr. Hoar there as an envoy, on a purely legal errand? Mr. Hedrick, Professor of Political Economy in the University of North Carolina, had a constitutional right to reside in that State. What regard was paid to that right, when he was driven from his home merely for declaring that he considered slavery an impolitic system, injurious to the prosperity of States? What respect for constitutional rights was manifested by Alabama, when a bookseller in Mobile was compelled to flee for his life, because he had, at the special request of some of the citizens, imported a few copies of a novel that everybody was curious to read? Your own citizen, Mr. Underwood, had a constitutional right to live in Virginia and vote for whomsoever he pleased. What regard was paid to his rights, when he was driven from your State for declaring himself in favor of the election of Fremont? With these and a multitude of other examples before your eyes, it would seem as if the less that was said about respect for constitutional obligations at the South, the better. Slavery is, in fact, an infringement of all law, and adheres to no law, save for its own purposes of oppression.

You accuse Captain John Brown of "whetting knives of butchery for the mothers, sisters, daughters, and babes" of Virginia; and you inform me of the well-known fact, that he is "arraigned for the crimes of murder, robbery, and treason." I will not here stop to explain why I believe that old hero to be no criminal, but a martyr to righteous principles which he sought to advance by methods sanctioned by his own religious views, though not by mine. Allowing that Captain Brown did attempt a scheme in which mur der, robbery, and treason were, to his own consciousness, involved, I do not see how Governor Wise can consistently arraign him for crimes he has himself commended. *You* have threatened to trample on the Constitution, and break the Union, if a majority of the legal voters in these confederated States dared to elect a President unfavorable to the extension of slavery. Is not such a declaration proof of premeditated treason? In the spring of 1842 you made a speech in Congress, from which I copy the following: —

"Once set before the people of the great valley the conquest of the rich Mexican provinces, and you might as well attempt to stop the wind. This government might send its troops, but they would run over them like a herd of buffalo. Let the work once begin, and I do not know that this House would hold *me* very long. Give me five millions of dollars, and I would undertake to do it myself. Although I do not know how to set a single squadron in the field, I could find men to do it. Slavery should pour itself abroad, without restraint, and find no limit but the southern ocean. The Camanches should no longer hold the richest mines of Mexico. Every golden image which had received the profanation of a false worship should soon be melted down into good American eagles. I would cause as much gold to cross the Rio del Norte as the mules of Mexico could carry; aye, and I would make better use of it, too, than any lazy, bigoted priesthood under heaven."

When you thus boasted that you and your "booted loafers" would overrun the troops of the United States "like a herd of buffalo," if the government sent them to arrest your invasion of a neighboring nation, at peace with the United States, did you not pledge yourself to commit treason? Was it not by robbery, even of churches, that you proposed to load the mules of Mexico with gold for the United States? Was it not by the murder of unoffending Mexicans that you expected to advance those schemes of avarice and ambition? What humanity had you for Mexican "mothers and babes," whom you proposed to make childless and fatherless? And for what purpose was this wholesale massacre to take place? Not to right the wrongs of any oppressed class; not to sustain any great principles of justice, or of freedom; but merely to enable "slavery to pour itself forth without restraint."

Even if Captain Brown were as bad as you paint him, I should suppose he must naturally remind you of the words of Macbeth:—

> "We but teach
> Bloody instructions, which, being taught, return
> To plague the inventor: this even-handed justice
> Commends the ingredients of our poisoned chalice
> To our own lips."

If Captain Brown intended, as you say, to commit treason, robbery, and murder, I think I have shown that he could find ample authority for such proceedings in the public declarations of Governor Wise. And if, as he himself declares, he merely intended to free the oppressed, where could he read a more forcible lesson than is furnished by the state seal of Virginia? I looked at it thoughtfully before I opened your letter; and though it had always appeared to me very suggestive, it never seemed to me so much so as it now did in connection with Captain John Brown. A liberty-loving hero stands with his foot upon a prostrate despot; under his strong arm, manacles and chains lie broken; and the motto is, "*Sic Semper Tyrannis;*" "Thus be it ever done to tyrants." And this is the blazon of a State whose most profitable business is the internal slave-trade! — in whose highways coffles of human chattels, chained and manacled, are frequently seen! And the seal and the coffles are both looked upon by other chattels, constantly exposed to the same fate! What if some Vezey, or Nat Turner, should be growing up among those apparently quiet spectators? It is in no spirit of taunt or of exultation that I ask this question. I never think of it but with anxiety, sadness, and sympathy. I know that a slave-holding community necessarily lives in the midst of gunpowder; and, in this age, sparks of free thought are flying in every direction. You cannot quench the fires of free thought and human sympathy by any process of cunning or force; but there is a method by which you can effectually wet the gunpowder. England has already tried it, with safety and success. Would that you could be persuaded to set aside the prejudices of education, and candidly examine the actual working of that experiment! Virginia is so richly endowed by nature that free institutions alone are wanting to render her the most prosperous and powerful of the States.

In your letter you suggest that such a scheme as Captain Brown's is the natural result of the opinions with which I sympathize. Even if I thought this to be a correct statement, though I should deeply regret it, I could not draw the conclusion that humanity ought to be stifled, and truth struck dumb, for fear that long-successful despotism might be endangered by their utterance. But the fact is, you mistake the source of that strange outbreak. No abolition arguments or denunciations, however earnestly, loudly, or harshly proclaimed, would have produced that result.

It was the legitimate consequence of the continual and constantly-increasing aggressions of the slave power. The slave States, in their desperate efforts to sustain a bad and dangerous institution, have encroached more and more upon the liberties of the free States. Our inherent love of law and order, and our superstitious attachment to the Union, you have mistaken for cowardice; and rarely have you let slip any opportunity to add insult to aggression.

The manifested opposition to slavery began with the lectures and pamphlets of a few disinterested men and women, who based their movements upon purely moral and religious grounds; but their expostulations were met with a storm of rage, with tar and feathers, brickbats, demolished houses, and other applications of lynch law. When the dust of the conflict began to subside a little, their numbers were found to be greatly increased by the efforts to exterminate them. They had become an influence in the State too important to be overlooked by shrewd calculators. Political economists began to look at the subject from a lower point of view. They used their abilities to demonstrate that slavery was a wasteful system, and that the free States were taxed to an enormous extent to sustain an institution which, at heart, two thirds of them abhorred. The forty millions, or more, of dollars expended in hunting fugitive slaves in Florida, under the name of the Seminole War, were adduced, as one item of proof, to which many more were added. At last politicians were compelled to take some action on the subject. It soon became known to all the people that the slave States had always managed to hold in their hands the political power of the Union, and that while they constituted only one third of the white population of these States, they held more than two thirds of all the lucrative, and once honorable, offices; an indignity to which none but a subjugated people had ever before submitted. The knowledge also became generally diffused that, while the Southern States *owned* their Democracy at home, and voted for them, they also systematically *bribed* the nominally Democratic party at the North with the offices adroitly kept at their disposal.

Through these and other instrumentalities, the sentiments of the original Garrisonian abolitionists became very widely extended, in forms more or less diluted. But by far the most efficient co-laborers we have ever had have been the slave States themselves. By denying us the sacred right of petition, they roused the free spirit of the North as it never could have been roused by the loud trumpet of Garrison or the soul-animating bugle of Phillips. They bought the great slave, Daniel, and, according to their established usage, paid him no wages for his labor. By his coöperation they forced the Fugitive Slave Law upon us in violation of all our humane instincts and all our principles of justice. And what did they procure for the abolitionists by that despotic process? A deeper and wider detestation of slavery throughout the free States, and the publication of "Uncle Tom's Cabin," an eloquent outburst of moral indignation, whose echoes wakened the world to look upon their shame.

By filibustering and fraud they dismembered Mexico, and, having thus obtained the soil of Texas, they tried to introduce it as a slave State into the Union. Failing to effect their purpose by constitutional means, they accomplished it by a most open and palpable violation of the Constitution, and by obtaining the votes of senators on false pretenses.[1]

Soon afterward a Southern slave administration ceded to the powerful monarchy of Great Britain several hundred thousands of square miles that must have been made into free States, to which that same administration had declared that the United States had "an unquestionable right;" and then they turned upon the weak republic of Mexico, and, in order to make more slave States, wrested from her twice as many hundred thousands of square miles, to which we had not a shadow of right.

Notwithstanding all these extra efforts, they saw symptoms that the political power so long held with a firm grasp was in danger of slipping from their hands, by reason of the extension of abolition sentiments, and the greater prosperity of free States. Emboldened by continual success in aggression, they made use of the pretence of "squatter sovereignty" to break the league into which they had formerly cajoled the servile representatives of our blinded people, by which all the territory of the United States south of 36° 30' was guarantied to slavery, and all north of it to freedom. Thus Kansas became the battle-ground of the antagonistic elements in our government. Ruffians hired by the slave power were sent thither temporarily to do the voting and drive from the polls the legal voters, who were often murdered in the process. Names copied from the

---

[1] The following senators, Mr. Niles of Connecticut, Mr. Dix of New York, and Mr. Tappan of Ohio, published statements that their votes had been obtained by false representations; and they declared that the case was the same with Mr. Heywood of North Carolina.

directories of cities in other States were returned by thousands as legal voters in Kansas, in order to establish a Constitution abhorred by the people. This was their exemplification of squatter sovereignty. A Massachusetts senator, distinguished for candor, courtesy, and stainless integrity, was half murdered by slave-holders merely for having the manliness to state these facts to the assembled Congress of the nation. Peaceful emigrants from the North, who went to Kansas for no other purpose than to till the soil, erect mills, and establish manufactories, schools, and churches, were robbed, outraged, and murdered. For many months a war more ferocious than the warfare of wild Indians was carried on against a people almost unresisting, because they relied upon the central government for aid. And all this while the power of the United States, wielded by the slave oligarchy, was on the side of the aggressors. This was the state of things when the hero of Ossawatomie and his brave sons went to the rescue. It was he who first turned the tide of border-ruffian triumph, by showing them that blows were to be taken as well as given.

You may believe it or not, Governor Wise, but it is certainly the truth that, because slave-holders so recklessly sowed the wind in Kansas, they reaped a whirlwind at Harper's Ferry.

The people of the North had a very strong attachment to the Union; but by your desperate measures you have weakened it beyond all power of restoration. They are not your enemies, as you suppose, but they cannot consent to be your tools for any ignoble task you may choose to propose. You must not judge of us by the crawling sinuosities of an Everett; or by our magnificent hound, whom you trained to hunt your poor cripples,[1] and then sent him sneaking into a corner to die — not with shame for the base purposes to which his strength had been applied, but with vexation because you withheld from him the promised bone. Not by such as these must you judge the free, enlightened yeomanry of New England. A majority of them would rejoice to have the slave States fulfil their oft-repeated threat of withdrawal from the Union. It has ceased to be a bugbear, for we begin to despair of being able, by any other process, to give the world the example of a real republic. The moral sense of these States is outraged by being accomplices in sustaining an institution vicious in all its aspects; and it is now generally understood that we purchase our disgrace at great pecuniary expense. If you would only make the offer of a separation in serious earnest, you would hear the hearty response of millions, "Go, gentlemen, and

> 'Stand not upon the order of your going,
> But go at once!'"

Yours, with all due respect,

L. MARIA CHILD.

EXPLANATORY LETTER.

TO THE EDITOR OF THE NEW YORK TRIBUNE:

SIR, — I was much surprised to see my correspondence with Governor Wise published in your columns. As I have never given any person a copy, I presume you must have obtained it from Virginia. My proposal to go and nurse that brave and generous old man, who so willingly gives his life a sacrifice for God's oppressed poor, originated in a very simple

---

[1] Alluding to Daniel Webster and the Fugitive Slave Law.

and unmeritorious impulse of kindness. I heard his friends inquiring, "Has he no wife, or sister, that can go to nurse him? We are trying to ascertain, for he needs some one." My niece said she would go at once, if her health were strong enough to be trusted. I replied that my age and state of health rendered me a more suitable person to go, and that I would go most gladly. I accordingly wrote to Captain Brown, and inclosed the letter to Governor Wise. My intention was to slip away quietly, without having the affair made public. I packed my trunk and collected a quantity of old linen for lint, and awaited tidings from Virginia. When Governor Wise answered, he suggested the "imprudence of trying any experiment upon the peace of a society already greatly excited," etc. My husband and I took counsel together, and we both concluded that, as the noble old veteran was said to be fast recovering from his wounds, and as my presence might create a popular excitement unfavorable to such chance as the prisoner had for a fair trial, I had better wait until I received a reply from Captain Brown himself. Fearing to do him more harm than good by following my impulse, I waited for his own sanction. Meanwhile, his wife, said to be a brave-hearted Roman matron, worthy of such a mate, has gone to him, and I have received the following reply.

Respectfully yours,

L. Maria Child.

Boston, November 10, 1859.

MRS. CHILD TO JOHN BROWN.

WAYLAND [Mass.], October 26, 1859.

DEAR CAPTAIN BROWN: Though personally unknown to you, you will recognize in my name an earnest friend of Kansas, when circumstances made that Territory the battle-ground between the antagonistic principles of slavery and freedom, which politicians so vainly strive to reconcile in the government of the United States.

Believing in peace principles, I cannot sympathize with the method you chose to advance the cause of freedom. But I honor your generous intentions, — I admire your courage, moral and physical. I reverence you for the humanity which tempered your zeal. I sympathize with you in your cruel bereavement, your sufferings, and your wrongs. In brief, I love you and bless you.

Thousands of hearts are throbbing with sympathy as warm as mine. I think of you night and day, bleeding in prison, surrounded by hostile faces, sustained only by trust in God and your own strong heart. I long to nurse you — to speak to you sisterly words of sympathy and consolation. I have asked permission of Governor Wise to do so. If the request is not granted, I cherish the hope that these few words may at least reach your hands, and afford you some little solace. May you be strengthened by the conviction that no honest man ever sheds blood for freedom in vain, however much he may be mistaken in his efforts. May God sustain you, and carry you through whatsoever may be in store for you! Yours, with heartfelt respect, sympathy and affection, L. MARIA CHILD.

REPLY OF JOHN BROWN.

Mrs. L. Maria Child:

My Dear Friend, — Such you prove to be, though a stranger, — your most kind letter has reached me, with the kind offer to come here and take care of me. Allow me to express my gratitude for your great sympathy, and at the same time to propose to you a different course, together with my reasons for wishing it. I should certainly be greatly pleased to become personally acquainted with one so gifted and so kind, but I cannot avoid seeing some objections to it, under present circumstances. First, I am in charge of a most humane gentleman, who, with his family, has rendered me every possible attention I have desired, or that could be of the least advantage; and I am so recovered of my wounds as no longer to require nursing. Then, again, it would subject you to great personal inconvenience and heavy expense, without doing me any good. Allow me to name to you another channel through which you may reach me with your sympathies much more effectually. I have at home a wife and three young daughters, the youngest but little over five years old, the oldest nearly sixteen. I have also two daughters-in-law, whose husbands have both fallen near me here. There is also another widow, Mrs. Thompson, whose husband fell here. Whether she is a mother or not, I cannot say. All these, my wife included, live at North Elba, Essex county, New York. I have a middle-aged son, who has been, in some degree, a cripple from his childhood, who would have as much as he could well do to earn a living. He was a most dreadful sufferer in Kansas, and lost all he had laid up. He has not enough to clothe himself for the winter comfortably. I have no living son, or son-in-law, who did not suffer terribly in Kansas.

Now, dear friend, would you not as soon contribute fifty cents now, and a like sum yearly, for the relief of those very poor and deeply afflicted persons, to enable them to supply themselves and their children with bread and very plain clothing, and to enable the children to receive a common English education? Will you also devote your own energies to induce others to join you in giving a like amount, or any other amount, to constitute a little fund for the purpose named?

I cannot see how your coming here can do me the least good; and I am quite certain you can do immense good where you are. I am quite cheerful under all my afflicting circumstances and prospects; having, as I humbly trust, "the peace of God which passeth all understanding" to rule in my heart. You may make such use of this as you see fit. God Almighty bless and reward you a thousand fold!

Yours in sincerity and truth,
JOHN BROWN.

LETTER OF MRS. MASON.

ALTO, King George's Co., Va., November 11, 1859.

Do you read your Bible, Mrs. Child? If you do, read there, "Woe unto you, hypocrites," and take to yourself with twofold damnation that terrible sentence; for, rest assured, in the day of judgment it shall be more tolerable for those thus scathed by the awful denunciation of the Son of God, than for you. *You* would soothe with sisterly and motherly care the hoary-headed murderer of Harper's Ferry! A man whose aim and intention was to incite the horrors of a servile war — to condemn women of your own race, ere death closed their eyes on their sufferings from violence and outrage, to see their husbands and fathers murdered, their children butchered, the ground strewed with the brains of their babes. The antecedents of Brown's band proved them to have been the offscourings of the earth; and what would have been our fate had they found as many sympathizers in Virginia as they seem to have in Massachusetts?

Now, compare yourself with those your "sympathy" would devote to such ruthless ruin, and say, on that "word of honor, which never has been broken," would *you* stand by the bedside of an old negro, dying of a hopeless disease, to alleviate his suffering as far as human aid could? Have *you* ever watched the last, lingering illness of a consumptive, to soothe, as far as in you lay, the inevitable fate? Do *you* soften the pangs of maternity in those around you by all the care and comfort you can give? Do *you* grieve with those *near* you, even though their sorrows resulted from their own misconduct? Did *you* ever sit up until the "wee hours" to complete a dress for a motherless child, that she might appear on Christmas Day in a new one, along with her more fortunate companions? *We* do these and more for our servants, and why? Because we endeavor *to do our duty in that state of life it has pleased God to place us.* In his revealed word we read our duties to them — theirs to us are there also — "Not only to the good and gentle, but also to the froward." (1 Peter ii. 18.) Go thou and do likewise, and keep away from Charlestown. If the stories read in the public prints be true, of the sufferings of the poor of the North, you need not go far for objects of charity. "Thou hypocrite! take first the beam out of thine own eye, then shalt thou see clearly to pull the mote out of thy neighbor's." But if, indeed, you do lack objects of sympathy near you, go to Jefferson County, to the family of George Turner, a noble, true-hearted man, whose devotion to his friend (Colonel Washington) causing him to risk his life, was shot down like a dog. Or to that of old Beckham, whose grief at the murder of his negro subordinate made him needlessly expose himself to the aim of the assassin Brown. And when you can equal in deeds of love and charity to those *around* you, what is shown by nine tenths of the Virginia plantations, then by your "sympathy" whet the knives for our throats, and kindle the torch that fires our homes. *You* reverence Brown for his clemency to his prisoners! Prisoners! and how taken? Unsuspecting workmen, going to their daily duties; unarmed gentlemen, taken from their beds at the dead hour of the night, by six men doubly and trebly armed. Suppose he had hurt a hair of their heads, do you suppose one of the band of desperadoes would have left the engine-house alive? And did he not know that his treatment of them was his only hope of life then, or of clemency afterward? Of course he did. The United States troops could not have prevented him from being torn limb from limb.

I will add, in conclusion, no Southerner ought, after your letter to Governor Wise and to Brown, to read a line of your composition, or to touch a magazine which bears your name in its lists of contributors; and in this we hope for the "sympathy" at least of those at the North who deserve the name of woman.

M. J. C. MASON.

REPLY OF MRS. CHILD.

WAYLAND [Mass.], December 17, 1859.

Prolonged absence from home has prevented my answering your letter so soon as I intended. I have no disposition to retort upon you the "twofold damnation" to which you consign me. On the contrary, I sincerely wish you well, both in this world and the next. If the anathema proved a safety valve to your own boiling spirit, it did some good to you, while it fell harmless upon me. Fortunately for all of us, the Heavenly Father rules his universe by laws, which the passions or the prejudices of mortals have no power to change.

As for John Brown, his reputation may be safely trusted to the impartial pen of history; and his motives will be righteously judged by him who knoweth the secrets of all hearts. Men, however great they may be, are of small consequence in comparison with principles; and the principle for which John Brown died is the question at issue between us.

You refer me to the Bible, from which you quote the favorite text of slave-holders: —

" Servants, be subject to your masters with all fear; not only to the good and gentle, but also to the froward." — 1 Peter ii. 18.

Abolitionists also have favorite texts, to some of which I would call your attention: —

" Remember them that are in bonds, as bound with them. — Heb. xiii. 3.

" Hide the outcasts; bewray not him that wandereth. Let mine outcasts dwell with thee. Be thou a covert to them from the face of the spoiler." — Isa. xvi. 3, 4.

" Thou shalt not deliver unto his master the servant which

is escaped from his master unto thee: he shall dwell with thee ... where it liketh him best: thou shalt not oppress him." — Deut. xxiii. 15, 16.

"Open thy mouth for the dumb in the cause of all such as are appointed to destruction. Open thy mouth, judge righteously, and plead the cause of the poor and needy." — Prov. xxxi. 8, 9.

"Cry aloud, spare not, lift up thy voice like a trumpet, and show my people their transgression, and the house of Jacob their sins." — Isa. lviii. 1.

I would especially commend to slave-holders the following portions of that volume wherein you say God has revealed the duty of masters: —

"Masters, give unto your servants that which is just and equal; knowing that ye also have a Master in heaven." — Col. iv. 1.

"Neither be ye called masters: for one is your Master, even Christ; and all ye are brethren." — Matt. xxiii. 10.

"Whatsoever ye would that men should do to you, do ye even so to them." — Matt. vii. 12.

"Is not this the fast that I have chosen? to loose the bands of wickedness, to undo the heavy burdens, and to let the oppressed go free, and that ye break every yoke?" — Isa. lviii. 6.

They "have given a boy for an harlot, and sold a girl for wine, that they might drink." — Joel iii. 3.

"He that oppresseth the poor reproacheth his Maker." — Prov. xiv. 31.

"Rob not the poor, because he is poor: neither oppress the afflicted. For the Lord will plead their cause, and spoil the soul of those who spoiled them." — Prov. xxii. 22, 23.

"Woe unto him ... that useth his neighbor's service without wages, and giveth him not for his work." — Jer. xxii. 13.

"Let him that stole, steal no more: but rather let him labor, working with his hands." — Eph. iv. 28.

"Woe unto them that decree unrighteous decrees, and that write grievousness which they have prescribed; to turn aside the needy from judgment, and to take away the right from the poor of my people, that widows may be their prey, and that they may rob the fatherless!" — Isa. x. 1, 2.

"If I did despise the cause of my man-servant or of my maid-servant, when they contend with me; what then shall I do when God riseth up? and when he visiteth, what shall I answer him?" — Job xxxi. 13, 14.

"Thou hast sent widows away empty, and the arms of the fatherless have been broken. Therefore snares are round about thee, and sudden fear troubleth thee; or darkness, that thou canst not see." — Job xxii. 9–11.

"Behold, the hire of the laborers who have reaped down your fields, which is of you kept back by fraud, crieth; and the cries of them which have reaped are entered into the ears of the Lord of Sabaoth. Ye have lived in pleasure on the earth, and been wanton; ye have nourished your hearts, as in a day of slaughter. Ye have condemned and killed the just." — James v. 4.

If the appropriateness of these texts is not apparent, I will try to make it so, by evidence drawn entirely from *Southern* sources. The abolitionists are not such an ignorant set of fanatics as you suppose. They *know* whereof they affirm. They are familiar with the laws of the slave States, which are alone sufficient to inspire abhorrence in any humane heart or reflecting mind not perverted by the prejudices of education and custom. I might fill many letters with significant extracts from your statute books; but I have space only to glance at a few, which indicate the leading features of the system you cherish so tenaciously.

The universal rule of the slave State is, that "the child follows the condition of its *mother*." This is an index to many things. Marriages between white and colored people are forbidden by law; yet a very large number of the slaves are brown or yellow. When Lafayette visited this country in his old age, he said he was very much struck by the great change in the colored population of Virginia; that in the time of the Revolution nearly all the household slaves were black, but when he returned to America, he found very few of them black. The advertisements in Southern newspapers often describe runaway slaves that " pass themselves for white men." Sometimes they are described as having " straight, light hair, blue eyes, and clear complexion." This could not be, unless their fathers, grandfathers, and great-grandfathers had been white men. But as their *mothers* were slaves, the law pronounces *them* slaves, subject to be sold on the auction-block whenever the necessities or convenience of their masters or mistresses require it. The sale of one's own children, brothers, or sisters, has an ugly aspect to those who are unaccustomed to it; and, obviously, it cannot have a good moral influence, that law and custom should render licentiousness a *profitable* vice.

Throughout the slave States, the testimony of no colored person, bond or free, can be received against a white man. You have some laws, which, on the face of them, would seem to restrain inhuman men from murdering or mutilating slaves; but they are rendered nearly null by the law I have cited. Any drunken master, overseer, or patrol may go into the negro cabins, and commit what outrages he pleases, with perfect impunity, if no white person is present who chooses to witness against him. North Carolina and Georgia leave a large loop-hole for escape, even if white persons are present, when murder is committed. A law to punish persons for "maliciously killing a slave" has this remarkable qualification: "Always provided that this act shall not extend to any slave dying of moderate correction." We at the North find it difficult to understand how *moderate* punishment can cause *death*. I have read several of your law books attentively, and I find no cases of punishment for the murder of a slave, except by fines paid to the *owner*, to indemnify him for the loss of his *property*: the same as if his horse or cow had been killed. In the South Carolina Reports is a case where the State had indicted Guy Raines for the murder of a slave named Isaac. It was proved that William Gray, the owner of Isaac, had given him a *thousand lashes*. The poor creature made his escape, but was caught, and delivered to the custody of Raines, to be carried to the county jail. Because he refused to go, Raines gave him five hundred lashes, and he died soon after. The counsel for Raines proposed that he should be allowed to acquit himself by his *own oath*. The court decided against it, because *white witnesses* had testified; but the Court of Appeals afterward decided he *ought* to have been exculpated by his own oath, and he was *acquitted*. Small indeed is the chance for justice to a slave, when his own color are not allowed to testify, if they see him maimed or his children murdered; when he has slave-holders for judges and jurors; when the murderer can exculpate himself by his own oath; and when the law provides that it is no murder to kill a slave by "moderate correction!"

Your laws uniformly declare that "a slave shall be deemed a chattel personal in the hands of his owner, to all intents, constructions, and purposes whatsoever." This, of course, involves the right to sell his children, as if they were pigs; also, to take his wife from him "for any intent or purpose whatsoever." Your laws also make it death for him to resist a white man, however brutally he may be treated, or however much his family may be outraged before his eyes. If he attempts to run away, your laws allow any man to shoot him.

By your laws, all a slave's earnings belong to his master. He can neither receive donations nor transmit property. If his master allows him some hours to work for himself, and by great energy and perseverance he earns enough to buy his own bones and sinews, his master may make him pay two or three times over, and he has no redress. Three such cases have come within my own knowledge. Even a written promise from his master has no legal value, because a slave can make no contracts.

Your laws also systematically aim at keeping the minds of the colored people in the most abject state of ignorance. If white people attempt to teach them to read or write, they are punished by imprisonment or fines; if they attempt to teach each other, they are punished with from twenty to thirty-nine lashes each. It cannot be said that the anti-slavery agitation produced such laws, for they date much farther back; many of them when we were Provinces. They are the *necessities* of the system, which, being itself an outrage upon human nature, can be sustained only by perpetual outrages.

The next reliable source of information is the advertisements in the Southern papers. In the North Carolina (Raleigh) "Standard," Mr. Micajah Ricks advertises, " Runaway, a negro woman and two children.

A few days before she went off, I burned her with a hot iron on the left side of her face. I tried to make the letter M." In the Natchez "Courier," Mr. J. P. Ashford advertises a runaway negro girl, with " a good many teeth missing, and the letter A branded on her cheek and forehead." In the Lexington (Ky.) " Observer," Mr. William Overstreet advertises a runaway negro with " his left eye out, scars from a dirk on his left arm, and much scarred with the whip." I might quote from hundreds of such advertisements, offering rewards for runaways, " dead or alive," and describing them with " ears cut off," " jaws broken," " scarred by rifle-balls," etc.

Another source of information is afforded by your " fugitives from injustice," with many of whom I have conversed freely. I have seen scars of the whip and marks of the branding-iron, and I have listened to their heart-breaking sobs, while they told of " piccaninnies " torn from their arms and sold.

Another source of information is furnished by emancipated slave-holders. Sarah M. Grimké, daughter of the late Judge Grimké, of the Supreme Court of South Carolina, testifies as follows: " As I left my native State on account of slavery, and deserted the home of my fathers to escape the sound of the lash and the shrieks of tortured victims, I would gladly bury in oblivion the recollection of those scenes with which I have been familiar. But this cannot be. They come over my memory like gory spectres, and implore me, with resistless power, in the name of a God of mercy, in the name of a crucified Saviour, in the name of humanity, for the sake of the slaveholder, as well as the slave, to bear witness to the horrors of the Southern prison-house." She proceeds to describe dreadful tragedies, the actors in which she says were " men and women of the first families in South Carolina ; " and that their cruelties did not, in the slightest degree, affect their standing in society. Her sister, Angelina Grimké, declared : " While I live, and slavery lives, I *must* testify against it. Not merely for the sake of my poor brothers and sisters in bonds; for even were slavery no curse to its victims, the exercise of arbitrary power works such fearful ruin upon the hearts of slave-holders, that I should feel impelled to labor and pray for its overthrow with my latest breath." Among the horrible barbarities she enumerates is the case of a girl thirteen years old, who was flogged to death by her master. She says : " I asked a prominent lawyer, who belonged to one of the first families in the State, whether the murderer of this helpless child could not be indicted, and he coolly replied that the slave was Mr. ——'s property, and if he chose to suffer the *loss*, no one else had anything to do with it." She proceeds to say : " I felt there could be for me no rest in the midst of such outrages and pollutions. Yet I saw nothing of slavery in its most vulgar and repulsive forms. I saw it in the city, among the fashionable and the honorable, where it was garnished by refinement and decked out for show. It is my deep, solemn, deliberate conviction, that this is a cause worth dying for. I say so from what I have seen, and heard, and known, in a land of slavery, whereon rest the darkness of Egypt and the sin of Sodom." I once asked Miss Angelina if she thought abolitionists exaggerated the horrors of slavery. She replied, with earnest emphasis : " They *cannot* be **exaggerated**. It is impossible for imagination to go beyond the facts." To a lady who observed that the time had not yet come for agitating the subject, she answered: " I apprehend if thou wert a *slave*, toiling in the fields of Carolina, thou wouldst think the time had *fully* come."

Mr. Thome of Kentucky, in the course of his eloquent lectures on this subject, said: " I breathed my first breath in an atmosphere of slavery. But though I am heir to a slave inheritance, I am bold to denounce the whole system as an outrage, a complication of crimes, and wrongs, and cruelties, that make angels weep."

Mr. Allen of Alabama, in a discussion with the students at Lane Seminary, in 1834, told of a slave who was tied up and beaten all day, with a paddle full of holes. "At night, his flesh was literally pounded to a jelly. The punishment was inflicted within hearing of the academy and the public green. But no one took any notice of it. No one thought any wrong was done. At our house, it is so common to hear screams from a neighboring plantation that we think nothing of it. Lest any one should think that the slaves are *generally* well treated, and that the cases I mentioned are exceptions, let me be distinctly understood that cruelty is the *rule*, and kindness is the exception."

In the same discussion, a student from Virginia, after relating cases of great cruelty, said: "Such things are common all over Virginia; at least, so far as I am acquainted. But the planters generally avoid punishing their slaves before *strangers*."

Miss Mattie Griffith of Kentucky, whose entire property consisted in slaves, emancipated them all. The noble-hearted girl wrote to me: " I shall go forth into the world penniless; but I shall work with a light heart, and, best of all, I shall live with an easy conscience." Previous to this generous resolution, she had never read any abolition document, and entertained the common Southern prejudice against them. But her own observation so deeply impressed her with the enormities of slavery, that she was impelled to publish a book, called "The Autobiography of a Female Slave." I read it with thrilling interest; but some of the scenes made my nerves quiver so painfully that I told her I hoped they were too highly colored. She shook her head sadly, and replied: "I am sorry to say that every incident in the book has come within my own knowledge."

St. George Tucker, Judge and Professor of Law in Virginia, speaking of the legalized murder of runaways, said: "Such are the cruelties to which a state of slavery gives birth — such the horrors to which the human mind is capable of being reconciled by its adoption." Alluding to our struggle in '76, he said: "While we proclaimed our resolution to live free or die, we imposed on our fellow-men of different complexion a slavery ten thousand times worse than the utmost extremity of the oppressions of which we complained."

Governor Giles, in a message to the Legislature of Virginia, referring to the custom of selling free colored people into slavery, as a punishment for offences not capital, said: "Slavery must be admitted to be a *punishment of the highest order;* and, according to the just rule for the apportionment of punishment to crimes, it ought to be applied only to *crimes of the highest order.* The most distressing reflection in the application of this punishment to female offenders is, that it extends to their offspring; and the innocent are thus punished with the guilty." Yet one hundred and twenty thousand innocent babes in this country are annually subjected to a punishment which your governor declared " ought to be applied only to crimes of the highest order."

Jefferson said: " One *day* of American slavery is worse than a *thousand years* of that which we rose in arms to oppose." Alluding to insurrections, he said: " The Almighty has no attribute that can take side with us in such a contest."

John Randolph declared: " Every planter is a sentinel at his own door. Every Southern mother, when she hears an alarm of fire in the night, instinctively presses her infant closer to her bosom."

Looking at the system of slavery in the light of all this evidence, do you candidly think we deserve " twofold damnation " for detesting it? Can you not believe that we may hate the system, and yet be truly your friends? I make allowance for the excited state of your mind, and for the prejudices induced by education. I do not care to change your opinion of me; but I do wish you could be persuaded to examine this subject dispassionately, for the sake of the prosperity of Virginia, and the welfare of unborn generations, both white and colored. For thirty years, abolitionists have been trying to reason with slave-holders, through the press, and in the halls of Congress. Their efforts, though directed to the *masters only*, have been met with violence and abuse almost equal to that poured on the head of John Brown. Yet surely we, as a portion of the Union, involved in the expense, the degeneracy, the danger, and the disgrace of this iniquitous and fatal system, have a *right* to speak about it, and a right to be *heard* also. At the North, we willingly publish pro-slavery arguments, and ask only a fair field and no favor for the other side. But you will not even allow your own citizens a chance to examine this important subject. Your letter to me is published in Northern papers, as well as Southern; but my reply will not be allowed to appear in any Southern paper. The despotic measures you take to silence investigation, and shut out the light from your own white population, prove how little reliance you have on the strength of your cause. In this enlightened age, all despotisms *ought* to come to an end by the agency of moral and rational means. But if they resist such agencies, it is in the order of Providence that they *must* come to an end by violence. History is full of such lessons.

Would that the veil of prejudice could be removed from your eyes. If you would candidly examine the statements of Governor Hincks of the British West Indies, and of the Rev. Mr. Bleby, long time a missionary in those islands, both before and after emancipation, you could not fail to be convinced that Cash is a more powerful incentive to labor than the Lash, and far safer also. One fact in relation to those islands is very significant. While the working people were slaves, it was always necessary to order out the military during the Christmas holidays; but, since emancipation, not a soldier is to be seen. A hundred John Browns might land there without exciting the slightest alarm.

To the personal questions you ask me, I will reply in the name of all the women of New England. It would be extremely difficult to find any woman in our villages who does *not* sew for the poor, and watch with the sick, whenever occasion requires. We pay our domestics generous wages, with which they can purchase as many Christmas gowns as they please; a process far better for their characters, as well as our own, than to receive their clothing as a charity, after being deprived of just payment for their labor. I have never known an instance where the "pangs of maternity" did not meet with requisite assistance; and here at the North, after we have helped the mothers, *we do not sell the babies.*

I readily believe what you state concerning the kindness of many Virginia matrons. It is creditable to their hearts: but after all, the best that can be done in that way is a poor equivalent for the perpetual wrong done to the slaves, and the terrible liabilities to which they are always subject. Kind masters and mistresses among you are merely lucky accidents. If any one *chooses* to be a brutal despot, your laws and customs give him complete power to do so. And the lot of those slaves who have the kindest masters is exceedingly precarious. In case of death, or pecuniary difficulties, or marriages in the family, they may at any time be suddenly transferred from protection and indulgence to personal degradation, or extreme severity; and if they should try to escape from such sufferings, anybody is authorized to shoot them down like dogs.

With regard to your declaration that "no Southerner ought henceforth to read a line of my composition," I reply that I have great satisfaction in the consciousness of having nothing to lose in that quarter. Twenty-seven years ago I published a book called "An Appeal in Behalf of that Class of Americans called Africans." It influenced the minds of several young men afterward conspicuous in public life, through whose agency the cause was better served than it could have been by me. From that time to this, I have labored too earnestly for the slave to be agreeable to slave-holders. Literary popularity was never a paramount object with me, even in my youth; and, now that I am old, I am utterly indifferent to it. But, if I cared for the exclusion you threaten, I should at least have the consolation of being exiled with honorable company. Dr. Channing's writings, mild and candid as they are, breathe what you would call arrant treason. William C. Bryant, in his capacity of editor, is openly on our side. The inspired muse of Whittier has incessantly sounded the trumpet for moral warfare with your iniquitous institution; and his stirring tones have been answered, more or less loudly, by Pierpont, Lowell, and Longfellow. Emerson, the Plato of America, leaves the scholastic seclusion he loves so well, and, disliking noise with all his poetic soul, bravely takes his stand among the trumpeters. George W. Curtis, the brilliant writer, the eloquent lecturer, the elegant man of the world, lays the wealth of his talent on the altar of Freedom, and makes common cause with rough-shod reformers.

The genius of Mrs. Stowe carried the outworks of your institution at one dash, and left the citadel open to besiegers, who are pouring in amain. In the church, on the ultra-liberal side, it is assailed by the powerful battering-ram of Theodore Parker's eloquence. On the extreme orthodox side is set a huge fire, kindled by the burning words of Dr. Cheever. Between them is Henry Ward Beecher, sending a shower of keen arrows into your intrenchments; and with him ride a troop of sharp-shooters from all sects. If you turn to the literature of England or France, you will find your institution treated with as little favor. The fact is, the whole civilized world proclaims slavery an outlaw, and the best intellect of the age is active in hunting it down.

L. MARIA CHILD.

TO MRS. S. M. PARSONS.

WAYLAND, December, 1859.

I thank you very cordially for your affectionate letter, and I am right glad you and your husband were so much pleased with my doings. Recent events have renewed my youth and strength, and filled me with electricity, and one word of apology for slavery makes the sparks fly. What a sublime martyrdom was that of old John Brown! There was nothing wanting in the details of his conduct. There was a grand simplicity and harmony throughout.

I reverenced him for refusing to be prayed over by slave-holding priests; and how my heart jumped toward him, when I read of his kissing the little colored child, on his way to the gallows! In last night's "Liberator" there is a very touching letter, which I received from a colored man in Ohio, about John Brown. You will see it, for I hear you have subscribed for that paper. The colored people in Boston held a prayer-meeting all day, on the 2d[1] of December, and I chose to spend that solemn day with them. There was nothing there to jar upon the tender sadness of my feelings. There was no one to

---

[1] The 2d of December, 1859, was the day on which John Brown was hanged.

question the old hero's claims to reverence, or to doubt his sanity of mind. All they knew about it was, that he was the friend of their oppressed race, and that he proved it by dying for them. It was very touching to hear them sing appropriate Methodist hymns so plaintively. Some of their prayers were uncouth, of course, because the pride and prejudice of white men have prevented their having a chance for mental culture; but many of them were eloquent, from the simple effect of earnestness. One old black man who informed the Lord that he "had been a slave, and knew how bitter it was," ejaculated with great fervor, "and since it has pleased thee to take away our Moses, oh! Lord God! raise us up a Joshua." To which all the congregation responded with a loud "Amen!" The 16th of December was more painful to me than the 2d. Those other victims were young, and wanted to live; and they had not so many manifestations of sympathy to sustain them as their grand old leader had. If Brown had not taken the arsenal, but had simply taken off such slaves as wanted to go, as he did in Missouri, and had died for that, I should be more completely satisfied with his martyrdom. But he liked Old Testament heroes better than I do. He had his mind filled with the idea of founding a "city of refuge;" and as he acted from his own conscientious convictions, I have no disposition to blame him, though I wish it had been otherwise. The lesson I learn from it is to try to act up to my own standard of duty as faithfully as he did to his. In a moral point of view his failure will prove a magnificent success, worth a thousand such as he planned.

"God moves in a mysterious way,
His wonders to perform."

TO MISS LUCY OSGOOD.

WAYLAND, 1859.

Your package arrived on Saturday evening, but Theodore Parker had the start of you. He had sent me the sermon the Thursday before, accompanied by a brief little farewell note in pencil, which I shall treasure among my "sacred relics;" for my heart misgives me that I shall never look upon that Socratic head again. I read the sermon, forthwith, to Mr. Child, and a jewel of a sermon we both thought it. Though not a farewell discourse, it seems to have a farewell sadness about it. . . . Newman's book on The Soul seemed to me a very admirable work. The Phases of Faith pleased me by the honesty of its confessions, and I read it with all the eagerness we all so naturally feel to arrive at the inmost spiritual secrets of another soul; but the conclusion left me very uncomfortable. It seemed, as the collegian said in his theme, "to land me in the great ocean of eternity." I had travelled so far, and so confidently, with him, to arrive — nowhere! I cannot say, as Lessing did, that if God offered him the truth with one hand, and the investigation with the other, he would choose the latter. I want to believe. Above all things, I want to believe. If I can only be sure that I do not accept delusion for truth. Different qualities of my mind so nearly balance each other that they cause me severe conflicts. No mortal will ever know through what long deserts I have passed; how bitter have proved the waters wherewith I have tried to slake my mighty thirst; and what hordes of Philistines have come out to do battle. Whether I shall ever get a sight of Canaan before I die, I know not.

TO MRS. S. B. SHAW.

WAYLAND, 1859.

I would gladly come to meet you, to save you trouble; but for no other reason. As for turning us out of our chamber, we transfer only our bodies; and should you consider that any great trouble, for the sight of a precious friend? Moreover, suppose it was any trouble, be it known to you that I would turn myself out of my house, and live in a tree, any time, for you. Please put quite out of your head all idea that your coming will give me trouble. In the first place, I will promise not to take trouble. In the next place, I would inform you that the world is divided into two classes: those who love to minister to others, and those who like to be ministered unto. I think I belong to the first class. I also belong to the class described in "Counterparts:" those to whom it is more necessary to love than to be loved; though both are essential to my happiness. Bad, is n't it? for a childless woman of sixty years. But then my good David serves me for husband and "baby and all." What a singular book is that "Counterparts." It has some of the inspiration of the tripod, and some of the confusion also. The philosophy is sometimes unintelligible, and the moral influence in some degree dubious. How gorgeous is the style; how the embroidery and the jewels are piled on! It made me think of Madame Bishop's singing. She was so fond of *fioritune* in music, that when she sang some common, simple air, even Rosa was sometimes puzzled to recognize it. Yet Madame Bishop charmed me with her tone-embroidery, and so does this woman with her word-embroidery. Some of her comparisons sparkle with poetry; but it is "sparkle," not glow. It is from outward, not inward light. They tell me she is a German, resident in England; and that accounts for the un-Englishness of some of her phraseology. A Jewess she is, of course. I am always pleased to have the Jews do anything great; as I am to have the colored people, or any other persecuted race. I was so glad the Rothschilds and others compelled the Emperor of Austria to repeal his contemptuous law, by resolving to have no commercial relations with Austrians! The silly despot concluded it was safer to offend the Pope than to displease the wealthy Jews.

TO MRS. S. B. SHAW.

1860.

I have made an excursion lately, which is unusual for me. Miss L. wanted to go to Newbury to see her sister, and was too feeble to go alone, and asked me to go with her. Her sister owns a mill, where the Artichoke joins the Merrimack. . . .

Friend Whittier lives about four miles from the mill, across the river. The bridge was being repaired, which made it necessary to go a long way round. I was not sorry, for the scenery was lovely. We rode along the Merrimack nearly all the way. The sunshine was rippling it with gold, and the oars of various little boats and rafts were dropping silver as they went. I think nature never made such a vivid impression on me as it has this summer. I don't know whether it is because I have so very few human ties, or whether it is that I feel a sort of farewell tenderness for the earth, because I am growing old.

Friend Whittier and his gentle Quakerly sister seemed delighted to see me, or, rather, he seemed delighted and she seemed pleased. There was a Republican meeting that evening, at which he felt obliged to show himself; but he came back before long, having indiscreetly excused himself by stating that I was at his house. The result was, that a posse of Republicans came, after the meeting was over, to look at the woman who "fired hot shot at Governor Wise." In the interim, however, I had some cosy chat with Friend Whittier, and it was right pleasant going over our anti-slavery reminiscences. Oh, those were glorious times! working shoulder to shoulder, in such a glow of faith! — too eager working for humanity to care a fig whether our helpers were priests or infidels. That's the service that is pleasing in the sight of God.

Whittier made piteous complaints of time wasted and strength exhausted by the numerous loafers who came to see him out of mere idle curiosity, or to put up with him to save a penny. I was amused to hear his sister describe some of these irruptions in her slow, Quakerly fashion. "Thee has no idea," said she, "how much time Greenleaf spends in trying to lose these people in the streets. Sometimes he comes home and says, 'Well, sister, I had hard work to lose him, but I have lost him.'" "But I can never lose a *her*," said Whittier. "The women are more pertinacious than the men; don't thee find 'em so, Maria?" I told him I did. "How does thee manage to get time to do anything?" said he. I told him I took care to live away from the railroad, and kept a bull-dog and a pitch-fork, and advised him to do the same.

TO SAMUEL E. SEWALL.

WAYLAND, September 20, 1860.

I expect to be in Boston in a few days, and should like to look at Rantoul's speech, if you have the volume at your office. . . .

It seems as if slavery would be the death of me. If all I suffer on the subject counts as vicarious atonement for the slave-holders, they are in a hopeful way. My indignation rises higher than it used to in my younger days. According to the general rule, I ought to grow calmer, but I do not. If the monster had one head, assuredly I should be a Charlotte Corday.

TO MISS LUCY OSGOOD.

WAYLAND, 1860.

You are almost constantly present with me, in these days of this declining year, and to-morrow I am sure my first waking thought will be of you and the dear one who a year ago passed behind the veil; that veil so dark and heavy, with merely a line of golden light around its edges, intimating the inner, invisible glory. More and more strongly do I feel, as I grow older, that this unsatisfactory existence is the mere threshold of a palace of glories; but reason is importunate with its questions of how and where. I strive to attain to an habitual state of child-like trust, to feel always, as I do sometimes, like a little one that places its hand within its father's, and is satisfied to be led, it knows not whither.

Mr. —— is a great, good man, and when he lets doctrines alone his preaching always edifies and strengthens me. But he has no logic in his composition; not a jot; and sometimes I wish I had not.

Sometimes I think the light from God's own throne is best transmitted through the transparent golden veil of poesy. But there stands <u>my reason, a stubborn fact; and it will not accept any supernatural mediums between my soul and its Heavenly Father</u>; whether the mediums be Virgin Mothers, or Divine Humanities. There is undoubtedly a sense in which the doctrine of Divine Humanity is true; for in its highest ideal all humanity is divine. But that sense would be very unsatisfactory to Mr. ———.

How I should like to know what your sister's active soul is now thinking of all these things! Perhaps she has introduced Theodore Parker to Dr. Hopkins; and perhaps Luther comes up behind them "with the sound of iron shoes upon a stone pavement," as Swedenborg describes his walk in the spiritual world. It bears considerable resemblance to his walk in this world, I think. If Dr. Channing joins them, it will be in velvet slippers, on the softest carpet.

TO MRS. S. B. SHAW.

MEDFORD, 1860.

You doubtless remember Thomas Sims, the fugitive slave, who was surrendered in Boston, in 1852. I saw a letter from him to his sister expressing an intense longing for his freedom, and I swore "by the Eternal," as General Jackson used to say, that as Massachusetts had sent him into slavery, Massachusetts should bring him back. I resolved, also, that it should all be done with *pro-slavery* money. They told me that I had undertaken to "hoe a very hard row." I laughed, and said, "It *shall* be done: General Jackson never retracts." I expected to have to write at least a hundred letters, and to have to station myself on the steps of the State House this winter, to besiege people. Sims is a skilful mechanic and his master asks $1,800 for him. A large sum for an abolitionist to get out of pro-slavery purses! But I got it! I got it! I got it! Hurrah! I had written only eighteen letters, when one gentleman promised to pay the whole sum, provided I would not mention his name.

TO HON. LEMUEL SHAW.

MEDFORD, January 3, 1861.

TO THE HON. LEMUEL SHAW, — By this mail I send you three pamphlets, for which I ask a candid perusal. With deep sadness I saw your respected and influential name signed to an address in favor of repealing the Personal Liberty Bill. I trust you will not deem me disrespectful if I ask whether you have reflected well on all the bearings of this important subject. Perhaps you may consider me, and those with whom I labor, as persons prone to look only on one side. Grant that it is so — is it not the neglected side? is it not the right side? And are not you yourself, in common with all human beings, liable to look upon things too much from one point of view? I presume that your social environment is almost entirely conservative; and conservative of habits and stereotyped sayings, rather than of the original principles on which the government of this country was founded. Have you carefully examined and duly considered the other side? This mutual agreement between North and South to keep millions of fellow-beings in abject degradation and misery cannot possibly be right. No sophistry can make it appear so to hearts and minds not frozen or blinded by the influence of trade or politics.

If the common plea of the inferiority of the African race be true, that only adds meanness to our guilt; the magnanimous strong are ashamed not to protect the weak. But then everybody knows that an immense proportion of American slaves are not black. Thousands upon thousands of them are lighter than Italians, Spanish, Portuguese, Greeks, etc. They are the sons and daughters of our presidents, governors, judges, senators, and generals. The much vaunted Anglo-Saxon blood is coursing in their veins, through generations after generations.

If you set aside heart and conscience as appropriate guides for women only, and assume pure cold intellect for a standard of action, what answer will enlightened reason give, if you ask whether free institutions in one part of the country can possibly survive continual compromises with despotism in another part? If the lowest person in the community is legally oppressed, is not the highest endangered thereby? And does not the process inevitably demoralize the people by taking away from law that which renders it sacred, namely, equal and impartial justice? I again ask you, respectfully and earnestly, to read my pamphlets with candid attention. If the request seems to you obtrusive or presumptuous, my apology is that I believe you to be an upright and kind man, and therefore infer that your heart and conscience are not in fault, but only the blinding influences of your social environment. Yours respectfully,

L. MARIA CHILD.

TO MRS. S. B. SHAW.

MEDFORD, January, 1861.

Tired in mind and body, I sit down to write to you and tell you all about it. On Wednesday evening I went to Mrs. Chapman's reception. The hall inside was beautiful with light and banners; and outside the street was beautiful with moonlight and prismatic icicles. All went on quietly. People walked about and talked, occasionally enlivened by music of the Germania Band. They seemed to enjoy themselves, and I (being released from the care of unruly boys, demolishing cake and spilling slops as they did last year) did my best to help them have a good time. But what with being introduced to strangers, and chatting with old acquaintances half forgotten, I went home to Derne Street very weary, yet found it impossible for me to sleep. I knew there were very formidable preparations to mob the anti-slavery meeting the next day, and that the mayor was avowedly on the side of the mob. I would rather have given fifty dollars than attend the meeting; but conscience told me it was a duty. I was excited and anxious; not for myself, but for Wendell Phillips. Hour after hour of the night, I heard the clock strike, while visions were passing through my mind of that noble head assailed by murderous hands, and I obliged to stand by without the power to save him.

I went very early in the morning, and entered the Tremont Temple by a private labyrinthine passage. There I found a company of young men, a portion of the self-constituted body-guard of Mr. Phillips. They looked calm, but resolute and stern. I knew they were all armed, as well as hundreds of others; but their weapons were not visible. The women friends came in gradually by the same private passage. It was a solemn gathering, I assure you; for though there was a pledge not to use weapons unless Mr. Phillips or some other anti-slavery speaker was personally in danger, still nobody could foresee what might happen. The meeting opened well. The anti-slavery sentiment was there in strong force; but soon the mob began to yell from the galleries. They came tumbling in by hundreds. The papers will tell you of their goings on. Such yelling, screeching, stamping, and bellowing I never heard. It was a full realization of the old phrase, "All hell broke loose." Mr. Phillips stood on the front of the platform for a full hour, trying to be heard whenever the storm lulled a little. They cried, "Throw him out!" "Throw a brick-bat at him!" "Your house is a-fire; don't you know your house is a-fire? go put out your house!" Then they'd sing, with various bellowing and shrieking accompaniments, "Tell John Andrew, tell John Andrew, John Brown's dead." I should think there were four or five hundred of them. At one time they all rose up, many of them clattered down-stairs, and there was a surging forward towards the platform. My heart beat so fast I could hear it; for I did not then know how Mr. Phillips's armed friends were stationed at every door and in the middle of every aisle. They formed a firm wall which the mob could not pass. At last it was announced that the police were coming. I saw and heard nothing of them, but there was a lull. Mr. Phillips tried to speak, but his voice was again drowned. Then by a clever stroke of management he stooped forward and addressed his speech to the reporters stationed directly below him.

This tantalized the mob, and they began to call out, "Speak louder! We want to hear what you're saying." Whereupon he raised his voice, and for half an hour he seemed to hold them in the hollow of his hand. But as soon as he sat down they began to yell and sing again, to prevent any more speaking. But Higginson made himself heard through the storm, and spoke in very manly and effective style; the purport of which was that to-day he would set aside the subject of slavery, and take his stand upon the right of free speech, which the members of this society were determined to maintain at every hazard. I forgot to mention that Wendell Phillips was preceded by James Freeman Clarke, whom the mob treated with such boisterous insults that he was often obliged to pause in his remarks. After Mr. Phillips, R. W. Emerson tried to address the people, but his voice was completely drowned. After the meeting adjourned, a large mob outside waited for Mr. Phillips, but he went out by the private entrance, and arrived home safely.

In the afternoon meeting the uproar was greater than it had been in the forenoon. The mob cheered and hurrahed for the Union, and for Edward Everett, for Mayor Wightman, and for Charles Francis Adams. The mayor came at last, and, mounting the platform, informed his "fellow-citizens" in the galleries that the trustees of the building had requested him to disperse the meeting and clear the hall. Turning the meeting out-of-doors was precisely what they wanted him to do.

[The remainder of this letter has been lost, but the purport of it was, that on the mayor's complying with the demand that he should read the letter aloud to the meeting, it appeared that the trustees had desired him to disperse the *mob*, and not the meeting. The presiding officer (Mr. Edmund Quincy) thereupon called upon him to fulfil his duty and eject the mob from the hall, which was done within ten minutes, to the intense chagrin of the rioters and the discomfiture of the mayor, and the meeting proceeded without further serious interruption. The mayor, on leaving the hall, promised that an adequate police force should be sent to protect the evening meeting, and he then returned to the City Hall to issue an order that the hall should be closed and no meeting permitted there that evening. These events took place at the annual meeting of the Massachusetts Anti-Slavery Society, on the 24th of January, 1861. — Eds.]

TO THE SAME.

WAYLAND, May 5, 1861.

I am glad to witness the universal enthusiasm for the U. S. flag, though the sight of that flag always inspires a degree of sadness in my own breast. I should so delight in having it thoroughly worthy of being honored! But every flap of the stars and stripes repeats to me the story of those poor slaves who, through great perils and sufferings, succeeded in making their way to Fort Pickens, strengthened by the faith that President Lincoln was their friend, and that his soldiers would protect them. They were chained and sent back to their masters, who whipped them till they nearly died under the lash. When such things are done under the U. S. flag, I cannot and I will not say, "God bless it!" Nay, unless it ceases from this iniquity, I say, deliberately and solemnly, "May the curse of God rest upon it! May it be trampled in the dust, kicked by rebels, and spit upon by tyrants!" But I think it will cease from this iniquity. These wicked things that have happened at Fort Pickens and Fort Monroe, occurred during the twenty days before hostilities commenced. The U. S. government, having offered the rebels twenty days during which they might make up their minds to lay down their arms, perhaps thought it necessary to obey that hateful clause in the Constitution. But now the offered term of grace has expired. If they continue in arms, they are no longer a part of the Union, and none of those devilish obligations of the Union can be considered as any longer binding upon us; not even by men who have no other consciences than legal consciences. . . . Twenty years ago, John Quincy Adams maintained on the floor of Congress the constitutional right of the United States to proclaim emancipation to all the slaves in time of war, either foreign or civil. He maintained that it was in strict conformity to the law of nations and the laws of war, and he challenged any man to prove to the contrary. No one attempted to do it. Let us hope and trust that a great good is coming out of this seeming evil. Meanwhile, I wait to see how the United States will deport itself. When it treats the colored people with justice and humanity, I will mount its flag in my great elm-tree, and I will thank you to present me with a flag for a breast-pin; but, until then, I would as soon wear the rattlesnake upon my bosom as the eagle. I have raved and I have wept about that Fort Pickens affair. When one puts one's self in the slave's stead, pity and indignation will boil over in rage, in view of such enormities.

TO MISS LUCY SEARLE.

WAYLAND, June 5, 1861.

I return "Silas Marner" with cordial thanks. It entertained me greatly. His honest attempts at education were extremely amusing. What a genuine touch of nature was " Eppie in the tole hole!" What a significant fact it is in modern literature, that the working class are so generally the heroes. No princes in disguise are necessary now to excite an interest in the reader. The popular mind is educated up to the point of perceiving that carpenters, weavers, etc., are often real princes in disguise. The longer I live, the more entirely and intensely do my sympathies go with the masses.

I am glad to see some amendment with regard to sending back fugitive slaves. Those at Fort Monroe are to be protected so long as Virginia continues in rebellion. God grant that all the slave-holders may rebel, and remain in rebellion, till the emancipation of their slaves is accomplished! Success to Jeff. Davis, till he goads the free States into doing, from policy and revenge, what they have not manhood to do from justice and humanity! It is a dreadful thing, a most demoralizing thing, to have the laws of one's country at such variance with the laws of God. I never realized it so fully as when I heard your good, conscientious, intelligent friend say that he would send back a fugitive slave because the Constitution required it. When our fathers joined hands with slave-holders to form the Constitution, with their feet on the prostrate and helpless slaves, they did sad work for their descendants. If my father had made a compact with a rich neighbor that I would help him rob a poor one, I should break the compact. Law is not law, if it violates principles of eternal justice. If drunken foreigners are hired to vote for a member of Congress, and the vote of that member causes the enactment of the Fugitive Slave Law, probably because he wishes to obtain some still higher office, am I bound to sell my soul to perdition because the iniquity has been framed into a law? The dictionary does not contain words enough to express my detestation of all laws framed for the support of tyranny. To keep that unrighteous compact with fellow-citizens was bad enough, but to keep it with rebels, who have over and over again violated all their part of the compact, is adding imbecility and absurdity to wickedness.

TO MISS HENRIETTA SARGENT.

WAYLAND, July 26, 1861.

One can't think about anything else but the war; and where is the prophet inspired to see the end thereof? All seems to me a mass of dark thunder-clouds, illumined here and there with flashes of light that show God is behind the clouds. I have never in my life felt the presence of God as I do at this crisis. The nation is in his hand, and he is purging it by a fiery process. The people would not listen to the warnings and remonstrances of the abolitionists, uttered year after year in every variety of tone, from the gentle exhortations of May and Channing to the scathing rebukes of Garrison; from the close, hard logic of Goodell to the flowing eloquence of Phillips. More than a quarter of a century ago, Whittier's pen of fire wrote on the wall, —

"Oh! rouse ye, ere the storm comes forth, —
The gathered wrath of God and man!"

In vain. The people went on with their feasting and their merchandise, and lo! the storm is upon us!

Every instance of sending back poor fugitive slaves has cut into my heart like the stab of a bowie-knife, and made me dejected for days; not only because I pitied the poor wretches who trusted the government in vain, but because I felt that all moral dignity was taken out of the conflict by such incidents, and that the enthusiasm of the soldiers and the people must be diminished by it. A soldier needs a great idea to fight for; and how can the idea of freedom be otherwise than obscured by witnessing the wicked, mean, unmanly surrendering of poor trembling fugitives? The absurd policy of the thing is also provoking. To send back those who want to serve us, to be employed by rebels to help them in shooting us! It seems to me as if the eyes of the government were holden, that they cannot see. Still pursuing the old policy of years — willing to disregard the dictates of justice and humanity, for the sake of conciliating the few slave-holders we have left to be conciliated. I have said all along that we needed defeats and reverses to make us come up manfully to the work of freedom. . . . Yet these last battles, with all their terrible incidents, have made me almost down sick. Night and day I am thinking of those poor soldiers, stabbed after they were wounded, shot after they dropped down from fatigue. My heart bleeds for the mothers of those sons. And shall all this awful havoc be made without removing the cause of the war? without abolishing that detestable institution which will always be marring our prosperity and troubling our peace, so long as it is allowed to exist? But my belief is that order is to be brought out of this chaos. My faith is founded upon the fact that God has so wonderfully ordered events that it is plainly for a purpose. Only look at the sort of men who are now talking real fanatical abolitionism! Men who, a few months ago, were the hardest hunkers, the most pro-slavery demagogues! Verily, "it is the Lord's doing, and it is marvellous in our eyes."

TO MISS LUCY SEARLE.

WAYLAND, August 22, 1861.

Three weeks ago I set out to come to see you and broke down half way. It was the hottest day we have had this summer, and I wilted under it so that I had no energy left. I took refuge in the anti-slavery office, and there remained in the shade till the hour arrived for returning home. It was the second day of August, and many anti-slavery friends were returning from the celebration of the first at Abington, so that quite a levee was held at the office the last hour I was there. I know of nothing that stirs up my whole being like meeting with old friends by whose side I entered into the great moral battle thirty years ago. It seems to me the early Christians must have experienced similar emotions when they met each other. Glorious old Paul! What an anti-slavery man he would have made, if his earthly lot had been cast in these times! Well, his friends were mobbed and despised by the world; but nevertheless, Christianity sat on the throne of the Cæsars, and even the selfishness of men paid homage to it. Our cause also is going to mount the throne of popular favor. Then I shall bid good-by to it, and take hold of something else that is unpopular. I never work on the winning side, because I know there will always be a plenty ready to do such work.

TO MISS HENRIETTA SARGENT.

WAYLAND, August 24, 1861.

I should have been cheerful in my solitude, had it not been for my irrepressible anxiety about public affairs.

I made, and quilted on my lap, the prettiest little crib-quilt you ever saw. The outside had ninety-nine little pink stars of French calico, on a white ground, with a rose-wreath trimming all round for a border; and the lining was a very delicate rose-colored French brilliant. It took one month of industrious sewing to complete it. I sent it to my dear friend, Mrs. S., in honor of her first grand-daughter. It was really a relief to my mind to be doing something for an innocent little baby in these dreadful times. One other recreation I have had this summer. My loved and honored friend, S. J. May, spent a few weeks in Boston, and wrote to me to meet him at his cousin's, S. E. Sewall's. I went after dinner, and left after breakfast next morning. How much we did talk! Sometimes laughing over old reminiscences, sometimes serious even to sadness in view of the great struggle between despotism and freedom. None of us had much faith in men, or in any political party; but we all agreed that the will of God was manifestly overruling the will of man, and making even his wrath to praise him. All thought that emancipation would be the result of the war; the forced result, not the chosen one. Miss R. complained of the exceeding slowness with which things tended to that result. I told her of the consolation an old nurse gave to a mother whose child was very sick. The mother said, "The medicine don't seem to work as you thought it would." The nurse replied, "It *will* work. Trust in God, ma'am; he's tedious, but he's sure." We did n't any of us realize in those early days the extent of our privilege in having engaged in a cause so righteous, with so many earnest, true-hearted, all-alive people.

TO JOHN G. WHITTIER.

WAYLAND, September 10, 1861.

DEAR FRIEND WHITTIER, — . . . Nothing on earth has such effect on the popular heart as songs, which the soldiers would take up with enthusiasm, and which it would thereby become the fashion to whistle and sing at the street corners. "Old John Brown, Hallelujah!" is performing a wonderful mission now. Where the words came from, nobody knows, and the tune is an exciting, spirit-stirring thing, hitherto unknown outside of Methodist conventicles. But it warms up soldiers and boys, and the air is full of it; just as France was of the Marseillaise, whose author was for years unknown.

If the soldiers only had a song, to some spirit-stirring tune, proclaiming what they went to fight for, or thought they went to fight for, — for home, country and liberty, and indignantly announcing that they did not go to hunt slaves, to send back to their tyrants poor lacerated workmen who for years had been toiling for the rich without wages; if they had such a song to a tune that excited them, how rapidly it would educate them! . . . Dr. Furness wrote me that a young friend of his was a volunteer in a wealthy aristocratic company that went from Philadelphia.

They returned much worked up about slavery. The young man told Dr. F. that he one day met a rude, rough man, a corporal, crying right out, blubbering like a school-boy. When asked what was the matter, he replied, "They've just sent a poor fellow back into slavery. I didn't leave my home to do such work as this, and I won't do it. I come here to fight for the country and the flag, not to hunt slaves; and if the colonel orders any more such work, I'm afraid I shall shoot him."

Another who was ordered on picket-duty, of course at unusual risk of his life, was told that while he was sentinel, if any slave attempted to pass the lines, he must turn him back. He replied, "That is an order I will not obey." Being reminded of his duty to obey orders, he replied, "I know the penalty I incur, and am ready to submit to it, but I did not enlist to do such work and I will not do it." The officers, being aware that his feeling would easily become contagious, modified the order thus: "If anybody tries to pass, ascertain that all's right before you allow them to pass." That night the moon shone brightly, and the sentinel on duty saw a moving in the bushes before him. "Who goes there? Answer quickly!" Up rose a tall ebony man. "Who are you?" "A fugitive." "Are you all right?" "Yes, massa." "Then run quick."

Another time, a lordly Virginian rode up to the United States lines with a pass to the other side. He curled his lip contemptuously when a United States sentinel barred the course of his stylish chariot. "Where's your pass?" The Virginian, scorning to acknowledge authority from a "greasy mechanic" of the North, did not deign to make any reply, but motioned to the slave who was driving his barouche to deliver the paper to the soldier. The slave dismounted and gave the sentinel the required pass. The sentinel seized him, and by a quick motion set him twirling down the hill, at the bottom of which were marshalled the United States forces. "Now you can turn back," said the sentinel. "But I obtained an order allowing me to pass. How dare you hinder me?" "Where is your order?" "My servant just gave it to you." "Oh, that was an order to pass only one, and he has already gone with it."

The Virginian swore roundly, and called vociferously to his slave to come back. The bewildered slave attempted to do so, but the mischievous sentinel put his musket across the path. "Show the paper!" shouted the master. The slave did so. The sentinel read it, and coolly replied, "This is a pass from Norfolk. You must obtain another to go *to* Norfolk." And so the haughty Southerner was obliged to guide his own horses back again whence he came.

TO THE SAME.

WAYLAND, January 21, 1862.

You will make me write to you, you keep doing so many things that delight me! I was moved to write you my thanks for "The Two Watchers;" but I was busy working for the "contrabands" at Fortress Monroe, and so I kept the thanks warm in my heart, without giving them an airing. But that Negro Boat Song at Port Royal! How I have chuckled over it and sighed over it! I keep repeating it morning, noon, and night; and, I believe, with almost as much satisfaction as the slaves themselves would do. It is a complete embodiment of African humor, and expressed as they would express it, if they were learned in the mysteries of rhyme and rhythm. I have only one criticism on the negro dialect. They would not say, "He 'leab' de land." They would say, He "leff" de land. At least, so speak all the slaves I have talked with, or whose talk I have seen reported.

What a glorious, blessed gift is this gift of song, with which you are so lavishly endowed! Who can calculate its influence, which you exert always for good! My David, who always rejoices over your writings, was especially pleased with the Boat Song, which he prophesies will be sung ere long by thousands of darkies. He bids me say to you that

> "One bugle note from Whittier's pen
> Is worth at least ten thousand men."

So you see that you are at least equal to a major-general in the forces you lead into the field, and your laurels are bloodless.

You have of course read "The Rejected Stone," for it is the most powerful utterance the crisis has called forth. God sends us so many great prophets that it seems as if he thought us worth saving; but latterly I fear greatly that there is not virtue enough left in the country to make salvation possible. Slavery seems to have poisoned the fountains of our national life. I do not know whether it is in the providence of God to allow us to be an example to the nations, or whether he intends to use us as a warning. If we are saved, it will be better than we deserve. I would sacrifice everything in life, and life itself, to preserve our free institutions; but if we must have the noble structure pulled down about our ears by the blind giant Slavery, I hope the poor negroes will have a rollicking good time over its ruins.

[1] *The Rejected Stone; or, Insurrection vs. Resurrection in America* By a Native of Virginia. (M. D. Conway.) Boston, 1861.

You have doubtless heard of Harriet Tubman, whom they call Moses, on account of the multitude she has brought out of bondage by her courage and ingenuity. She talks politics sometimes, and her uncouth utterance is wiser than the plans of politicians. She said the other day: "Dey may send de flower ob dair young men down South, to die ob de fever in de summer, and de agoo in de winter. (Fur 't is cold down dar, dough 't is down South.) Dey may send dem one year, two year, tree year, till dey tired ob sendin', or till dey use up all de young men. All no use! God's ahead ob Massa Linkum. God won't let Massa Linkum beat de South till he do de right ting. Massa Linkum he great man, and I'se poor nigger; but dis nigger can tell Massa Linkum how to save de money and de young men. He do it by setting de niggers free. S'pose dar was awfu' big snake down dar, on de floor. He bite you. Folks all skeered, cause you die. You send for doctor to cut de bite; but snake he rolled up dar, and while doctor dwine it, he bite you agin. De doctor cut out dat bite; but while he dwine it, de snake he spring up and bite you agin, and so he keep dwine, till you kill him. Dat's what Massa Linkum orter know." . . .

This winter I have for the first time been knitting for the army; but I do it only for Kansas troops. I can trust them, for they have vowed a vow unto the Lord that no fugitive shall ever be surrendered in their camps. There is a nephew of Kossuth in Colonel Montgomery's regiment. A few weeks ago when he was on scout duty a mulatto woman implored him to take her to the Yankee camp where her husband was. The mistress rushed out in hot pursuit. The young Hungarian reined in his horse, and called to the slave, "Jump up, and hold on by me!" She sprang on the horse, and they galloped away, under a shower of wrathful words from the mistress. When they rode into the Kansas camp, all the soldiers threw up their caps and hurrahed, and Colonel Montgomery called out, "Three cheers for the Union!" The young Hungarian, Cassimir, is a sort of adopted son of one of my relatives, to whom he wrote the story.

It is well that war has some pleasant pictures.

TO MISS LUCY OSGOOD.

WAYLAND, 1862.

I thank you heartily for thinking of me at New Year's time. The echo of "hand clapping," which you heard when news came of the capture of Port Royal, was not from me. I have had but one approach to a pleasurable sensation connected with public affairs since this war began, and that was when I read Fremont's proclamation. He acknowledged the slaves as "men." Nobody else, except the old Garrisonian abolitionists, seems to have the faintest idea that they have any rights which we are bound to recognize. They are to be freed or not, according to our necessities or convenience, and then we are to do what we please with them, without consulting their interest or convenience. It is the same hateful pro-slavery spirit everywhere. I felt very little interest in the capture of Mason and Slidell. It did not seem to me of much consequence, especially as their dispatches were carried to Europe. Living up here in Wayland, at a distance from cities and railroads, is very conducive to quietude of mind, which is in

fact in some danger of approaching to drowsiness.
The prospect of a war with England, superadded to
our present troubles, made me almost down sick.
The pacific policy of our government was an immense relief to my mind. I did not see any call for
"astuteness" about it. It was simply a question
whether we had infringed upon the law of nations;
and since the lawyers and statesmen all round agreed
that we had violated it, at least in form, I think it
was as manly in the nation to acknowledge the mistake as it would have been in an individual. It
would have been something worse than absurd to go
to blowing out each other's brains about a mere legal
technicality. I think Charles Sumner takes the true
ground. How calm and strong he is! I know of no
one who so well deserves the title of Serene Highness.

I have written a letter to the "Anti-Slavery Standard;" but it is so long that I doubt whether they
will get it into the next paper. You will think that
I " roar like any sucking dove." I tried to do so, for
it did not seem to me right to do anything to increase
the inflammable state of things. Conscience is apt
to plague me about acting out my total depravity.
I thought of several sarcasms which some readers
might have thought smart, but I suppressed them.

Ah, how often I have had your thought: " Would
that increasing nearness to the spiritual world abated
one jot of its mystery." To me the mystery thickens
the more I contemplate it. Brother Convers, writing
to me of the death of his wife, says: " Mysterious
ocean of Silence! whence not a sound reaches the ear
of one who walks on its shores and listens with an agony of desire. Yet I often say to myself, what mat-

ters this, if the soul can only keep its balance of repose and trust? Questions and doubts are mostly the devil's work. While we are with God, we know little or nothing of them. True it is,

> ' The Sphinx sits at the gate of life,
> With the old question on her awful lips;'

but she cannot now devour us, if we do not solve the question. The heart has its answer; an answer which God has placed there; and blessed are those who rest content with that. I know of no other faith than this of the heart that is worth much. I love the simple beauty of old Richard Baxter's expression: 'The jingling of too much philosophy often drowns the music of Aaron's bells.'" I sympathize with these expressions of my brother's feelings.

TO MRS. S. B. SHAW.

WAYLAND, 1862.

I had planned writing to you a few days hence; deferring it for the important reason that I could then write on my birthday, and inform you that I was sixty years old. But there comes along a package from you and Mrs. C——, followed by your letter, and I am so charmed with " John Brent " that I must write " right away," as the children say. How all-alive the book is! Glowing and effervescing, like champagne poured out in the sunshine! I had formed the idea that Mr. Winthrop was an uncommon man; but I had no idea he was so overflowing with genius. Alas, that such a rich and noble life should have been cut off in its full vigor by the ruthless hand of slavery! I took a great interest in him because he was a dear friend of yours; but since a portion of his vivacious and beautiful mind has been transmitted to me through the pages of his book, I feel as if he were my friend, — as if I had known and loved him. When I was in Boston, last week, I stopped and looked at the advertisement of " John Brent " in the windows of Ticknor & Fields. I wanted it very much, and was on the point of stepping in and buying it. But I thought of the " contrabands," and of other claims upon me, still nearer, so far as natural relationship goes, and I said to myself, " No unnecessary expense till the war is over." I walked away very well satisfied with my decision; but I was amazing glad to have the book, and I thank Mrs. C—— a thousand times. It is very curious how often it happens so. My wants are few, but when I do want anything very much it is very apt to come to me, from some source, without my expressing the wish to any one. I wonder whether there is any spiritual magnetism in it?

TO FRANCIS G. SHAW.

WAYLAND, 1862.

I inclose twenty dollars, which I wish you would use for the " contrabands " in any way you think best. I did think of purchasing shoes, of which I understand they are much in need, but I concluded it was best to send to you to appropriate it as you choose. In November I expended eighteen dollars for clothing, mostly for women and children, and picked up all the garments, blankets, etc., that I could spare. I sent them to Fortress Monroe. Last week I gave A. L. twenty dollars toward a great box she is filling for Port Royal. My interest in the " contrabands," everywhere, is exceedingly great; and at this crisis I feel that every one ought to be willing to do their utmost. I still have forty dollars left of a fund I have set apart for the "contrabands." I keep it for future contingencies; but if you think it is more needed now, say the word and you shall have it.

TO MISS LUCY SEARLE.

WAYLAND, 1862.

So you dispute Gerrit Smith's testimony about my being "wise and candid"? I cannot say I have much respect for my wisdom. I think less and less of it every year I live. But when I write for the public, I think I am generally candid. I do not profess to be so in my talk, because that bubbles up, and I do not take time to examine its spirit. We all present different phases of character, according to circumstances, and I think I do so more than most people. It is natural enough that Gerrit Smith should deem me "wise." When I approach him, I don't go dancing on a slack rope, decorated with spangles and Psyche-wings; I walk on solid ground, as demurely as if I were going to meeting, with psalm book in hand. If I happen to catch a glimpse of a fairy by the way, she and I wink at each other, but I never "let on." He supposes the chosen teachers of my mind to be profound statesmen and pious Christian Fathers. I never introduce to him any of my acquaintances of light character. I have a consciousness that fairies are not the most respectable company for a woman of my venerable years (I shall be sixty to-morrow), and it is only to a few that I manifest my predilection for such volatile visitors. Dear Sarah Shaw likes to see fanciful dancing on moon-beams, and when I write to her I sometimes caracole in a fashion that would make good, sensible Gerrit Smith wonder what had become of the "wisdom" of his sage friend. . . .

I suppose George's indignation against England is not abated by her recent manifestations. I thought perhaps you would read Harriet Martineau's letter in the "Standard" aloud for his especial edification, and I amused myself with imagining its effect. I didn't know but it would make each particular hair on his head stand up on end, charged brimful with the electricity of righteous wrath.

TO THE SAME.

1862.

Since I saw you, I have often thought of the fear you seem to have of Spiritualism. You appear to regard it as something uncanny. I cannot feel so about it. I don't believe there is any miracle or any deviltry about it. I simply believe that the union of our spiritual nature with our material is governed by laws which we do not understand, and which lie beyond the region of any tests we are as yet able to apply. I don't think the devil has anything to do with Spiritualism, any more than he has with comets. I rather think I don't believe in the devil. I certainly never think of him in connection with any mysteries that interest me. . . . Now there is electricity! That is an everlasting puzzle to me. I am always asking questions about it, and never get any of them answered. I have a vague idea that it is "the spiritual body" of the universe. I have a great many questions laid up to ask Plato when I see him. He has been at the high school so long, he must know a great deal. . . . My soul goes about "pervading" all departments of the universe, "wanting to know;" and the only answer I get is, "Go about your business." So I go about it. I have just done fifteen pair of mittens and three pair of socks for the Kansas troops. I can trust them never to surrender a fugitive slave; so I work for them with a will. Conway of Kansas has made a magnificent speech in Congress. It seems to me one of the greatest speeches I ever read. I rejoiced also in Boutwell's speech before the Emancipation League. It was ably argued, well arranged, excellent in its spirit, judicious and practical in its suggestions.

TO MISS HENRIETTA SARGENT.

WAYLAND, 1862.

The broad meadow lies very beautiful before me; for the frequent rains have kept it fresh and green. The sky is a beautiful clear blue, with a light, floating tracery of silvery clouds. All looks so serene and smiling that it is difficult to realize the scenes of violence and destruction going on in other parts of the country. A little striped squirrel that has for weeks come to the stone wall near my back window, to eat the breakfast I daily placed for him there, has disappeared for several days, and the fear that some evil beast has devoured him makes me sad. When so many mothers are mourning for their sons, not knowing where or how they died, I am ashamed to say that I have cried a little for the loss of my squirrel. I had learned to love the pretty little creature. He came so confidingly and sat up so prettily, nibbling a kernel of corn in his paws. I learned many of the little ways of squirrels, which I had never known before. He would scratch his ears and wash his face like a kitten, and even fold his paws under him and go to sleep, within reach of my arm. All innocent and peaceful things seem peculiarly attractive in these times of bloodshed and hatred, and I cannot help mourning some for my little squirrel.

TO MISS LUCY OSGOOD.

WAYLAND, December, 1862.

Your letter did me an "unco deal o' gude," as your letters always do. I agree with you entirely about the "buss fuss" of metaphysics. It has always been my aversion. More than thirty years ago, when Mrs. R. was intimate at my brother's, I used to hear her discuss Kant's philosophy with collegian visitors, until I went to bed without knowing whether or not I had " hung myself over the chair and put my clothes into bed." I met Mrs. R. in the cars several days ago, after an interval of twenty years, and what do you think? In ten minutes she had plunged into the depths of Kant's philosophy, and was trying to pull me after her. But I resisted stoutly. I do sometimes like a bank of fog to look at, if there are plenty of rainbows on it; but I have no fancy for sailing through it. Circumstances afterward made me acquainted with the transcendentallists, and I attended some of their meetings, where I saw plenty of fog with rainbows flitting over it. I remember once after a long silence, when everybody was looking in the fire expecting something great to come by and by, Mr. —— turned toward us, with that serene glance of his, and said slowly: " Why do we rummage about with memory in the Past, to ascertain our whereabouts and our whatabouts?" He paused for a reply, and receiving none, he continued: " Why do we rummage about in the Past to ascertain it? I am it; and it is I; is it not?"

TO MISS LUCY SEARLE.

WAYLAND, December 21, 1862.

We live almost like dormice in the winter. Very few people are so completely isolated. But I warm up my little den with bright little pictures, and rainbow glories from prisms suspended in the windows. I am amused twenty times a day with their fantastic variations. Sometimes the portrait of Charles Sumner is transfigured by the splendid light, and sometimes the ears of my little white kitten, in the picture opposite, are all aglow. The moss on a stick of wood in the corner suddenly becomes iridescent, and then the ashes on the hearth look like the glittering soil where the metallic gnomes live. I am childish enough to find pleasure in all this, and to talk aloud to the picture of a baby that is being washed. But you must not infer from this that I live for amusement. On the contrary, I work like a beaver the whole time. Just now I am making a hood for a poor neighbor; last week I was making flannels for the hospitals; odd minutes are filled up with ravelling lint; every string that I can get sight of, I pull for my poor oppressed brother Sambo. I write to the " Tribune " about him; I write to the " Transcript " about him; I write to private individuals about him; and I write to the President and Members of Congress about him; I write to Western Virginia and Missouri about him, and I get the articles published too. That shows what progress the cause of freedom is making. You see even the grave Historical Society of Massachusetts comes up to the work, in Mr. Livermore's valuable pamphlet entitled " Historical Researches." The manner in which poor Sambo's cause gets argued and listened to in all quarters now is the most encouraging feature of the times. I try to forget Bull Runs and Fredericksburg retreats, and think only of the increasing rapidity of moral progress. Human hands blunder shockingly; but the Divine Hand is overruling all in infinite wisdom.

TO MRS. S. B. SHAW.

1863.

As for the President's proclamation, I was thankful for it, but it excited no enthusiasm in my mind. With my gratitude to God was mixed an under-tone of sadness that the moral sense of the people was so low that the thing could not be done nobly. However we may inflate the emancipation balloon, it will never ascend among the constellations. The ugly fact cannot be concealed that it was done reluctantly and stintedly, and that even the degree that was accomplished was done selfishly; was merely a war measure, to which we were forced by our own perils and necessities; and that no recognition of principles of justice or humanity surrounded the politic act with a halo of moral glory. This war has furnished many instances of individual nobility, but our national record is mean.

But notwithstanding these misgivings, I am truly thankful for the proclamation. It is doing us a great good in Europe, and will be a powerful agent in helping on the change of feeling in England. I have always put a good deal of trust in the common people of England.

Speaking of individual nobility, how beautifully and bravely young Russell behaved when Savage was wounded! I murmured that he was a prisoner when his parents had been such consistent and generous friends of freedom; but after all, they have their reward in having a son to whom opportunities for moral greatness came not in vain. Your Robert, too, — people say the war has ripened in him all manly qualities. God bless and protect the two young heroes! They told me in Boston that they had both offered to lead colored soldiers. Is it so?

I thank you very much for the lovely photograph of S——. What a pity it is that the ancients were ignorant of this wonderful process! How I should like a photograph of Plato! and how I should like to have a representation of the Venus of Milo unmutilated. Nothing within my limited knowledge of ancient art affects me like that miraculous statue. Is it a Venus? Always it seems to me like the heroic Antigone proclaiming to the tyrant Creon that there is a "higher law" than that of kings. The physical beauty of the woman is wonderfully inspired with moral majesty.

TO THE SAME.

WAYLAND, 1863.

I have been travelling through dark and thorny places, dear, where there were no roses of thought to send to you; and ever overhead has been the great murky cloud of public affairs that will not scatter and let the sunshine through.

I am glad, dear, that new bright links are being continually added to your life. To me there come no changes but sad ones; no new links — only the continually dropping away, one after another, of the old ones. The decease of my brother adds greatly to my loneliness. In my isolated position, he was almost my only medium with the world of intellect. How much my mind has owed to him can never be described. I loved him, too, and this separation, so utterly unexpected, rouses up a thousand memories of childhood and youth. During the last month of his life I was going backward and forward often to see him. I was with him the last eight days, and with him when his soul departed on its mysterious journey to the unknown. Oh, how I suffered! It tore me all to pieces. And now, in the spring-time, I cannot make the renovation of nature seem cheerful. But why should I cast my shadow over you? I told you of my sad experiences mainly to account for my neglected correspondence.

I am rejoiced that Robert is so well pleased with his regiment. The Lord seems to have inspired the colored people to behave remarkably well all through this terrible conflict. When I was in Boston, last week, I said to Edmund Quincy that never in the course of my observation, or in my reading of human history, had I seen the hand of Providence so signally manifested as in the events of this war. He replied in a very characteristic way: "Well, Mrs. Child, when the job is done up, I hope it will prove creditable to Providence." My own belief is that it will. Think of Victor Hugo's writing a tragedy with John Brown for its hero! A French John Brown! It is too funny. I wonder what the old captain himself would think of it if he were present in Paris at its representation. I fancy he would be as much surprised at the portraiture as would the honest wife of Joseph the carpenter, with her troop of dark-eyed girls and boys, Joses and James and Jude, etc., if she were told that the image of the "immaculate

Virgin" Mary, with spangled robe and tinselled crown, was a likeness of her.

TO MISS LUCY OSGOOD.

WAYLAND, 1863.

I am glad your Philadelphia campaign proved so glorious. I hope you will enjoy many such. After all, I think the careful housewife was the largest element in your good time at Philadelphia. The older I grow the more I respect the "careful Marthas." I would rather have one for a household companion than ten devout and contemplative Marys. They did very well in the days when saints went barefoot and wore a perennial suit of hair-cloth: but the Marthas are decidedly preferable in these days of nicely-ironed linen, daily renewed, and stockings so flimsy that they need continual looking after. Devout, poetic saints must have careful Marthas to provide for them if they would be comfortable themselves, or be able to promote the happiness of others. Mr. S—— says his wife is a careful Martha. I wonder what would have become of him and the boys if she had been of the Mary pattern. All hail to the careful Marthas! say I. If I had one I would kiss her very shoe-ties.

TO MISS ELIZA SCUDDER.

WAYLAND, 1863.

Was n't I as proud as a peacock, and did n't it make me spread all my feathers, to have a "pair o' vairses" written to me in my old age? and such verses, too! Seriously, dear friend, I was never so touched and so pleased by any tribute in my life. I cried over the verses, and I smiled over them. I wanted to show them to everybody; but I did n't dare to show them to anybody — they were so complimentary. I knew I did n't deserve them; but I also knew that you thought I did, and that made me happy.

TO L. M. CHILD.

They cannot know, who only know
    Thy wise sweet written word,
Whose willing ears thy genial flow
    Of speech have never heard,

Who have not in thy soul's true face
    Traced each familiar line, —
The spirit's all informing grace
    That moulds a life like thine.

But I, belovéd, who have read,
    As one God's book who reads,
The power by purest purpose shed
    O'er homeliest ways and deeds;

Who know thy love's most royal power,
    With largesse free and brave,
Which crowns thee helper of the poor,
    The suffering and the slave;

Yet springs as freely and as warm
    To greet the near and small,
The prosy neighbor at the farm,
    The squirrel on the wall;

Which strengthens thee in hope to bear
    And toil and strive alone,
And lift another's load of care,
    While wearied 'neath thine own;

> So apt to know, so wise to guide,
> So tender to redress, —
> O friend, with whom such charms abide,
> How can I love thee less?
>
> E. S.

TO MRS. S. B. SHAW.

WAYLAND, July, 1863.

Oh, darling! darling! if the newspaper rumor be true,[1] what I have so long dreaded has come upon you. But rumor very often exaggerates and sometimes invents; so I still hope, though with a heart that bleeds for you. If the report be true, may our Heavenly Father sustain you under this heavy sorrow. Severe as the blow must be, it is not altogether without consolation. If your beautiful and brave boy has died, he died nobly in the defence of great principles, and he has gone to join the glorious army of martyrs; and how much more sacred and dear to memory is such a life and such a death, than a life spent in self-indulgence, gradually impairing the health and weakening the mental powers. Your darling Robert made the most of the powers and advantages God had given him by consecrating them to the defence of freedom and humanity. Such a son in the spirit-world is worth ten living here for themselves alone. Besides, dear, the separation is only for a little while. You parted from him a young man, but rendered thoughtful and anxious beyond his years by reason of the heavy responsibilities that devolved upon him. You will meet him a serene angel, endowed with larger vision and better understanding why it is that we are doomed to suffer here. Ah, darling, my words fall coldly upon your bereaved

---

[1] Report of the death of Colonel Robert G. Shaw.

heart. God comfort you! He alone can carry you through this dark passage. He has given you beautiful little grandchildren to love, and I trust their soft arms will help to bear you up. Most sincerely do I wish that my old life could have been sacrificed to save your brave and beautiful boy. But the Heavenly Father ordereth all things in wisdom and in mercy, too; as we should acknowledge if we could only see the end from the beginning.

In your last but one you wrote as if I might think you did not pity me enough. I was going to answer that you pitied me more than enough; more than I pity myself. I was going to ask you what was my misfortune[1] compared with that of the poor wretches driven from their homes by murderous mobs; or what was it compared with the anxiety of a mother whose only son was leading a colored regiment into South Carolina. But now in view of this terrible rumor, how utterly insignificant and contemptible seem all my troubles! I thank Mrs. Gay very much for her hearty sympathy; but tell her that at a crisis like this it is merely as if a mosquito had stung me.

Ought I not to be taking care of the sick and wounded soldiers? Sometimes that thought worries me. Yours with a heart brimful of love and sympathy.

TO FRANCIS G. SHAW.

July, 1863.

Words are inadequate to express what I feel for you. The same faith that made you willing to sacrifice your only son in defence of righteous principles will help to sustain you under this sorrowful bereavement. But oh, how hard it would be for our poor

---

[1] A fire had burned a part of her house.

human hearts, were it not for the hope of reunion in that other world, where all the shocking discords are resolved into harmony!

Dear friend, I herewith return you the remaining check for two hundred dollars. Since those horrible New York mobs, I cannot keep it with an easy conscience. Do not understand me as returning it to you, but to your fund for the relief of poor wretches whose need is so much greater than mine. Besides this feeling, there are other personal considerations which, in part, induce me to return your bounty. I have met with two unexpected lucky incidents. I have also just recovered fifty dollars which I supposed was lost by the failure of my bookseller. I also hope to make three or four hundred dollars by my forthcoming book for old people.

Under these circumstances, I think you will see that I ought not to receive help when there are so many sufferers in the land who need it more than I do. You will see that it is not pride, dearest friend, but conscience. Never, never shall I forget your kindness in sending it. It did me a world of good, when I felt so stunned and desolate. But I am getting bravely over all that now. I reproach myself for having cared so much about a home, when so many homes are ruthlessly broken up. The débris of a fire is bad, but what is it compared with the desolation wrought by a mob? I am most sincerely sorry for James Gibbons and his family.[1] Miss Osgood told me they had one room consecrated to interesting souvenirs of their lost Willie. How dreadful it must have been to have that pillaged by a mob!

---

[1] Mr. Gibbons's house in New York city was gutted by the mob during the draft riots of July, 1863.

MISS LUCY OSGOOD.

WAYLAND, 1864.

I joyfully hailed the sight of your hand-writing; more joyfully even than usual; because I conjectured that you would write about the biography of Theodore Parker. It is an inspiring book, making one feel that there is nobleness in the battle of life when a true man girds on his armor for the fight. This record confirms my impression that Theodore Parker was the greatest man, morally and intellectually, that our country has ever produced. The manner in which the book is made up is, I think, open to some criticism. In the first place, there is the general fault of containing too much. It seems to me that if one half, or at least one third, had been omitted, the remaining portion would have been more unqualifiedly interesting. In the second place, the arrangement is not orderly. In the third place, the sentences of Mr. Weiss sometimes need studying to discover his meaning. I have great respect and admiration for Mr. Weiss, but I do not like his style. I often wish that his large and noble thoughts were expressed with more simplicity. He reminds me of an anecdote of Mr. Berrien of Georgia. A stranger, who had just been hearing Foote of Mississippi speak in Congress, remarked to Mr. Berrien, "Foote has great command of language." "On the contrary," replied Berrien, "I think language has great command of him." I think scorn of simplicity and directness is the crying sin of writers of the present day.

TO MISS ELIZA SCUDDER.

WAYLAND, 1864.

Another encouraging thing is the marvellous and constantly increasing change in public opinion on the subject of slavery. Only think of George Thompson's speaking in the Halls of Congress, and of John Brown's Hallelujah being performed there! Captain —— of the United States Navy, has been a bitter pro-slavery man, violent in his talk against abolitionists and " niggers." He has been serving in the vicinity of New Orleans, and has come home on a furlough, an outspoken abolitionist. He not only says it in private, but has delivered three lectures in town, in which he has publicly announced the total change in his sentiments since he had "an opportunity to know something on the subject." A few days ago he was going in the cars from Boston to Roxbury, when a colored soldier entered the car. Attempting to seat himself, he was repulsed by a white man, who rudely exclaimed, " I'm not going to ride with niggers." Captain W., who sat a few seats farther forward, rose up, in all the gilded glory of his naval uniform, and called out, " Come here, my good fellow! I've been fighting alongside of people of your color, and glad enough I was to have 'em by my side. Come sit by me." Two years ago I would not have believed such a thing possible of him. So the work goes on in all directions.

TO MRS. S. B. SHAW.

1864.

I suppose you will hear of George Thompson while he is in New York, if you do not see him. How wonderful it is that he should be received in this manner, when twenty-nine years ago he had to hustle away privately to Halifax to take passage for England, because his life was in danger in our cities! Now a great deal of the respectability of Boston unites with us to give him a grand reception, and his entrance is greeted with hurrahs!

> "To-day abhorred, to-morrow adored,
> So round and round we run;
> And ever the Truth comes uppermost,
> And ever is Justice done."

I met Mr. Thompson at the Anti-slavery Office. In talking with him, I told him how wrathy I had been with England. "You should remember, Mrs. Child," said he, "how your cause was made to appear in the eyes of the world. First, your President's inaugural was largely taken up with assurances that fugitive slaves would be returned to their masters, and that those who attempted to interfere would be punished; secondly, two of your generals volunteered offers to put down insurrections of the slaves, should they try to obtain their freedom; thirdly, slaves who escaped into your lines were sent back and cruelly scourged by the tyrants from whose power they had sought your protection; fourthly, Mr. Seward charged Mr. Adams not to speak of slavery, and, through him, gave assurance that 'the status of no class of people in America would be changed by the war;' fifthly, President Lincoln, after the war had continued more than a year, offered the slave-holders a hundred days to consider whether they would come back with their chattels, or still fight for their independence at the risk of the abolition of slavery. Was there anything in this to excite the enthusiasm of the

English people about your war?" I was obliged to confess that there was not, and that I had myself often apologized for the common people of England in that very way; saying, I felt " sure their hearts would sympathize with any war for freedom and humanity." " Now that freedom appears to be the dominant idea, the common people of England do sympathize with you most heartily," replied he. " As for the aristocratic classes, a desire to see the grand experiment of a republic fail underlies all their hostility to the North." I admitted the truth of all this; but after all, it must be remembered that our haughty step-dame England hastened to recognize the rebels as belligerents before we had given any of the alleged signs of subservience to slavery. Did you see Kingsley's exultation over the idea that the pages he was writing might meet the eyes of that great hero and statesman, Jeff. Davis? It was miserable twaddle, to say nothing of its want of principle. It does seem to me remarkable that the literary men of England should so favor a cause avowedly founded on despotism.

TO MISS ELIZA SCUDDER.

WAYLAND, 1864.

I wish there were not such a wall of partition between us and the animal world. It would be so curious and entertaining to understand what they are about, and to help them in emergencies by our superior strength and wisdom. The swallow's nest in the sitting-room chimney fell down a few days ago. Four of the little birds were dead, but one was alive and lusty, though its eyes were not yet opened. The mother, not knowing what to do, flew up chimney, and left it to its fate. I tried to feed it with flies on

a pin; but it was of no use. I did not understand its
ways. The poor little thing scrambled round with so
much energy, called its mother so loudly, and manifested such a determination to live, that it made me
very sorry to be unable to help it. But it was better
for it to die; for if I had succeeded in bringing it up
by hand, the foolish little thing would have been bewildered in all its instincts, and never have known
how to bring up a family. . . . One of the pictures,
" The Trumpeting Angel of Fra Angelico," charmed
me extremely. But after all, the angels, I apprehend, are something very superior to all that. We
know as little about them and their ways as the
chimney swallows know about us. Walls of partition
rise up everywhere, above and below.

TO THE SAME.

WAYLAND, 1864.

I am a happy woman since the election.[1] It makes
me feel that our republican form of government rests
on more secure foundations. There was no enthusiasm for honest old Abe. There is no beauty in him,
that men should desire him; there is no insinuating,
polished manner, to beguile the senses of the people;
there is no dazzling military renown; no silver flow
of rhetoric; in fact, no glittering prestige of any kind
surrounds him; yet the people triumphantly elected
him, in spite of all manner of machinations, and notwithstanding the long, long drag upon their patience
and their resources which this war has produced. I
call this the triumph of free schools; for it was the
intelligence and reason of the people that reëlected
Abraham Lincoln. He has his faults, and I have

[1] The second election of President Lincoln.

sometimes been out of patience with him; but I will say of him that I have constantly gone on liking him better and better. His recent reply to some people who serenaded him charmed me exceedingly. A most beautiful spirit pervaded it. As for Andy Johnson, he has completely taken me captive by his speech at Nashville. To think of that colored procession going through the streets of Nashville, greeted from the windows with hurrahs, and waving of hats and handkerchiefs! To think of the Vice President of the United States promising to be their Moses, to lead them out of bondage, telling them, "Remember they who would be free, themselves must strike the blow!" And all this in Nashville where Amos Dresser, thirty years ago, was publicly flogged for having an abolition tract in his carpet-bag! Then to think of Maryland wheeling into the circle of free States, with ringing of bells and waving of banners! To think of the triumphal arch in the streets of Baltimore, whereon, with many honored historical names, were inscribed the names of Benjamin Banneker and R. R. Forten, two colored men! , Glory to God! This is marvellous progress. Glory to God! Hallelujah!

Miss Cobbe's introduction to the "Life of Theodore Parker" I like extremely. It is a truly manly production; thus we are obliged to compliment the "superior sex" when we seek to praise our own. I have also been reading her "Broken Lights." Her analysis of the present state of the churches is very clear and complete. Concerning her "Church of the Future" I am more doubtful. Sterne says, very truly, "A philosophic religion is fit for philosphers only." Miss Cobbe, and minds that are kindred to hers, will be satisfied with the "internal consciousness of God;" but will the masses of men ever arrive at that height? For myself, I think the church of the future is to be a church of deeds, not of doctrines of any kind. Men will combine together to work for each other, as children of the Universal Father; and these combinations will be to them as churches.

TO MISS LUCY OSGOOD.

WAYLAND, 1865.

I thank you for your two right pleasant letters. I have several times been amused at being charged with totally different deficiencies by different people. You accuse me of "being indifferent to externals," whereas the common charge against me is that I think too much of beauty, and say too much about it. I myself think it is one of my greatest weaknesses. A handsome man, woman, or child, can always make a fool and a pack-horse of me. My next neighbor's little boy has me completely under his thumb, merely by virtue of his beautiful eyes and sweet voice.

I have been a very happy woman since this year came in. My Sunset book [1] has had most unexpected success. The edition of 4,000 sold before New Year's Day, and they say they might have sold 2,000 more if they had been ready. This pleases me beyond measure, for the proceeds, whether more or less, were vowed to the freedmen; and cheering old folks with one hand, and helping the wronged and suffering with the other, is the highest recreation I ever enjoyed. Nobles or princes cannot discover, or invent, any pleasure equal to earning with one hand and giving with the other. I seldom have a passing wish

---

[1] *Looking towards Sunset. From Sources Old and New, Original and Selected.* By L. Maria Child. Boston, 1864.

for enlarged means except for the sake of doing more for others. My own wants are very few and simple. I am glad you approve of the book. I am not surprised that the "Mysterious Pilgrimage" seemed to you "fanciful." You know there is a practical side and a poetic side to me. In a book designed for general readers, I thought it best to show both sides. What most pleases one class of readers will be less pleasing to others. I am surprised that you say nothing about Bernard Palissy. He is perfectly charming to me. My prime object in making the Sunset book was to present old people with something wholly cheerful. Human nature, as the years pass on, more and more requires cheerful influences. Memory has a superabounding stock of sadness for all, and any addition to it in books or conversation is an unwelcome excess. To everything there is a bright side and a dark side; and I hold it to be unwise, unphilosophic, unkind to others, and unhealthy for one's own soul, to form the habit of looking on the dark side. Cheerfulness is to the spiritual atmosphere what sunshine is to the earthly landscape. I am resolved to cherish cheerfulness with might and main.

William C. Bryant wrote me a charming note about the book. I will quote part of it to you, because I know you like to hear of anything pleasant that happens to me. He says: "My dear Mrs. Child, you are like some artists, who excel in 'sunset' views. You give the closing stage of human life an atmosphere of the richest lights and warmest hues, and make even its clouds add to its glory. My wife and I have read your book with great delight.' And while I am talking of the pleasant things that have happened to me lately I will ask, "What do you think I had for a New Year's present?" Mrs. L., bless her kind soul! sent me Milmore's bust of Charles Sumner. Now the fact is, I had a private longing for that bust, though I never mentioned it to any mortal. I did once think about inquiring the price; but I remembered the freedmen and the soldiers, and resolved not to put myself in the way of temptation. It is not only a good likeness, but it is a wonderfully speaking likeness, full of the noble soul of the man.

TO HON. GEORGE W. JULIAN.

April 8, 1865.

We must not forget that all great revolutions and reformations would look mean and meagre if examined in detail as they occurred at the time. We talk of Constantine as the "Christian" Emperor; but it is more than doubtful whether he ever adopted, or even understood, the first principles of Christianity. The converts to the new religion had become so numerous that they were an element of power; and if he did not avail himself of their influence, rivals would. If their church could prop up his throne, he was very willing it should become the religion of the state.

If we examine into the Protestant reformation we shall find that the sincere and earnest men engaged in it bore no greater proportion to the time-serving and self-seeking than do the thorough anti-slavery men to the politicians of our own time. And then what base agents helped on that great work! Who would have supposed that Henry the Eighth could have been turned to any good account? It is marvellous by how small a force this world is moved, in point of numbers, when God is on their side. Still more wonderful is it to observe what poor, mean cattle God yokes to the car of progress, and makes them draw in a direction they are striving to avoid. It has been most strikingly illustrated in the course of this war. The details are often ludicrous exhibitions of human inconsistency and selfishness, but the result is a sublime manifestation of an overruling Providence.

TO MISS LUCY OSGOOD.

WAYLAND, 1865.

I received a letter last week from William H. Channing, in acknowledgment of funds sent to the freedmen in his department. He is the same infinite glow that he was when he took my heart captive twenty years ago. He writes: "You ought to have been in Congress on the ever-to-be-remembered 31st of January 1865.[1] Such an outburst of the people's heart has never been seen in the Capitol since the nation was born. It was the sunrise of a new day for the republic. I was standing by John Jay, and as we shook hands over the glorious vote I could not but say, 'Are not our fathers and grandfathers here with us? They surely must be here to share our joy in thus gathering the fruit of which they planted the seed.' Yes! and our blessed, great-hearted Theodore Parker was there, with a band of witnesses. Selah!"

[1] The day on which the Thirteenth Amendment to the Constitution, abolishing slavery in the United States, passed the House of Representatives, and (having previously passed the Senate) went to the Legislatures of the several States for ratification.

Yesterday I walked up to see Mr. and Mrs. S., where I have not been for a year. He is full of the great Convocation of Unitarians at New York, to which he is sent as delegate. He seems to think it will be very easy to settle "a few fundamental principles, in which all can agree, while sufficient room for progress will be left in unsettled minor opinions." But his very first " fundamental principle " concerning the divine origin of Jesus puts up a bar that stops the chariot wheels. There is a large class of minds that cannot see in Unitarianism a mere half-way house, where spiritual travellers find themselves well accommodated for the night, but where they grow weary of spending the day. And many of them will not even spend a night there, when they discover a new road, so shortened and straightened, that when they want to call upon the Father, they are under no necessity of going roundabout to call upon the Son.

TO MRS. S. B. SHAW.

1865.

You were curious to know who it was that offered to pay $1,800 for the redemption of Thomas Sims. It was Major-General Devens, who was United States marshal at the time of the rendition of Sims. He made the offer unasked; and when Sims found his way North again he sent him, through me, $100 to assist him till he could get into business. It seems to me a singularly noble proceeding. I suppose that his idea of the necessity of sustaining law, and his great admiration of Daniel Webster, led him to do what pained his heart at the time and troubled his conscience afterward. But you would rarely find a man who would atone so nobly for an error. Now that the war is over, and slavery is abolished, I think his reason for enjoining secresy no longer exists. When I urged upon him that the moral influence of the action might do good, he did not renew his prohibition. In a recent letter to me he expresses great satisfaction that he has been enabled to take an active part in the struggle that has resulted in the emancipation of the slaves. How I wish that your darling Robert had survived to look back upon the Revolution as a thing completed, and to glory in his share of it! Yet perhaps it would not have been better so. I am glad it is proposed to erect a statue to him in Boston; but I hope they will not place it in the vicinity of Daniel Webster. If Webster had done his duty, there would have been no storming of Fort Wagner.

TO THE SAME.

1865.

I agree with Garrison in thinking the Anti-Slavery Society had better dissolve when the States have ratified the amendment to the Constitution. But I think they ought to form themselves into a society for the protection of the freedmen. Those old slaveholders will "act like Cain" as long as they live. They will try to discourage, misrepresent, and harass the emancipated slave in every way, in order to prevent the new system of things from working well, just as the Jamaica planters did. It will not do to trust the interests of the emancipated to compromising politicians; their out-and-out radical friends must mount guard over them.

TO MRS. ANNA LORING DRESEL.

WAYLAND, February 13, 1866.

It takes Germans to make pictures of real, all-alive children, because they are an honest, child-like nation. The French make graceful puppets and fashionable dolls. I have laughed and laughed over that little book, and I dare say the sight of it will have a cheering influence all the year through, whenever I am inclined to be sad. It will be like having a play with children, with the great advantage of putting them away when I like. The literary portion of it is not above my comprehension, with the exception of three or four words which I suppose to be baby lingo. I thank your dear mother very much for the beautiful statuette. The more I look at it, the more I am impressed with the genius indicated by the conception and execution of the group. That craving for beauty lies too deep in my nature ever to be uprooted. Speaking of beauty, I wish you could have seen our great elm-tree, one morning, when a cold night had completely incrusted it with the frozen vapor of the preceding warm day. Such great branches of pearls and diamonds lifted up high in the air, with the darkest and clearest blue sky for a back-ground. I am a great admirer of winter scenery, but never in my life have I seen anything so beautiful as that. I shouted again and again, and I would have run two miles to have caught a poet to come and shout with me. David admired it greatly, and made divers superb comparisons in a quiet, philosophic way, but I could n't get him up to the shouting point.

TO REV. SAMUEL J. MAY.

WAYLAND, January, 1866.

I was greatly refreshed by your affectionate letter about "The Freedmen's Book." I live so entirely apart from the world that when I publish anything I rarely see or hear anything about the effect it produces. I sent the slave-holders, the year before the war, over twelve hundred copies of "The Right Way the Safe Way," directed them with my own hand, and paid the postage out of my own purse; and I received but one response. I had a feeling that such a book as the "Freedmen's Book" was needed at the present time and might do good. In order to adapt it carefully for them, I wrote over two hundred letter pages of manuscript copy; and then, despairing of getting it published, I paid $600 to get it through the press; which sum, if it ever returns, will be a fund to help in the education of the freedmen and their children. I have done what I could, and I hope a blessing will rest upon it. That you approve of it so heartily is one guaranty that it will be useful.

TO MISS LUCY OSGOOD.

WAYLAND, 1866.

It seems a long while since I received your very lively letter.

With regard to the comparative value of novels and sermons, you go farther for your side than I could go for mine. You confess to enjoying "a dullish sermon." I cannot wade through a dullish novel. A third-rate one I never read, unless I read it aloud, to oblige some one else; and I can scarcely tolerate even second-rate ones. A first-rate novel I do enjoy better than any other reading. I like them better now than I did in my youth; partly because the need of being entertained grows upon people in general as the sad experiences of life multiply, and partly because I live so much in solitude that pictures of society supply, in some degree, the place of society. I agree with you entirely with regard to public teaching at stated seasons. I think all classes of minds would be benefited by it. What I complain of is that they do not really get teaching. The habits and wants of society have changed, and preaching has not sufficiently changed with them.

Very little of the preaching is adapted to the wants of any class of minds. When people hear true living words spoken concerning the things they are doing and the thoughts they are thinking, they hear the words gladly. The magnetic power of Theodore Parker and Henry Ward Beecher, I think, is largely to be attributed to the fact that they meet the popular mind on its own plane instead of addressing it from a height. I do not want to see preaching abolished, but I do want to see its sphere enlarged. There must be some cause for the prevailing and ever-increasing feeling of its insufficiency. As for me, after struggling much with my disinclination to attend meeting, I have given up the contest.

I have n't, for years, attended any anti-slavery meetings, or lectures of any sort; I have such a dread of the constraint. Then, one has to go through so much to get so little at any of the conventions or great gatherings! It is necessary to listen to half-a-dozen commonplace speeches before a good one comes on. It is " swimming through the Mediterranean to catch a smelt," as old Dr. Allyne used to say.

I hope you have seen Bierstadt's "Storm on the Rocky Mountains." I went to look at it when I was last in Boston, and I wanted to stay all day; though I had an impression that the rain would pour down from those clouds, and the lightning flash through them, if I stayed there long. Such clouds I did not suppose to be possible on canvas. They seemed so distinctly to roll away that I was surprised to look up and find them still there.

TO REV. SAMUEL J. MAY.

WAYLAND, 1867.

Your anti-slavery sketches [1] carry me back pleasantly to those bygone days when our souls were raised above the level of common life by the glorious inspiration of unselfish zeal. It seems but a little while ago, and yet men speak of it as a "dead subject," so swiftly the world whirls round, carrying us, and all memory of us, with it!

In your very kind notice of me, you have exaggerated some things, and omitted others. I don't think I lost so much "per annum" by espousing the anti-slavery cause. At all events, I think the indefinite statement that my literary prospects were much injured by it would have been better. With regard to society, I was a gainer decidedly; for though the respectables, who had condescended to patronize me, forthwith sent me "to Coventry," anti-slavery intro-

---

[1] *Some Recollections of our Anti-Slavery Conflict,* by Samuel J. May. Boston, 1869. At the time this letter was written, however, they were appearing in regular installments in the *Christian Register* of Boston.

duced me to the noblest and best of the land, intellectually and morally, and knit us together in that firm friendship which grows out of sympathy in a good but unpopular cause. Besides, it is impossible to estimate how much one's own character gains by a warfare which keeps the intellect wide awake, and compels one to reflect upon moral principles. I was quite surprised, one day, by a note from the trustees of the Boston Athenæum, offering me the free use of the library, the same as if I owned a share. . . . I had never asked such a favor, and I am not aware that any friend of mine had ever solicited it. My husband was anti-slavery, and it was the theme of many of our conversations while Garrison was in prison. About the time of the unexpected attention from the trustees, Mr. Garrison came to Boston, and I had a talk with him. Consequently the first use I made of my Athenæum privilege was to take out some books on that subject, with a view to writing my "Appeal." A few weeks after the "Appeal" was published, I received another note from the trustees, informing me that at a recent meeting they had passed a vote to take away my privilege, lest it should prove an inconvenient precedent!

TO MRS. S. B. SHAW.

WAYLAND, 1868.

I did receive the "Breviary," but I had no idea of its coming from you. . . . I might answer your inquiries with some roundabout polite equivocation, but that is not my way. So I will e'en tell the plain truth. I never liked any of that sort of books. I would never reflect at all, if I had "Reflections for Every Day in the Year" marked out for me. I have a strong resistance to all sorts of ritual. Moreover, this book of Scheffer's seems to me uncommonly lugubrious of its kind. I read a few of the poems, and they made me feel so forlorn that I hastened to hide the book away in a receptacle that I keep for things not cheerful to read, and consequently not profitable to lend. The world is so full of sadness that I more and more make it a point to avoid all sadness that does not come within the sphere of my duty.

I read only "chipper" books. I hang prisms in my windows to fill the room with rainbows; I gaze at all the bright pictures in shop windows; I cultivate the gayest flowers; I seek cheerfulness in every possible way. This is my "necessity in being old." Then you know I never did like the things that "good people" like. Ritual was always antagonistic to my temperament; it interferes with my free-will, and my free-will grows more rampant every year I live. And now having blown my blast against the "saint's" book, I thank you sincerely for your friendly intention in sending it; that I shall cherish in my memory though I consign the book to oblivion. The poems are certainly pure, solid good sense; *dreadful* solid.

TO MISS ELIZA SCUDDER.

WAYLAND, 1868.

In our climate what a misnomer it is to call this season spring! very much like calling Calvinism religion. I don't care, I insist upon being glad that I was born in Massachusetts. As for anybody that prefers to have been born among mosquitoes and copperheads down South, or where the sun sets behind the Golden Gate, why let them go and be born again. I, being rather a Puritanic person, stand by old Massachusetts, if she is covered with snow in April. To speak seriously, I do think our climate is changing. For many years I have noticed that winter extends farther into spring than it used to do when I was young. They say that tusks of ivory dug up in Onalaska prove that region to have once been in the tropical zone. If so, perhaps we also are steering for the North Pole. It is comforting to know that I shall not be on board when the old ship Massachusetts anchors among the icebergs. That "precession of the equinoxes" is a mysterious business. What it is going to do with this earth of ours I don't know.

TO MRS. S. E. SEWALL.

WAYLAND, July 30, 1868.

As you and Mr. Sewall are one, and he is too busy to read rhapsodical letters, I will write to you to thank him for "The Gypsy," and I do thank him most fervently. I think some good brownie helps you two to find out what I most want. I have been hankering after that "Spanish Gypsy" and trying to borrow it, but I did not hint that to you, knowing your lavish turn of mind. Some of my friends think I make an exaggerated estimate of the author of "Adam Bede," but I have long ranked her as the greatest among women intellectually, and the moral tone of her writings seems to me always pure and elevated. I never expected to enjoy a poem again so much as I enjoyed "Aurora Leigh," but I think the Gypsy is fully equal, if not superior. I read it through at first ravenously, all aglow; then I read it through a second time slowly and carefully, to taste every drop of the sparkling nectar. The artistic construction cannot be too highly praised, and it is radiant throughout with poetic light. . . . That wonderful glorification of the juggler's exhibition made me so wild with delightful excitement that my soul heard the music, saw the transfiguring light of the setting sun, and went leaping through the dance with Fedalma. It is an immortal picture in my gallery for the other world.

TO FRANCIS G. SHAW.

WAYLAND, February 11, 1869.

DEAR FRIEND OF OLD TIMES AND OF ALL TIMES:

To-day I am sixty-seven years old. Living out of the world as I do, and keeping few holy-days, I have formed the habit of consecrating this day in my small way. When I feel like praying, I pray; and I generally do on this anniversary, so full of memories of the past, and of aspirations for the future, stretching into the eternal world. I look at the photographs of my intimate friends always with a swelling heart, but for the purpose of recalling everything pleasant associated with them, not to indulge in mourning for those who are separated from me by time, distance, or change of existence.

A few nights ago, after the sun had set, the broad sheet of ice on the meadows was all roseate and glowing with the reflected light. I strive to realize this in the state of my own soul. My sun is setting, and the ice of age is gathering around me, but light from above and warm flushes of memory fall on the wintry landscape and make it beautiful. . . .

I formerly thought that the New Church opened for us a view of the eternal city with its gold and precious gems. It was a pleasant vision, and it did much to help the growth of my soul; but happy as

the state was, I would not go back to it if I could. I
have stumbled over much in cold and darkness since
then, but I know that also is one of the appointed
means of growth. We do not choose our states, they
come upon us. The best we can do is to reverently
follow all the truth it is given us to see at any time.
My faith in theological doctrines of any kind has
diminished almost to vanishing, but my faith in eternal principles has grown ever stronger and stronger,
and more and more humble and reverent is my desire
to embody them in my life. . . .

I still think that Fourier was a great prophet of
the future. I am convinced that this troublesome
knot of employers and employed can never be disentangled except by some process of association which
shall apportion some manual labor to all, and some
culture and recreation to all. . . . The peace of God
be with you all!

TO MRS. S. B. SHAW.

WAYLAND, 1869.

The music-box arrived safely, and I thank you from
my inmost heart for thinking of your old friend, and
wishing to give her pleasure. The old music-box is
very dear to me. Its powers are limited, but what it
does say it says very sweetly; and the memories it
sings to me are the dearest of all. . . .

We had quite a glorification here over Grant's
election. We had a really handsome procession of
five hundred men bearing flags and gay-colored lanterns, and attended by a band of music from Boston.
I had no idea they would come up so far as our house;
but as we had subscribed, as they thought, liberally,
they concluded to pay us that compliment. When

we heard the sounds coming nearer and nearer, and saw the first torches pass our nearest neighbor's, I tore open the curtains, and scrambled to place fourteen lights in the front windows; being all I could get up on such short notice. Then I went to the front door and waved a great white cloth, and joined in the hurrahs of the procession like a "strong-minded" woman as I am. The fact is, I forget half the time whether I belong to the stronger or weaker sex.

While I was demonstrating at one door, David was exercising his lungs at another. A crowd of foreigners were following the procession in a discomfited state of mind, and seeing us so jubilant they called out, "Three cheers for the nigger President!" a curious title to bestow on Grant, who has never manifested the slightest interest in the colored people. But I don't want him to be a "nigger President." I simply want him to see that equal justice is administered to all classes of people, and I have great hopes he will do that. So unpretending a man must be substantially good and honest, I think. However, I did not shout from such enthusiasm for him so much as I did from a feeling of relief that we were rid of Seymour.

TO MISS LUCY OSGOOD.

WAYLAND, 1869.

I have read a good many of Taine's papers on Art, and always with great zest. His descriptions of Venice in "Les Deux Mondes" is wonderfully glowing and poetic. It was almost like seeing that city of enchantment. Max Müller's "Chips" I have never seen. The greatest extravagance I have committed for years was buying his "Science of Language," price seven dollars, as a birthday present for my philological mate. His habit of digging for the origin of words has proved contagious, and he often expresses surprise at the help my quick guesses afford him in his patient researches. I resolutely read Max Müller's "Science of Language," and picked up a good many new ideas and valuable suggestions; but to read it with full understanding required a great deal more learning than I possess.

A friend is accustomed to say that my " bark is worse than my bite ; " and it is something so with regard to my theological intolerance. For instance, I have given yearly to the American Missionary Association, ever since emancipation, twenty dollars a year, to help them support a teacher among the freedmen, true blue orthodox. Yet when I proposed to them to aid me in the circulation of my " Freedmen's Book," offering them several hundred volumes at the mere cost of materials, they were not willing to do it unless they could be allowed to cut out several articles, and in lieu thereof insert orthodox tracts about " redeeming blood," etc. Yet my book contained not one sectarian word, except here and there an orthodox phrase in articles written by colored people. I do sincerely believe that all creeds which make faith in doctrines of more importance than the practice of morality have an injurious effect on character, and I abominate them.

One of my neighbors told me there was a biographical sketch of me in the " Christian Register," copied from the " Chicago Tribune." But I did not wish to see it, having a great aversion to newspaper publicity. I care a good deal what my friends think of my performances, but I am singularly indifferent to notices of the press. They are so indiscriminate, and so much done up in a spirit of trade between publishers and editors, that they have little value. I do not see the "Westminster Review," but I care very little about being "respectfully cited" in it. The same honor befalls hundreds below the level of mediocrity. I think few things are more inconvenient and disagreeable than being a "small" lion. One loses the advantage of complete obscurity, without attaining to the advantages of great fame. If what I have written has been the means of doing any good in the world, I am thankful; but as for personal gratification in receiving, as a lion, what you call "the homage of smaller animals," I have none. All I want is to be left in peace to do quietly the work which my hands find to do.

I agree with you in thinking that there are many good things in the article, "New Chapter of Christian Evidences," in the "Atlantic." But if Christianity is, as the writer says, better adapted for a universal religion than any other, is it not simply because Christianity is an accretion of all the antecedent religious aspirations of mankind? How many rivulets of thought had been flowing from various parts of the world, and through continuous ages, all drawn toward each other by the extension of the Roman Empire! And in the midst of those gathering tides stood Paul! He was the man, by whose agency a Jewish reformation was widened into a world-religion. All the world being represented in the system, it may well be better adapted for a universal religion than any of its component parts. But it is still receiving accretions from present inspirations, and so it will go on. Swedenborg has not established a "*new* church,' but he has greatly modified the old one. I opine that Paul would recognize in the teachings of our day few of the distinctive features of Christianity as it presented itself to his mind. It is curious to read the sermons that were admired a hundred years ago, and compare them with the preaching of the present day. What congregations would now be edified by the thunder of those old guns of the Gospel? There is not a parish that would hear them as "candidates."

TO THE SAME.

WAYLAND, 1869.

I wish you joy of your "new Greek grammar." I eschew all grammars, because I cannot receive their contents by intuition. Perhaps if you were to confine your investigation to the Greek article, you would find it more "entertaining,' but still the result might not be satisfactory. I have read of a German philologist who expended the diligent labor of a long life on the study of the Greek article, and on his deathbed he said to his son, "Take warning by my example. Do not undertake too much. I ought to have confined myself to the dative case."

I cordially agree with the praises of "Unspoken Sermons." They are the only kind that interest me.

I was amused by the prematureness of Aggy; but of all the children I ever heard of, Susan L——'s eldest daughter has manifested the most precocious forecast. When she was about six years old, her father, in reading the newspaper aloud, read of a workman in a manufactory whose arm had been shockingly torn by the machinery. They did not suppose the little one understood it, or took any notice of it, but when she was put to bed she began to cry bitterly. When her mother asked what was the matter, she burst out vehemently, " Oh, what if I should marry a machine man ? What should I do ? " " Don't cry about that, dear," replied her mother, trying to repress laughter, " Perhaps you won't be married." " Oh yes I shall ! " exclaimed the little Mary (who ought to have been named the little Martha) ; " They will marry me to a machine man ; and then, if he tears his arm, I sha'n't know what to do." She is now fifteen or sixteen, and is always betraying the same forecasting tendencies. She has learned to swim, and is very expert in the water. A little while ago she swam up to a child on the bank of the river and said, " Please get on my back, and let me carry you across. I want to see if I could save you, if we should be aboard the same ship and get wrecked." The child consented, and Mary was exultant to find that she could swim with such a burden.

TO THE SAME.

1870.

Mrs. J——, the author of " Linda," spent a couple of nights here a few weeks ago. She told me one little anecdote which reminded me of the Puritan soldiers of old. She said that one day, during the war, she was gathering vegetables in the garden of the hospital where she was nursing the wounded. A soldier passed by, and seeing some roses in bloom he said, " Auntie, will you give me a rose ? " Mrs. J—— was sensitive about being called Auntie, that being the universal way of addressing middle-aged slaves. So she answered, " I will give you some roses with all my heart, for I am always willing to give anything to a soldier of the United States. But I am not your auntie; your mother was not my sister." "Was n't she, though?" rejoined the soldier. You 'd better ask General Christ about that. He was a great general, and I guess he would say that your mother was my mother's sister. My mother is a good woman. If you knew her, you would love her." Beautiful, was it not?

TO FRANCIS G. SHAW.

WAYLAND, 1870.

I thank you cordially for "M. Sylvestre." It is charmingly translated, in that free, flowing way that makes it seem as if it were written in English. It is far less exciting than "Consuelo" was, but it is very attractive, full of serene wisdom and gleams of simple beauty. I never can believe that George Sand is so debased and impure as many represent her to be. She may have committed grave errors, but I think they must have proceeded from the restless yearnings of unsatisfied affections, and the pursuit of an ideal which she could not find, rather than from unbridled sensuality. A woman of impure soul might write elaborate sentences in praise of virtue, but I deem it impossible for such a woman to write books that breathe such pure aspirations as many of hers do. And even her very worst ones, are they not true pictures of life as she has seen it in that false, corrupted France? And is it not the sincerity of her nature, rather than any delight in uncleanness, which makes it impossible for her to gloss over the corruptions which she sees all around her? Some people are so constituted that they must "tell the truth, and shame the Devil." Then again, admitting that George Sand has been as licentious as some say, is it quite just to condemn her and her writings as irredeemably bad, while Burns's poems are in every family, and the anniversaries of his birthday are kept as if they were festivals in honor of a saint?

TO MISS HENRIETTA SARGENT.

1870.

I promised to send you the lines I wrote about George Thompson in 1835. Here they are. Perhaps they will recall to you the feelings with which you used to listen to him in those old stirring times.

> I've heard thee when thy powerful words
>   Were like the cataract's roar,
> Or like the ocean's mighty waves
>   Resounding on the shore.
>
> But, even in reproof of sin,
>   Love brooded over all,
> As the mild rainbow's heavenly arch
>   Rests on the waterfall.
>
> I've heard thee in the hour of prayer,
>   When dangers were around;
> Thy voice was like the royal harp,
>   That breathed a charmèd sound.
>
> The evil spirit felt its power,
>   And howling turned away;
> And some, perchance, who "came to scoff,
>   Remained with thee to pray."
>
> I've seen thee, too, in playful mood,
>   When words of magic spell
> Dropped from thy lips like fairy gems,
>   That sparkled as they fell.

> Still great and good in every change,
> Magnificent and mild,
> As if a seraph's godlike power
> Dwelt in a little child.

TO CHARLES SUMNER.

WAYLAND, 1870.

DEAR AND HONORED MR. SUMNER, — If I were to write to you every time the spirit moves me to thank you for some good thing you have done, you would have a very voluminous correspondence. I lay the flattering unction to my soul that I am a very enlightened statesman, and my reasons for forming such a high opinion of myself are, that whenever I arrive at conclusions on any subjects which have occupied my mind, you are always sure to indorse my views. Many a time, after reading your speeches or debates aloud, I have exclaimed, " There it is again! You see Mr. Sumner says just what I have been hoping and expecting he would say." I differ from you often enough, however, to prove that my soul is my own.

In your speech you say, " The oppressiveness of a tax is not to be measured by the insensibility of the people on whose shoulders it is laid. It is a curiosity of depotism that the people are too often unconscious of their slavery, as they are also unconscious of bad laws. A wise and just government measures its duties, not by what the people will bear without a murmur, but by what is most for their welfare."

My dear Mr. Sumner, is not the same remark applicable to the assertion that the elective franchise ought not to be bestowed on women until the majority of them demand it? I have been often urged to write to you on what is called the "Woman Question," but I have foreborne, because I thought your shoulders (strong and willing as they are) were already loaded with sufficient weight. Moreover, when I have perfect confidence in the moral and intellectual insight of a man, I am not desirous to hurry his conclusions. You are so organized that you cannot help following principles, wheresoever they may lead; and, sooner or later, you will see clearly that our republican ideas cannot be consistently carried out while women are excluded from any share in the government. I reduce the argument to very simple elements. I pay taxes for property of my own earning and saving, and I do not believe in "taxation without representation." As for representation by proxy, that savors too much of the plantation-system, however kind the master may be. I am a human being; and every human being has a right to a voice in the laws which claim authority to tax him, to imprison him, or to hang him. The exercise of rights always has a more salutary effect on character than the enjoyment of privileges. Any class of human beings to whom a position of perpetual subordination is assigned, however much they may be petted and flattered, must inevitably be dwarfed, morally and intellectually.

But I will not enlarge on the theme. For forty years I have keenly felt my limitations as a woman, and have submitted to them under perpetual and indignant protest. It is too late for the subject to be of much interest to me personally. I have walked in fetters all my pilgrimage, and now I have but little farther to go. But I see so clearly that domestic and public life would be so much ennobled by the perfect equality and companionship of men and women in all the departments of life, that I long to see it accomplished, for the order and well-being of the world.

TO MISS LUCY OSGOOD.

1870.

You say you sometimes think we should "be greatly strengthened if we could be sure of a real *bonâ fide* 'Thus saith the Lord.'" I don't think so. If it had been good for us, Divine Providence would have so ordered it. It is obviously a part of his plan that we should work our own passage through in the darkness, or rather by the far-off gleam of a few guiding stars, and it seems to me that in no other way could we become educated for a higher plane of existence. You are mainly anxious for this *bonâ fide* revelation on account of the ignorant masses, which you think "need to lean on authority." You need not be concerned on that score, my friend. Just so long as the multitude need to believe that Jesus was God, they will believe it. You and I could n't take that faith from them while it was a necessity of their souls, even if we wished to do it. Divine Providence takes care that neither the old material nor spiritual skin shall fall off till a new one has formed under it. All that any of us have to do is to follow, fearlessly and faithfully, the light within our own souls. In no other way can the individual so help the race.

I doubtless have "more confidence in the common mind" than you have. I think I have historical ground for the confidence. Scientific progress begins with the educated; spiritual progress always originates with the unlearned. Look at Jesus and his fishermen; at Luther and his peasant followers. The scholars and the gentry of England would never have abolished slavery. It was the mass of working-people that compelled government to take that great step in human progress; and the movement has a similar history in this country.

TO JOHN G. WHITTIER.

WAYLAND, January 10, 1871.

I thank you, from my heart, for your volume of beautiful poems, and for the kind inscription. But what is the world coming to when a plain-coated Friend dates " Christmas " instead of Twelfth Month? If thou departest from the ancient testimonies in this way, friend John, thou wilt assuredly be dealt with. I am very indifferent to anything the world can give, either its pleasures or its honors; and I am very little prone to envy, but I do envy you your wide-spread popularity, because it furnishes you with such ample means to scatter abroad the living seeds of goodness and truth. Thanks to the Heavenly Father, that the great opportunity fell into hands that used it so conscientiously and so industriously! For myself, I cannot accomplish much; but I will try to deserve the acknowledgment, " She hath done what she could."

One of my old-time friends sent me, for a New Year's present, a book on Siam, by an English lady who was for several years governess there, in the king's family.[1] I found it extremely interesting. I have long felt that we Christians greatly wronged the Buddhists. The precepts of Buddha are wonderfully large and holy. Whoever he was, he was a man that dwelt near unto God. His religion is overrun with

[1] *An English Governess at the Siamese Court*, by Mrs. A. H. Leonowens. Boston, 1870.

superstitions and ceremonies, but I doubt whether it is more so than the religion of Jesus in that very large part of Christendom where the Roman Catholic Church is established. Those who have not examined into it curiously, as I have, are not aware how small a part of Christianity really emanated from Jesus or his apostles. It is a fact that troubles me not at all. If a truth is clear in my own soul, I care not that it has appeared to others in manifold varying aspects. I recognize and reverence an eternal principle, whatsoever garb it wears. What matters it that the good and the true come to us through a foreign faith?

> "Since everywhere the Spirit walks
> The garden of the heart, and talks
> With man, as under Eden's trees,
> In all his varied languages."

Thank you for that broad lesson. You are bringing precious stones to build up the great church of the future, the church of the All-Father. May his blessing be with you now and forever!

TO MISS LUCY OSGOOD.

WAYLAND, 1871.

I wish I had known when your eightieth birthday was. I would have made a fuss on the occasion, I assure you. I have often been tempted to ask when your birthday was, but I always remembered what were your sister's first words when I called to see her after she had her fall: "Now don't go to muching me! I don't like to be muched." I had an idea that you shared her aversion to being "muched," and so I concluded to let your birthday slide. I dare say, after all, that you were rather pleased with having the anniversary marked by so many kindly memorials. For my part I am delighted to find a few flowers on the mile-stones as I pass along. No matter how simple they are; a buttercup is as good as a japonica; somebody placed it there who remembered I was going by, and that is sufficient.

What a blessing it was for that dear good man, S. J. May, to pass away in the full possession of his faculties, and surrounded by such an atmosphere of love and blessing. Friend Whittier, writing to me the other day, says: "How many sweet and precious memories I have of my intercourse with him! Where is he now? What is he doing and thinking? Ah me! we beat in vain against the doors of that secret of God! But I am so certain of God's infinite goodness and love, that I think I can trust myself, and all I hold dear, to his love and care."

TO THE SAME.

1872.

Speaking of women, is it not wonderful how all the world seems to be moving on that question? Did you notice that the Pasha of Egypt has established a school for girls at Cairo? What is more, he compels the officials of his government to send their daughters for two years, to be instructed on European subjects after the European manner. After that, he stipulates that the girls shall be left free to choose whether they will veil themselves again and return to their former Egyptian modes of life, or not. Among the Mohammedans is a sect called The Bab, meaning The Gate, or Door. It appears to be a door that opens easily, for it is very courteous about letting in other religions, and urges that women should be educated and go about as freely as men. The Brama-Somadj is pleading for the similar emancipation and enlightenment of Hindoo women. Assuredly, the Millerites will have to wait a while. The world cannot be destroyed just yet; there is too much going on that needs to be completed.

I saw some extracts from Father Taylor's Biography in the papers. I was much amused with his answer to his nurse, when she sought to comfort him by saying, "You will soon be with the angels." "What do I care about angels!" he exclaimed; "I want to be with folks." That was a real outburst of nature.

TO MRS. S. B. SHAW.

WAYLAND, 1872.

I wanted to write a hurrah as soon as it was certain the ship of state had safely passed that coalition snag,[1] but was prevented from time to time. Then came that awful fire in Boston, and put one out of the mood of hurrahing. But that conflagration, terrible as it was, was not so disastrous as would have been the restoration of Democrats and rebels to power. And not only have we cause for congratulation that a present danger is escaped, but we have reason to be devoutly thankful for this new proof that the people are capable of self-government.

About the Society for the Prevention of Cruelty to Animals, you and I, as usual, agree. I have taken a lively interest in it, and have been a member of the Boston society from the beginning. I have not made up my mind about the Darwinian theory, but I have long felt that man does not sufficiently recognize his

[1] Referring to President Grant's reëlection.

kindred with animals. If they were tenderly and rationally treated from their birth, I believe it would make a vast change in the development of their faculties and feelings. I believe the principal reason why Arabian horses are so celebrated for intelligence and docility is that the Arab lives with his horse as with a companion and friend. I hope this widespread horse-distemper [1] will make men more thoughtful about the comfort of their horses; having learned the great inconvenience of doing without them.

TO MISS LUCY OSGOOD.

1873.

I wish to see Samuel Johnson's book,[2] and I thank you for the offer to send it to me. I will write 11th of February in it, and put it among my birthday offerings. It is very true that a philosophic religion is fit for philosophers only, but all that each individual has to do is to follow the truth as far as he sees it, without assuming that his boundary is necessarily the end of the universe. I opine that we have nothing to do with the question whether the views that seem to us true can meet the wants of the "ignorant, silly, sensuous, suffering masses." It is our business to seek truth reverentially, and utter it frankly, leaving it to its mission of educating "the masses" to a higher stand-point. It is never safe to look outside and calculate consequences in forming our estimate of any truths. What a muddy medley they made of Christianity by grafting upon it one superstition

---

[1] The epizoötic epidemic then prevailing in all the large cities of the United States.

[2] *Oriental Religions and their Relation to Universal Religion.* By Samuel Johnson. Boston, 1873.

which was important to the Jewish converts, another to the Greek, another to the Scandinavian, and so on! The Italian peasant woman is doubtless comforted by praying to a doll dressed up in tinsel, which she worships as the "Mother of God." I would not, if I had the power, make it illegal for her to comfort herself in that way; but shall I refrain from philosophic utterance, lest it should make her doll fall out of its shrine? The doll will not and cannot fall, so long as the "ignorant, sensual, suffering masses" have need of her. The work that needs to be done is to bring the world into such a state of order that there will be no "ignorant, sensual, suffering masses," and consequently no further use for consecrated dolls. Meanwhile, let them comfort themselves with their dolls. It is the business of grown people to lead children gently away from the necessity for toys. It is a long time since principles were all that commanded my implicit faith and reverence. Some would say regretfully that I believed less than formerly; but in my inmost soul I know that I believe more.

TO THE SAME.

WAYLAND, 1873.

New Year's Day shone very brightly out of heaven. A fine mist had frozen on the trees, and made them look like great chandeliers of crystallization sparkling in the clear blue sky. What can Alpine regions furnish more beautiful than this scene of fairy splendor? I thought of you and of the little feet that would be trotting through the snow to see what Miss Osgood had provided for them. They read of fairies that disguise themselves like old women, though they are in reality young and beautiful, and have all manner of flowers and jewels that they can shake out of their mantles when they choose. I should n't wonder if the Medford little folks suspected you of being one of those rich and beneficent beings, and would be on the look-out to catch a glimpse of your hidden rainbow-wings some day. I hope you and they had a pleasant time as usual. I devote my New Year's attentions to old folks. Two of the eight for whom I always try to do something pleasant on that anniversary have passed away since that season last came round. My *protégées* are likely to diminish while yours will increase; but I have fewer competitors in my department, and I find that the old are as much pleased by presents and tokens of remembrance as children are.

TO FRANCIS G. SHAW.

WAYLAND, 1873.

Very hearty, though somewhat tardy, thanks for your beautiful present at the close of the year. I feasted my eyes on the binding, so orientally gorgeous, yet so tasteful. The very colors are appropriate; black and gold and that tawny red. I shall not live to see the universally acknowledged brotherhood of the human race, but I rejoice over the ever-increasing indication of tendencies toward such a result; among which the mission of Mrs. Leonowens is very significant. The book, though unavoidably painful in some respects, was very fascinating to me. I read it right through, every word. How the proclamations of the young King of Siam concerning the abolition of slavery and the brotherhood of religions thrilled through me! God bless him! I want to send him something. And those tender-hearted women of the harem whose hearts melted over " Uncle Tom's Cabin, and whose reverence was bestowed both on Jesus and Buddha, because they recognized a tender self-sacrificing spirit in both! Those women are not degraded by polygamy as we should be, simply because they are not conscious of degradation. Some one said very wisely, " How unlike in character is the nakedness of a courtesan and the nakedness of a savage!" There are no gardens of the human soul anywhere so neglected that God has not placed in them " flaming cherubims that turn every way to guard the Tree of Life."

Did Mrs. Leonowens's first book ever reach Siam? If so, has she ever heard how it was received? I judge that the young king's desire to emulate President Lincoln must have been in a good degree owing to her influence, though she very modestly says nothing about it. What a blessing to be able to carry light into dark corners of the world, and then see from afar how the little candle spreads its rays! Christian missionaries might have done much to modify the laws and customs of all the world, if they had only been less theological. . . .

It sometimes seems rather hard that I should be so entirely shut out from all intellectual intercourse, but I don't know how to arrange it otherwise, consistently with the discharge of my duty. It is not "eccentricity," as many people call it; it is owing to peculiar circumstances not of my own creating, and which my energy and caution are powerless to change. Nobody could understand it unless they had experienced it. But I have many, many blessings; the chiefest of which are the dear friends I have. God bless them for illuminating and cheering my life as they have done.

TO THE SAME.

WAYLAND, 1873.

I thank you cordially for the Diana, which is full of life and spirit. Spiritually, it is far inferior to the Venus of Milo, but it has an all-alive physical beauty which is charming. Thank you, also, for the bas-relief from Thorwaldsen. The little heads are delightfully child-like, but to my eye their perpendicular position conveys an idea of walking on the clouds, rather than that of floating, or flying. As I never expect to see any of the galleries of sculpture, it is a great treat to me to form a small stereoscopic gallery of my own, which, with the aid of imagination, is almost like seeing the originals.

I agree with you that there are portions of the Old Testament too devout and sublime to be omitted in any Bible for the human soul. But I do not remember anything in the New Testament so demoralizing as Lot and his daughters, Noah's drunkenness, Jacob's dishonest trickery, and David's conduct to Uriah. I believe the constant reading of such monstrous things, as sacred writ, from God himself, has done much more to unsettle the moral principles of mankind than is generally supposed.

TO MRS. S. B. SHAW.

WAYLAND, 1873.

As for the poor Indians, would to heaven they had education and newspapers to tell their side of the story! The pages you inclosed scarcely give a glimpse of the real facts that caused the Seminole war. The Seminoles were adopting civilized modes of life. They were devoting themselves to agriculture, and had established a friendly relation with their neighbors. But the slave-holders of Georgia wanted to drive them out, because they coveted their lands, and still more because their slaves were prone to take refuge with them. This had been going on for generations, and the fugitives had largely intermarried with the Indians. The slave-holders not only claimed their slaves that had escaped, but their children and grandchildren and great-great-grandchildren, on the ground that "the child follows the condition of the mother." It was to satisfy them that Jackson got up the war. It was not Osceola's wife and children only that were seized and carried into slavery. Multitudes of their wives and children were carried off; and you may easily conjecture that no very nice care was always taken to ascertain whether they had descended from slaves in the United States or not. The pages you send contain the cool remark that "the seizure of Osceola's beautiful wife was an unfortunate affair." God of heaven grant me patience! What would he call it if the Indians had seized and carried off his beautiful wife, to sell her in the market for a mistress. I hope the writer is no relation of yours, for I have a vehement desire to cuff his ears. As for the Seminoles not removing after they had by treaty agreed to, I do not know the real facts of the case; but this I do know, that General Jackson was in the habit of making nominal treaties with any Indians who could be brought by grog to sign a paper, which was forthwith declared to be an official treaty concluded with the government of the tribe. Just the same as if the government of France or England should enter into negotiations with General Butler, or Boss Tweed, and then claim that the arrangement was binding on the government of the United States.

General Grant has disappointed me. His Indian policy looked candid and just on paper; but he does not seem to have taken adequate care that it should be carried out. The Modocs have formerly had a good name as peaceable neighbors; but they have been driven from place to place, and finally pushed into a barren corner, where the soil did not admit of their raising sufficient for a subsistence. They were driven to desperation by starvation, and wearied out with promises that were never fulfilled. Poor Captain Jack said, "To die by bullets not hurt much; but it hurts a heap to die by hunger." I regret the barbarities of Captain Jack, but not more than I regret the barbarities of Phil. Sheridan. I look upon Osceola and Captain Jack both as worthy of an historical place in the list of heroes that have died for their oppressed peoples. But I may as well stop writing on this theme, for it is a hopeless task to try to delineate the "general cussedness" of governments. It is a strange thing, but it seems impossible to convince politicians that it is not "visionary" to be guided by correct principles in the administration of affairs. Their idea is, the greater the indirectness and the double dealing, the greater the statesmanship. Yet, all the time, they make loud professions of following the teaching of him who said, "Let your yea be yea, and your nay, nay." Oh, Sarah, I am so tired of shams! It is very inconvenient to be habitually direct, in such a world of indirectness.

I pitied Mr. Curtis when I read his patient answers to the "interviewers." Really, those men, who have made a profession of audacity and impertinence, are as insufferable a nuisance as mosquitoes; and in these days there is no kind of netting that will keep the pests out. Certainly the prophesied day has arrived, when whatsoever is done in the house is proclaimed upon the house-top. Was Dr. Livingstone really "interviewed" by a Yankee "interviewer?" Why don't we hear further from him? What has become of the party headed by Dr. Livingstone's son, that set out in search of him before Stanley? Professional interviewers manufacture interviews when they do not succeed in finding the individual they propose to bore. Even such a small lion as I am has been served up in that style. Years ago there was a column in the "New York Tribune" describing me in a place where I never was, looking as I never looked, and saying things I never said or thought of. Even the heart of Africa is not a place of safety, and if one were to climb Himalaya, some sort of pulley would be contrived to hoist up an "interviewer"!

I am so sorry about the Modocs! I have no doubt the poor wretches had been goaded to desperation before they committed that wanton and most impolitic assault upon the Peace Commissioners. White men have so perpetually lied to them that they don't know whom, or what, to believe. And after all, we, who are so much more enlightened, and who profess to be so much more human, have again and again killed Indians who were decoyed into our power by a flag of truce. No mortal will ever know the accumulated wrongs of that poor people. No wonder they turn at bay, in their desperation and despair. . . .

You ask if I am in favor of the prohibitory law. I **am**. Its aim is, and its effect would be, to diminish, **if** not entirely to suppress, groggeries; and a large portion of the awful drunkenness that prevails is owing to the moral weakness that cannot withstand temptation continually placed right before the eyes. Unfortunately, alcohol is needed in medicine and in various arts, but for these purposes a few wholesale depositories are sufficient. I grow more and more strict about temperance. I do not now manufacture currant wine for the sick, as I used to do.

TO MRS. S. B. SHAW.

WAYLAND, 1874.

How cheering Mrs. Somerville's Life is, as a proof of the capabilities of woman! And how it makes me mourn over the frivolous, wasted life of women in general!

John Stuart Mill's biography made me sad for him. He had too much soul to have it entirely pressed to death; but I believe he would have been a much greater man, and certainly a much happier one, if it had not been for that loveless, dreary childhood, that incessant drilling, that cramming of his boyish brain, that pitiless crushing out of all spontaneity. With regard to his writings, I do not always like his tone, or always agree with his conclusions. It jarred upon my feelings to have him decide that because evil existed, therefore the Creator of the universe was either not all-good, or else he was not all-powerful. I grant that, taking the very limited view we finite beings are capable of, as many facts could, perhaps, be brought forward to prove that the world was made by a malevolent Being as that it was made by a benevolent Being; but we are such a small part of the whole, that it seems to me presumptuous to deny that the apparent discord may be "harmony not understood." Take Mill's writings all in all, they neither cheer nor strengthen me, though I greatly respect and admire the intellectual ability, the moral courage, and the perfect sincerity of the man; and as a woman, there is no limit to the gratitude I owe him. Anna D. has recently sent me a book which I like amazingly (you know you always laugh at me for my use of that word). It is "A Princess of Thule." The plan of it is original, even in these days, when one would think the invention of anything new in stories had become exhausted. The characters are well imagined and delineated with a good deal of power. Descriptions of scenery are apt to become tiresome; but these are not only graphic, but are finished with such exquisitely artistic touches, that I felt as if I had been sailing among the Hebrides through all their aspects of sunshine and storm. The book brought back very distinctly that overture of Mendelssohn's called "Fingal's Cave," so wonderfully full of winds and waves, and æolian whistlings through the fissures of the rocks.

There is something very queer and inexplicable about the manner in which music comes to me. I am lamentably deficient in time and tune; but in some way or other music says things to me which skilful musicians often do not hear. The first time I heard the overture of "Fingal's Cave," I was very much impressed by its sea-wildness, and I said: "Breathings of an æolian harp mingle with the voice of the ocean." The musician to whom I said it smiled in a way that said, "You are full of odd conceits." Several years after, when reading a description of Fingal's Cave, I found that there was a fissure in the rocks, through which, in certain states of the tide, the winds played

like a powerful æolian harp. I don't know whether
Mendelssohn ever went to Fingal's Cave and heard
the weird music, but the harp of the winds is in
his overture. When I meet him in another world,
I mean to ask him, for my own private satisfaction,
whether he did n't know he put it there. This fascinating
"Princess of Thule" brings back the overture
and the dream I once had of seeing Mendelssohn
at a concert in the other world.

TO THE SAME.

WAYLAND, 1874.

I have been wanting to write you these many days,
but I make it a rule not to write when I am sad,
and my soul has been greatly troubled. Since the
death of Ellis Gray Loring, no affliction has oppressed
me so heavily as the death of Charles Sumner.
I loved and reverenced him beyond any other
man in public life. He was my ideal of a hero, more
than any of the great men in our national history.
In fact I almost worshipped him. I see no hopes of
such another man to stem the overwhelming tide of
corruption in this country. But perhaps when a momentous
crisis comes, the hour will bring forth the
man. If so, it will be well for the nation and for the
world; but for myself I can never, never again feel
the implicit trust in any mortal man that I felt in
Charles Sumner. A feeling akin to remorse renders
my grief almost insupportable. Certainly it was not
my fault, that I could not view the last election in
the light he did; but I wept bitterly when he wrote
to me: "It makes the tears come to my eyes to find
that you do not sympathize with me in the stand I
have taken from motives the most conscientious that

have ever influenced my life." And now that he has gone, it seems as if it would kill me to think that my want of sympathy should ever have brought tears to his eyes. Then I have not written to him for some months past. I often wanted to, but his mind seemed full of the old vexed topic, and I knew, however tenderly and reverentially I might write, nothing would satisfy him but the acknowledgment that he had been entirely in the right; because he never for a moment ceased to believe himself so. It is true that President Grant, since his second election, has done many things, and left still more undone, which tend to confirm Mr. Sumner's estimate of him. But, as I again and again wrote to Mr. Sumner, the question was not whether General Grant was a fitting candidate for the presidency, but whether it was safe to restore power in our national councils to Democrats and rebels. He believed that Democrats and rebels had met with a great change of heart; but I thought, and still think, there was superabounding evidence that they were still essentially in the same state of mind as ever. I thought then, and I think now, that artful politicians could not have so imposed upon Mr. Sumner if it had not been for the state of his health. If he had been in perfect physical health he would never have believed that Mr. —— had cultivated the growth of a conscience, after doing without one for half a century. But the more I am convinced that his nervous system was in a shattered and excited state, the more keenly do I regret that I did not write to him frequently and affectionately. I am aware that my letters could not have been of much consequence to him, but perhaps they might have soothed him a little. It seems as if I had been ungrateful to him for all his magnificent services to freedom and public morals. In the anguish of my heart I cry out, "Enemies wrote to him, and friends did not! And all the while he was dying by inches!"

Processions and flowers and panegyrics have become so much a matter of custom that they are generally distasteful to me, as are all things that degenerate into forms without significance. But the homage to the memory of Charles Sumner seems to be really spontaneous and almost universal. It is a great consolation to me, not only because he richly deserved it, but because it is a good omen from the nation. There has been nothing like it except the mourning for Abraham Lincoln; and in both cases it was preeminently honesty of character to which the people paid spontaneous homage. They reverenced the men because they trusted them.

TO THE SAME.

1874.

I try not to be anxious about my future, and to feel a trust that "something will turn up." With regard to out-door work, something did "turn up," in a wonderful way, when dear David's hands became too lame to do his customary jobs. The husband of the woman who has washed and scoured for me has for many years acted "like Cain;" drinking up all his wages, and maltreating his wife; and at last he set fire to a barn, and burnt up a dozen cattle, because the man who had employed him hid his rum-bottle. He received the mild sentence of two years in the House of Correction. I hoped he would die there; I felt as if I could never endure the sight of him again. But when he came here of an errand, the day he had served his time out, he was so timid, and his eyes had such a beseeching look, as if his soul was hungry for a friend, that I could n't stand it; I shook hands with him, and invited him in. I had a long private talk with him, and told him that though he was sixty years old it was not too late to make a man of himself, if he would only resolve never to taste another drop of liquor; and I assured him that if he would only try, I would be a faithful friend to him. He promised me that he would try. It is now more than a year and a half ago. He has kept his promise, and I have kept mine. Every Sunday I prepare a good dinner for him, and give him a strong cup of tea. He works diligently, supplies his wife with everything comfortable, and makes her a present of what remains of his wages. The poor woman says she was never so happy in her life. He is very attentive to our wants; runs of errands, is ready to shovel snow, split kindlings, etc. In fact he is our "man Friday." If I could get such faithful, hearty service within doors, I should be set up for life. Of course he may fall back into his old habits, but so long a time has elapsed, and I seem to be such an object of worship to him, that I cannot but hope for the best. I have never in my life experienced any happiness to be compared to the consciousness of lifting a human soul out of the mire.[1]

[1] In her will, Mrs. Child left an annuity of fifty dollars a year to be paid in monthly instalments to the man mentioned in the above letter, so long as he should abstain from intoxicating drink.

TO JOHN G. WHITTIER.

WAYLAND, June 18, 1874.

I cannot help writing to thank you for the Lines you have written to the memory of Charles Sumner. They are very beautiful, and nothing could be more appropriate.

We went into Boston to hear Mr. Curtis's Memorial Address. I had been longing, amid all the fuss and formality, to hear just the right thing said about Mr. Sumner, and Mr. Curtis said it, and said it eloquently, from the heart. . . . Corruption is so widespread and so rampant, that I sometimes have gloomy forebodings concerning the future of this country; but the spontaneous and general homage to Charles Sumner's memory shows that there is still great respect for integrity deeply rooted in the popular mind.

I was reading over several of your poems last week, and for the thousandth time I felt myself consoled and strengthened by them, as well as delighted with their poetic beauty. It was a very precious gift you received, dear friend, to be such a benefactor to the souls of your fellow-beings. I know of no one man who I think has done so much in that way. That immortality you are sure of.

David and I are growing old. He will be eighty in three weeks, and I was seventy-two last February. But we keep young in our feelings. We are, in fact, like two old children; as much interested as ever in the birds and the wild flowers, and with sympathies as lively as ever in all that concerns the welfare of the world. Our habitual mood is serene and cheerful. The astonishing activity of evil sometimes make me despondent for a while, but my belief returns, as strong as ever, that there is more good than evil in the world, and that the All-wise Being is guiding the good to certain victory. How blest are those whom he employs as his agents!

TO MRS. S. M. PARSONS.

WAYLAND, 1874.

With regard to Dr. Clarke's book,[1] I do not believe his theory. Doubtless, women who are so much engrossed with study as to neglect physical exercise will lose their health, and so will men. I have known many more cases of young men who have injured their health in that way than young women. Every step in the world's progress, in any direction, is inevitably hindered by old customs and prejudices. It is necessary to bear this with patience, nay, to accept it, as in some sort a blessing. Everything must be disputed, that everything may be proved. The centrifugal force needs the centripetal, in spiritual, as well as in material affairs. Elizabeth Stuart Phelps, in an article in the "Independent," cut up Dr. Clarke with a sharp knife. But I think it needs a woman well versed in medical science to fight him with his own weapons.

TO MRS. S. B. SHAW.

MELROSE, October, 1874.

I have just received your loving letter of the 26th, which was forwarded to me here.

I have a longing to get to you, but I have many misgivings about going to New York. I was wonderfully calm at the time,[2] and for twenty-four hours

[1] *Sex in Education.* By Edward H. Clarke, M. D. Boston, 1874.
[2] The death of Mr. Child.

afterward, but since then I seem to get more and more sensitive and distressed. I try hard to overcome it, for I do not want to cast a shadow over others. Moreover, I feel that such states of mind are wrong. There are so many reasons for thankfulness to the Heavenly Father! And I do feel very thankful that he did not suffer for a very long time; that the powers of his mind were undimmed to the last; that my strength and faculties were preserved to take care of him to the last; and that the heavy burden of loneliness has fallen upon me, rather than upon him.

But at times it seems as if I could no longer bear the load. I keep breaking down. They told me I should feel better after I got away from Wayland, where memories haunted me at every step. But I do not feel better. On the contrary, I am more deeply sad. The coming and going of people talking about subjects of common interest makes life seem like a foreign land, where I do not understand the language. And I go back to my darling old mate with a more desperate and clinging tenderness. And when there comes no response but the memóry of that narrow little spot where I planted flowers the day before I left our quiet little nest, it seems to me as if all were gone, and as if I stood utterly alone on a solitary rock in mid-ocean; alone, in midnight darkness, hearing nothing but the surging of the cold waves.

How unfit I am for the company of others! It would be so painful to me to be a mar-plot to the pleasures of others! Thinking thus, I have great misgivings about going to New York. I long to get back to Wayland, to creep into a very private corner, and read stories to keep me from thinking. All this is morbid. But how to get over it is the question.

Dear Rosa thinks I may like to live near New York. But ah! how my heart would yearn for old Massachusetts, where I lived with dear David so many years! Years of struggle they have been, for the most part, but perhaps all the dearer for the trials we passed through together. I ought not to bring a shadow over your happy household. God bless you all!

TO MISS A. B. FRANCIS.

STATEN ISLAND, November 23, 1874.

I was received with the warmest of welcomes. I have a pretty, sunshiny room all to myself, hung with pictures, warmly carpeted, with soap-stone stove and every conceivable convenience.

From one window, I look out upon a lawn with trees and shubbery; from the other, upon a broad expanse of water, shimmering in the sunlight, with vessels and steamboats constantly passing, their bright flags fluttering in the breeze. The only trouble is that everything is too luxurious, and that I am waited upon more than suits my habits or inclinations.

I shall get used to it, in time; but at present I feel "like a cat in a strange garret," and, like a stray pussy, I would set off and run hundreds of miles, foot-sore and weary, if I could only get back to my humble little home and my darling old mate.

But there is no more of that for me, in this world and I ought to be thankful to the Heavenly Father for raising up such kind friends to hold me by the hand while I am passing through this valley of shadows. I am taken right into the bosom of the family, and am free to come and go, just as I please; and I like all the inmates extremely.

TO MR. AND MRS. S. E. SEWALL.

STATEN ISLAND, January 10, 1875.

You don't know how frequently and how affectionately I think of you, and how I long to have the light of your countenances shine upon me. Mr. and Mrs. S. go over to New York two or three times a week, and I sit alone in my little room and think, think, think. And there is but one who occupies my thoughts more than you two dear, good friends, whom he loved so well. Pope says, " The last years of life, like tickets left in the wheel, rise in value." It certainly is true of the last friends that remain to us. I have been eminently blest in my few intimate friends, and I think it is mainly owing to the fact that they were all sifted in the anti-slavery sieve. . . .

On Christmas Eve I went with R. H. to a gathering of O. B. Frothingham's Sunday-school scholars and a troop of poor children whom they had invited to partake with them of the manifold treasures on the Christmas-tree. Oliver Johnson personated Santa Claus, and did it very well, marching round and round in grotesque costume, to the lively tunes played by a colored fiddler. The little folks seemed to enjoy it highly. O. B. F. made a quaint little speech to them, in which he told them what a good baby Jesus was, never crying for what he ought not to have, never pulling his mother's hair, etc. . . .

That is all the pleasuring or visiting I have done since I parted from you. My days glide on very quietly and comfortably, and for the sake of others I try to keep from sadness as much as possible.

On Sundays I go to the Unitarian meeting, in an

extremely pretty little Gothic chapel, where George W. Curtis reads the best sermons of English and American liberal preachers. The walk of a mile is healthy exercise for me. They have a good organ, and Mr. Curtis reads admirably, so I find it a pleasant change.

TO MRS. S. B. SHAW.

WAYLAND, 1875.

My long visit to you was a great help to my heart and soul in many ways, and I was happier than I could have been anywhere else, under the circumstances. But you are right in supposing that I often felt "confused and bewildered." I feel so everywhere, dear friend, and I suppose it will be long before I get over it. Here in my native Massachusetts I feel like a hungry child lost in a dark wood. People are very kind to me, but I cannot banish the desolate feeling that I belong to nobody and that nobody belongs to me. . . .

Three days ago I went to my empty little shanty alone, opened doors and windows, and built fires with the wood dear David had so carefully provided. It was a very solemn and sad task. Every room was baptized with my tears. I have wavered a good deal about having my furniture carried back there, but nothing better seems to open for me, and when I inhabit the house, I hope the desolate feeling will gradually pass away. You cannot imagine anything more still and secluded than my life here. Luckily, I have been obliged to be very busy, most of the time. It was a job to get things back and arrange them. I sleep in the same old chamber, where I slept so many years with my dear old mate; where we were wont to amuse our waking hours reciting German poetry, and talking over all the affairs of the universe. I don't look into a German book, for there is nobody to hear me " speak my pieces " now.

TO MRS. S. E. SEWALL.

June 11, 1875.

Finding Robert F. Wallcut very desirous of a photograph of me, and having none to give him, I went to have some taken. A neighbor here told me wonderful stories about a spirit-photographer. So I thought I would go to him to have my photograph taken, and, without saying anything, see what would happen. When he showed me the negative, I said, " There is no other figure than my own on the plate." " Did you wish for any other ? " he asked. I thought to myself, " So they don't come unless they are bargained for ! " But I merely said, " If any departed friends had been reflected on the plate, it would have been gratifying, of course."

" It takes a longer time to procure the photographs of spirits," he replied, "and therefore I charge as much for six as I do for twelve of the common kind." I told him I would like to have him try, on condition that I neither took them, nor paid for them, unless there came the likeness of somebody I had known. He demurred, and said people must take their chance. A young clerk in the establishment looked at me twice and smiled very significantly during our conversation. The photographer seemed embarrassed and impatient; but he finally consented to my terms. He took the second plate out and carried it into another room, where he remained three times as long as he had done with the negative of my first photograph. When he brought it to me, at last, there were two heads behind my own; one of them a vulgar-looking man, the other a fat-faced girl with fluffy hair; neither of them faces I had ever seen before, or ever desired to see again. The whole proceeding indicated trickery. Still, notwithstanding the great amount of trickery practised, and the unsatisfactory nature of all the communications, there are real phenomena connected with the subject which are to me inexplicable, and which indicate some laws of the universe at present unknown to us.

TO JOHN G. WHITTIER.

WAYLAND, January 20, 1876.

You remember Charles Sprague's description of scenes he witnessed from a window near State Street? First, Garrison dragged through the streets by a mob; second, Burns carried back to slavery by United States troops, through the same street; third, a black regiment marching down the same street to the tune of "John Brown," to join the United States army for the emancipation of their race. What a thrilling historical poem might be made of that! I have always thought that no incident in the anti-slavery conflict, including the war, was at once so sublime and romantic as Robert G. Shaw riding through Washington Street at the head of that black regiment. He, so young, so fair, so graceful in his motions, so delicately nurtured, so high-bred in his manners, waving his sword to friends at the windows, like a brave young knight going forth to "deeds of high emprise;" followed by that dark-faced train, so long trampled in the dust, and now awakened by the trumpet-tones of freedom! How I wish a grand historical painting could be made of it! Mr. Sears, in a sermon he preached at the time of the attack on Fort Wagner, said: "The mere conflict of brute forces is so much murder and slaughter, and nothing more. Whichever side is victorious, there is cause for humiliation, and not for thanksgiving. But in the great conflict of ideas, of civilization against barbarism, of universal emancipation against the slavery of a race, it were a shame not to see the sword of God's mighty angel flashing like sunbeams over the field, and lighting our way to a glorious future."

TO THE SAME.

WAYLAND, January 28, 1876.

A few days ago, " the spirit moved " me to write to you; and to-day I am again moved to write to you some little incidents which I think will interest you.

I spent last winter with the parents of Colonel Shaw. . . . The flag of the 54th Regiment was in their hall, and the sword of Colonel Shaw. There is a history about that sword. It is very handsome, being richly damascened with the United States coat-of-arms, and the letters R. G. S. beneath. It was a present from a wealthy uncle in England, and he received it a few days before the attack on Fort Wagner. You know of his instantaneous death, and the manner of his burial. When it was suggested to his father and mother to ask for his body, to be buried at the North, they replied; "No. Let it remain where it fell. No monument can be so honorable to him, as to lie among the brave followers whom he was leading in the cause of freedom." When he went South, he of course had many parting keepsakes. For the sake of tender associations, his family made earnest efforts to obtain some of these; but amid the turmoil and reckless robbery of war they had all vanished. They could not obtain even the smallest memorial of him. But, months after, an officer of the United States heard that his sword was in possession of a Confederate family. He took a small band of soldiers and went to their dwelling to ask for the sword to send to Colonel Shaw's parents. No one was at home but a few colored servants, who of course were not very reluctant to admit the United States officers. He searched the premises, found the sword, and carried it off, without taking any other article from the house. It nearly escaped their notice, on account of being concealed in an old worn scabbard. The elegant sheath which belonged to it was probably fastened to Colonel Shaw's body, and thrown into the pit with him. When his mother showed me the weapon she said: " This is the sword that Robert waved over his followers, as he urged them to the attack. I am so glad it was never used in battle! Not a drop of blood was ever on it. He had received it but a few days before he died." These noble-hearted people manifested the same spirit about the burning of Darien. Colonel Shaw was strongly opposed to that measure, and publicly expressed his disapprobation of it as a wanton abuse of power, and an unnecessary addition to the horrors and sufferings of war. But the Georgians, by mistake or otherwise, accused him of having instigated it. His father took great pains to prove to them that Colonel Shaw and his family entirely disapproved of the conflagration, and years after peace was declared he sent them a generous donation towards rebuilding a small Episcopal church which had been burned.

I will tell you another touching incident, not without its beauty. Years after the war was over, a rumor reached the North that the embankment at Fort Wagner had broken away, and that some of the bones buried there were falling through. A connection of Colonel Shaw's, who was going South for her health, resolved to ascertain whether this report were true. Accordingly she procured a boat and was rowed to Fort Wagner. The embankment was not broken, and the place where Robert was " buried with his niggers " was one mass of white blossoms! It had happened thus : Hay had been carried from the North for the horses of the United States troops, and with the hay was carried seed of the Northern "whiteweed," a large starry flower with a golden heart. The weed had been unknown at the South, and, handsome as it is, it will certainly prove no blessing there. But was it not beautiful that the spot they strove to desecrate should be spontaneously, and, as it were, fondly beautified by Mother Nature with this profusion of white flowers from the North, shining in the warm sunlight of the South? You and I have the same feelings about war. But when I looked at that sword, and the flag of the 54th, I thought of those brave colored men facing death in the cause of their oppressed brethren, and of their leader leaving behind him all the fascinations of love, luxury, and refinement, and laying down his life in the cause of the poor and the despised ; and, with all my detestation of war, that sword did seem to me holy. He was acting out his convictions of duty in a manner that seemed to him noble and right, and which was so in the opinion of an immense majority of Christendom.

TO MRS. S. B. SHAW.

WAYLAND, 1876.

I have been gadding unusually for me. I went to the meeting of the Free Religious Association, where I was sorely tempted to speak, because the only woman who did speak was so flippant and conceited that I was ashamed of her. In the same excursion, I spent a day and night at Concord, with the Alcotts. Mrs. Alcott was a friend of my youth, and the sister of my dear friend, S. J. May. We had a charming time, talking over the dear old eventful times. I like L. and her artist-sister, M., very much. Some people complain that they are brusque; but it is merely because they are very straightforward and sincere. They have a Christian hatred of lionizing; and the Leo Hunters are a very numerous and impertinent family. Moreover, they don't like conventional fetters any better than I do. There have been many attempts to saddle and bridle me, and teach me to keep step in respectable processions; but they have never got the lasso over my neck yet, and "old hoss" as I am now, if I see the lasso in the air, I snort and gallop off, determined to be a free horse to the last, and put up with the consequent lack of grooming and stabling.

The house of the Alcotts took my fancy greatly. When they bought the place the house was so very old that it was thrown into the bargain, with the supposition that it was fit for nothing but fire-wood. But Mr. Alcott has an architectural taste more intelligible than his Orphic Sayings. He let every old rafter and beam stay in its place, changed old ovens and ash-holes into Saxon-arched alcoves, and added a wash-woman's old shanty to the rear. The result is a house full of queer nooks and corners, and all manner of juttings in and out. It seems as if the spirit of some old architect had brought it from the Middle Ages and dropped it down in Concord; preserving much better resemblance to the place whence it was brought than does the Virgin Mary's house, which the angel carried from Bethlehem to Loretto. The capable Alcott daughters painted and papered the interior themselves. And gradually the artist-daughter filled up all the nooks and corners with panels on which she had painted birds or flowers; and over the open fire-places she painted mottoes in ancient English characters. Owls blink at you and faces peep from the most unexpected places. The whole leaves a general impression of harmony, of a medieval sort, though different parts of the house seem to have stopped in a dance that became confused because some of the party did not keep time. The walls are covered with choice engravings, and paintings by the artist-daughter. She really is an artist.

TO THE SAME.

WAYLAND, 1876.

Whittier, in one of his letters to me, expresses himself about your beloved Robert, thus: "I know of nothing nobler or grander than the heroic self-sacrifice of young Colonel Shaw. The only regiment I ever looked upon during the war was the 54th, on its departure for the South. I shall never forget the scene. As he rode at the head of his troops, the very flower of grace and chivalry, he seemed to me beautiful and awful as an angel of God come down to lead the host of freedom to victory. I have longed to speak the emotions of that hour, but I dared not, lest I should indirectly give a new impulse to war. For his parents I feel that reverence which belongs to the highest manifestation of devotion to duty and forgetfulness of self, in view of the mighty interests of humanity. There must be a noble pride in their great sorrow. I am sure they would not exchange their dead son for any living one."

TO THE SAME.

WAYLAND, 1876.

The books arrived safely; for which I thank you. I must now tell you of something pleasant that has happened to me. Miss Osgood left $2,000 for the colored people, and appointed me trustee. I gave $1,000 to the Home for old colored women, and with the remainder I founded a scholarship at Hampton College, Va. Soon after, I chanced to see a letter from a young colored man in Georgia, to a lady who had been his teacher. He had been working very industriously to earn money to go to Hampton College, and had for that purpose placed $300 in the Freedman's Bank, and lost it all by the dishonesty of the managers. His letter impressed me very favorably, not only because it was uncommonly well written, but especially because he wrote: " Don't beg for me at the North, my good friend. I will go to work and try again. I want to row my own boat." I sent the letter to General Armstrong, and asked that the " Osgood Scholarship " might be bestowed upon him. That would defray the expense of his education, and if he was unable to pay for board, necessary books, etc., I agreed to be responsible therefor; with the request that he might not know there was any one to help him "row his boat." A few days ago I had a letter from General Armstrong, in which he says: "Forsyth is an uncommonly intelligent, sensible, and every way satisfactory pupil; and I have no doubt he will make a good record of himself hereafter." That had a very happyfying influence. I have so often been unsuccessful in my efforts to help others.

TO MRS. S. M. PARSONS.

BOSTON, December, 1876.

Your parcel arrived Christmas forenoon, and was most welcome. For nine days I had been unable to stir out of the house, on account of the fearfully slippery walking, and I was feeling very forlorn among strangers. The weather also was cloudy and chilly, and your little parcel came in like a sunbeam through a fog. Thank you a thousand times. The views are very fine. Perhaps the lady who carved the beautiful head in butter took the hint from Canova, who, as a boy, first attracted attention by the beautiful ornaments he carved in butter for a nobleman's table. I thank Henry cordially for the little book of poems. I always read eagerly any poem I see signed "J. W. Chadwick." The one entitled "The Two Waitings" is about the loveliest poem I ever read. I copied it into my extract book long ago. The lines "No more Sea" are beautiful. They seemed to bear my drooping spirits up on angel's wings.

As for our national affairs, I submit, as one must do, to things that cannot be helped. I am greatly disheartened, but not much disappointed. I have no patience with Republicans who refrained from voting on the plea that both parties were so corrupt there was nothing to choose between them. I am very weary of the fashionable optimism which calls one thing as good as another thing, thus undermining all distinctions between right and wrong. The "Good Lord and Good Devil" style, so habitually adopted by Mr —— does not suit my taste. I liked Garrison's earnest, straightforward letter to James Freeman Clarke.

TO THE SAME.

Boston, February 10, 1877.

Your bundle of views has just arrived. I think only three of them are duplicates. Thank you a thousand times for the kind remembrance. I am a little childish about liking to be remembered on my birthday. Seventy-five years old! What a long time to be wandering about this planet!

I think every individual, and every society, is perfected just in proportion to the combination, and co-operation, of masculine and feminine elements of character. He is the most perfect man who is affectionate as well as intellectual; and she is the most perfect woman who is intellectual as well as affectionate. Every art and science becomes more interesting, viewed both from the masculine and feminine points of view. Not of marriage only may it be justly said, "What God has joined together, let not man put asunder." I think God intended a participation of the masculine and feminine element in every relation and every duty of life. Politics form no exception to this universal rule. There are many ways in which women could do good service to their country by thoughtful and conscientious action in politics. By urging more enlightened laws, and voting for those who will sustain such laws, they may do much to shield their sons and brothers from the dangerous temptations of intemperance and licentiousness. By advocating and voting for a peaceable international settlement of difficulties, they may do much to prevent husbands, sons, and brothers from being butchered in battle. War is a horrid barbarism, which ought to cease throughout the civilized world. But even war is no exception to the rule that masculine and feminine elements should everywhere coöperate together. None can help so efficiently as women in the hospital department of war, and their usefulness might also be great in the commissary department. The more the sphere of woman's activity of thought enlarges, the more her character and capabilities enlarge. The more her attention is taken up with important subjects, the less time and thought will she expend on fashion and frivolous amusements. During the War of the Rebellion, there were sudden changes of character in mere worldly women, that seemed almost miraculous. Ladies, who had been accustomed to while away the hours of life with fancy work, manifested a degree of executive ability in the sanitary commission, and in the hospitals, which astonished their husbands and brothers. The power had always been in them, but it had not been developed, because they had not been called upon to use it. The women of Asia have the same human nature, and the same natural capabilities, that we have; but in those countries they spend their time playing with dolls and chattering with parrots. If they had been brought to New England as soon as they were born, they would have become clerks, authors, doctors, painters, and sculptors, and enlightened domestic companions for intelligent men, and sensible, judicious mothers of coming generations.

The civilization of any country may always be measured by the degree of equality between men and women; and society will never come truly into order until there is perfect equality and copartnership between them in every department of human life. . . .

TO MRS. S. B. SHAW.

BOSTON, 1878.

I get fresh reinforcement of courage, trust, and hope whenever I hear Mr. Savage preach. He is a genuine, all-alive man, and in his earnest, straightforward way, he is doing a great work. He fills my soul so full of electricity that the sparks fly when any sham touches me.

I have been reading all sorts of books: Renan's Jesus, Herbert Spencer's Philosophy, Omar Khéyam, etc. What a very French Jesus Renan portrays. To think of its being all arranged to raise Lazarus, to produce an effect, because public opinion required that he should prove himself a prophet by restoring a dead man to life.

There is a charm about the book, the descriptions are so home-like. But it is curious to observe how he fluctuates between the decisions of his own reason and his fear of making Jesus seem too human to please his readers. He represents Jesus as occasionally "tacking and veering," adroitly, according to the popular breeze; and he certainly does so himself. I suppose it seems to a Frenchman the most natural thing in the world for even the holiest man to diverge from the straight line for the purposes of temporary expediency.

TO THE SAME.

Boston, 1878.

I have three times been to such lectures as are given in the afternoon. One on "Japanese Ways" entertained me much. It was by Professor Morse, lately returned from Japan. He said he was struck with the peculiar cleanliness of all persons, and all places, in Japan. Their tea houses, or restaurants, were scrupulously neat, made cheerful by a few bright pictures of birds, or flowers, and ornamented mottoes from Buddhist Scriptures, such as "Forgive all injuries;" "Speak ill of no one," etc. "When I came back to our depots and restaurants," said he, "and saw on the walls, 'Beware of pickpockets!' and coarse pictures of pugilists, I thought that we might learn some salutary lessons from Japan. But they are an extremely courteous people; they are too polite to send us missionaries."

This hit brought cordial applause.

TO MRS. S. B. RUSSELL.

Wayland, May 24, 1878.

Thanks for your affectionate, cheerful letter. I am as pleased as a child with a new doll, to think you liked my little book [1] "entirely." In this secluded place, where people take little or no interest in anything, I have no means of knowing what effect the book produces. My motive was good, and I tried to write in a candid and kindly spirit. I leave it to its fate, merely hoping that it may do somewhat to enlarge the bands of human brotherhood. Personally

---

[1] *Aspirations of the World. A Chain of Opals.* Collected, with an Introduction, by L. Maria Child. Boston, 1878.

I have never expected any advantage from the publication of it. If it pays its own expenses I shall be satisfied. It would mortify me to have the publishers incur debt by it.

It is wonderful how shy even liberal ministers generally are about trusting people with the plain truth concerning their religion. They want to veil it in a supernatural haze. They are very reluctant to part with the old idea that God has given to Jews and Christians a peculiar monopoly of truth. It is a selfish view of God's government of the world, and it is time that we knew enough to outgrow it.

TO MISS ANNE WHITNEY.

1878.

You were right in your prediction about your poems. Many of them are too metaphysical for my simple, practical mind.

I cannot soar so high, or dive so deep; so I stand looking and wondering where you have gone, like a cow watching a bird or a dolphin. A wag said that when Emerson was in Egypt, the Sphinx said to him, "You're another." I imagine the Sphinx would address you in the same way. I find great beauty in the poems; and of those which I do not understand, I say, as was said of Madame de Staël, "Would that the Pythoness were less inspired, or I more intelligent." My favorites are the "Cyba," the "Yaguey," the "Prospect," and "Evening;" all of them, you see, characterized by the plainness of their meaning.

TO THE SAME.

Boston, November 25, 1878.

DEAR SAUCEBOX, — I dined with —— yesterday, and I expect to do it again next Sunday; and I do not intend to enter upon a course of promiscuous visiting. I have been a Bohemian for nearly seventy-seven years, and I have resolved to remain a Bohemian. Society has never yet got me into harness, and there is still enough of the colt in me to run at sight of a halter. So you may hang up your lasso, my lady.

I hope you are careful about going too near your windows. I have no temptation to such pitch-poling myself, but as your imagination seems active on the subject, it behooves you to take care. I certainly could not throw myself out without considerable forethought and preparation. Therefore, if such a somersault should occur, you may inform the interviewers of the press that you have my authority for declaring that it was done on purpose. Thereupon paragraphs will appear stating that Mrs. Child was the author of several books of water-color reputation, and though a somewhat eccentric old woman, was generally considered to have common sense; and, as it was not known that any peculiarly heavy trouble weighed upon her mind, her friends were at a loss how to explain her rash proceeding. You, perhaps, knowing that I think I have a soul (excuse the word), may conclude I was in a hurry to go and see what was to become of it. I remain, your truly attached

BIRD O'FREEDOM.

MRS. CHILD'S REMINISCENCES OF GEORGE THOMPSON. READ BY MR. GARRISON AT A MEETING IN COMMEMORATION OF GEORGE THOMPSON, BOSTON, FEBRUARY 2, 1879.

My most vivid recollection of George Thompson is of his speaking at Julian Hall, on a memorable occasion. Mr. Stetson, then keeper of the Tremont

House, was present with a large number of his slaveholding guests, who had come to Boston to make their annual purchases of the merchants. Their presence seemed to inspire Mr. Thompson. Never, even from his eloquent lips, did I hear such scathing denunciations of slavery. The exasperated Southerners could not contain their wrath. Their lips were tightly compressed, their hands clenched; and now and then a muttered curse was audible. Finally, one of them shouted, "If we had you down South, we'd cut off your ears." Mr. Thompson folded his arms in his characteristic manner, looked calmly at the speaker, and replied, "Well, sir, if you did cut off my ears, I should still cry aloud, 'he that *hath* ears to hear, let him hear.'"

Meanwhile my heart was thumping like a sledgehammer, for, before the speaking began, Samuel J. May had come to me and said in a very low tone, "Do you see how the walls are lined by stout truckmen, brandishing their whips? They are part of a large mob around the entrance in Federal Street, employed by the Southerners to seize George Thompson and carry him to a South Carolina vessel in waiting at Long Wharf. A carriage with swift horses is at the door, and these Southerners are now exulting in the anticipation of lynching him. But behind that large green curtain at the back of the platform there is a door leading to the chamber of a warehouse. We have the key to that door, which leads to a rear entrance of the building on Milk Street. There the abolitionists have stationed a carriage with swift horses and a colored driver, who of course will do his best for George Thompson. Now as soon as Mr. Thompson ceases speaking, we want the anti-slavery women to gather round him and appear to detain him in eager conversation. He will listen and reply, but keep imperceptibly moving backward toward the green curtain. You will all follow him, and when he vanishes behind the curtain you will continue to stand close together and appear to be still talking with him."

At the close of the meeting, twenty-five or thirty of us women clustered round Mr. Thompson and obeyed the directions we had received. When he had disappeared from our midst, there was quiet for two or three minutes, interrupted only by our busy talking. But the Southerners soon began to stand on tiptoe and survey the platform anxiously. Soon a loud oath was heard, accompanied by the exclamation, "He's gone!" Then such a thundering stampede as there was down the front stairs I have never heard. We remained in the hall, and presently Samuel J. May came to us so agitated that he was pale to the very lips. "Thank God, he is saved!" he exclaimed; and we wrung his hand with hearts too full for speech.

The Boston newspaper press, as usual, presented a united front in sympathy with the slave-holders. They were full of indignation against the impudent Englishman who dared to suggest to enlightened Americans that there was a contradiction between their slave-laws and the Declaration of Independence. The "Boston Post," preëminent in that sort of advocacy of democratic dignity, was very facetious about the cowardly Englishman and his female militia. But they were all in the dark concerning the manner of his escape; for as the door behind the curtain was known to very few, it remained a mystery to all except the abolitionists.   L. MARIA CHILD.

TO MISS A. B. FRANCIS IN EUROPE.

BOSTON, February 21, 1879.

Your letter came, followed by the picture, which arrived two days before my birthday. The little Picciola is a perfect beauty. It will be a "joy forever" to look at it. I have always been in love with Richter's delineation of children. Indeed, the Germans generally excel all other artists in pictures of children. They give them an indescribable air of naturalness and simplicity, which I like far better than the theatrical gracefulness of the French.

I should think one might have rather too much of art galleries. I always supposed that it would be confusing to my mind to wander about in a wilderness of pictures. As for "dead Christs and crucifixions," and saints stuck full of arrows, and women carrying a dead man's head, and other lugubrious subjects, I dislike them all. One "glorious human boy" is worth the whole host; to say nothing of my charming little Picciola.

The labor question continues to seethe and grumble, like a volcano about to explode. Laborers, instead of serving their own interests by leaving off smoking and drinking, are clamoring for the expulsion of the industrious and frugal Chinese. A great force is brought to bear upon Congress to procure the abolition of our treaty with China; a measure which would be dishonest and disgraceful to the United States, and extremely injurious to our trade with China.

Garrison, Phillips, Ward Beecher, and others are trying their utmost to prevent such a violation of principle. H. W. Beecher, in one of his public speeches, said, in his facetious way: "It is complained that the Chinese are idolaters, and therefore not fit to associate with Christians. We have stoned them, and clubbed them, and persecuted them, and tried religion upon them in almost every shape, and still they won't embrace it!"

TO MRS. S. B. SHAW.

BOSTON, 1879.

I keep working, because I am quite sure that no particle of goodness or truth is ever really lost, however appearances may be to the contrary. But in trying to help others, it is sometimes difficult to decide what is good. I have several poor souls in tow, trying to guide them into comfort through righteous paths. But I make them so dependent that I sometimes feel I do them harm rather than good. Yet what is to be done? They are so ignorant and weak-minded, they cannot rely upon themselves.

I admired the spirit of Mr. Curtis's Letter, and I entirely agree with the principle he inculcates. I have always resisted the idea of conventions and caucuses dictating to individuals how they shall vote. It is utterly subversive of republicanism, and would make an oligarchy of the government. I thank him cordially for speaking a true word, which greatly needed to be spoken.

TO THE SAME.

WAYLAND, 1879.

I think there is sufficient evidence of another state of existence, and of the possibility of communication. But beyond this glimpse, I think it is all precarious and unreliable. One had better spend his life in chasing shadows than in seeking for these "manifestations." But I agree with Victor Hugo, who says: "To elude a phenomenon, to turn our backs upon it laughing, is to make bankruptcy of truth. The phenomenon of the ancient tripod, and of the modern table-turning, has a claim to be observed, like all other phenomena. Root out the worthless weeds of error, but harvest the facts. When was chaff made a pretext for refusing the wheat?"

Science pronounces it entirely illogical to suppose that we exist as individuals after our bodies are resolved into the elements. But logic is a science extremely narrow in its limitations. There may be phases of existence as much beyond its cognizance as birds are beyond the observation of fishes. Since Emerson and Tennyson have been evolved out of the original cave men, it does not seem to me irrational to suppose that a continuity of the process may produce seraphs. I know that the theory of evolution is a continual changing of forms, and that each form, in giving place to another, loses its own identity. But when evolution has arrived at such a stage as man, a being capable of conceiving of higher planes of existence, may it not have produced a state of things in which continued consciousness through changing forms becomes possible? There is nothing supernatural. All things are produced and governed by universal laws. But the trouble is, an immense domain of those laws is beyond our knowledge. I bow respectfully to Science and I think she is the safest guide we have. But, after all, she does not go very far.

TO MRS. S. E. SEWALL.

WAYLAND, June 17, 1879.

During these weeks, so filled with memories of our friend Garrison, I have seemed to feel the presence of you and your dear, good husband, as you say you have felt mine. I thought of you continually on the day of the funeral, and while reading the beautiful tributes offered by Phillips and Weld and Whittier. If his spirit was there, how happy he must have been! The general laudation in the newspapers was truly wonderful. If any prophet had foretold it thirty years ago, who would have believed him? It seems to me there never was so great a moral revolution in so short a time. It was elevating and thrilling to read the funeral services, and it must have been much more so to have heard them. If Mr. Garrison was mistaken in his strong belief that individual, conscious existence continued elsewhere, he will never know of his mistake; but I think he was not mistaken. I suppose you noticed that Whittier recognized his spirit as still active in defending the right. How could such a spirit die? . . .

I should think that painful Pocasset tragedy might open people's eyes to the absurdity of taking the records of a semi-barbarous people for an inspired rule of life in the nineteenth century. Monstrous as the act seems, it is a legitimate result of eulogizing Abraham for his readiness to sacrifice his son, and of ascribing the same thing to God.

TO MISS ANNE WHITNEY.

WAYLAND, June, 1879.

I am glad you had such a pleasant evening with

Garrison. He has been a singularly fortunate man.
Fortunate in accomplishing his purposes; fortunate
in drawing around him the best spirits of his time;
fortunate in having an amiable, sympathizing wife;
fortunate in having excellent, devoted children, whose
marriages have suited him, and who have lived in
proximity to him; fortunate in having his energies
developed by struggle in early life; fortunate in later
years in being at ease in his worldly circumstances;
and most fortunate of all in dying before his mind
became weakened. Death will be to him merely
passing out of one room filled with friends into another room still more full of friends.

It is wonderful how one mortal may affect the destiny of a multitude. I remember very distinctly the
first time I ever saw Garrison. I little thought then
that the whole pattern of my life-web would be
changed by that introduction. I was then all absorbed in poetry and painting, soaring aloft on
Psyche-wings into the ethereal regions of mysticism.
He got hold of the strings of my conscience and
pulled me into reforms. It is of no use to imagine
what might have been, if I had never met him. Old
dreams vanished, old associates departed, and all
things became new. But the new surroundings were
all alive, and they brought a moral discipline worth
ten times the sacrifice they cost. But why use the
word sacrifice? I was never conscious of any sacrifice. A new stimulus seized my whole being, and
carried me whithersoever it would. "I could not
otherwise, so help me God!" How the same circumstances changed the whole coloring of life for Charles
Sumner and Wendell Phillips! The hour of nations'
expiation had come, and men and women must needs

obey the summons to accomplish the work through means they could not foresee.

TO MRS. H. W. SEWALL.

WAYLAND, August 25, 1879.

That Mrs. —— is the plague of my life. It is the fourth or fifth time she has been "pervading my department, wanting to know." I don't remember when the "Juvenile Miscellany" began, and what sort of interest can it have for the public? An impertinent reporter of the —— interviewed me, and in that paper last June informed the public of the figures in my carpet and the color of my gown, to which he appended some literary dates.

Few things "rile me up" like this impertinent curiosity, which, after all, is only a fashionable way of earning a penny without work. There is nothing in my personal history either "new, useful, or entertaining."

I thank you cordially for the books. . . . You say you "like human beings better than books." I like some human beings better than books, but not many. Books have one very great advantage over people; you can put them aside whenever you don't care to be with them any longer. Moreover, I can make up a contemptuous mouth and say, "Pshaw! all bosh!" when a book says what I don't like, but it won't do to treat people with so much freedom.

TO MISS A. B. FRANCIS.

BOSTON, December 24, 1879.

I know of nothing very interesting in the literary world," except a small volume called the "Light of Asia," by the English Mr. Arnold, who married W.

H. Channing's daughter. It recites the well-known legends about Buddha, in a form of singular poetic beauty. He made a great mistake, that good "Lord Buddha." It would have been more wise to have taught his fellow-creatures how to raise more grain, weave more cloth, and take better care of their health, than it was to descend into beggary with them. But there is something very touching and sublime in his determination to quit regal splendor and luxury, and live among the poor and suffering like a brother. The book sells well on account of its literary merit, and is helping many other quiet influences to enable human souls to recognize their spiritual kinship.

TO MRS. S. B. SHAW.

1880.

I wish you could see Miss Whitney's Sam. Adams. I never saw an image so full of life; not even the Minute Man at Concord. An acquaintance sent a very human-looking doll to a little friend, five years old. When a neighbor exclaimed, "What a pretty doll!" the child said, "You must n't call it doll, it's a little girl. She can't walk and talk now, but she will by and by." When I returned from Miss Whitney's studio, I was asked, "How did you like the statue?" I replied, "You must not call it a statue, it's a man. It will walk and talk by and by."

TO THEODORE D. WELD.

WAYLAND, July 10, 1880.

I thank you cordially for the interesting Memorial of your excellent wife.[1] Such a benediction is rarely bestowed on any man as to have loved and been be-

[1] Mrs. Angelina Grimké Weld.

loved by such a woman. How dim and cold all the pictures of the old saints seem, when brought into comparison with the clear light of her conscience, and the glowing warmth of her love for her fellow-creatures.

The memory of the early anti-slavery days is very sacred to me. The Holy Spirit did actually descend upon men and women in tongues of flame. Political and theological prejudices and personal ambitions were forgotten in sympathy for the wrongs of the helpless, and in the enthusiasm to keep the fire of freedom from being extinguished on our national altar.

All suppression of selfishness makes the moment great; and mortals were never more sublimely forgetful of self than were the abolitionists in those early days, before the moral force which emanated from them had become available as a political power. Ah, my friend, that is the only true church organization, when heads and hearts unite in working for the welfare of the human race!

And how wonderfully everything came as it was wanted! How quickly the "mingled flute and trumpet eloquence" of Phillips responded to the clarion call of Garrison! How the clear, rich bugle-tones of Whittier wakened echoes in all living souls! How wealth poured from the ever-open hands of Arthur Tappan, Gerrit Smith, the Winslows, and thousands of others who gave even more largely in proportion to their smaller means!

How the time-serving policy of Dr. Beecher drove the bold, brave boys of Lane Seminary into the battle-field! Politicians said, "The abolitionists exaggerate the evil; they do not know whereof they affirm;" and in response up rose Angelina and her sister Sarah, shrinking from the task imposed upon them by conscience, but upheld by the divine power of truth to deliver this message to the world: "We know whereof we affirm; for we were born and bred in South Carolina; and we know that abolitionists have not told, and could not tell, half the horrors of slavery."

Then, like a cloud full of thunder and lightning, Frederick Douglass loomed above the horizon. He knew whereof he affirmed, for he had been a slave. Congress seemed in danger of becoming a mere "den of thieves," when Daniel Webster walked out with Ichabod written on his garments; and, strong in moral majesty, in walked Charles Sumner, a man so honest and pure that he could not see any other line than a straight one. What if the pulpits were silent? Theodore Parker, that Boanerges of the clerical ranks, spoke in tones strong and far-reaching as a thousand voices.

Those were indeed inspiring days. I look back lovingly upon them; and I find it very hard to realize that so much of it has passed into oblivion, and that whatever remains is merely the cold record of history.

Your good and great Angelina and yourself are prominent in these memory pictures of a thrilling and exalting period. How well I remember her pale countenance and trembling limbs, when she rose to address the Legislature of Massachusetts! The feminine shrinking was soon overcome by her sense of the duty before her, and her words flowed forth, free, forcible, and well-arranged. Those who went from that hall unconverted were those who, being "convinced against their will, were of the same opinion still."

TO FRANCIS G. SHAW.

WAYLAND, September, 1880.

I thank you for the "Life of General Garfield." I did not think I should ever again take so much interest in a political campaign as I do in his election. I read every word of his speech on "Honest Money," eight columns long. I am not well posted upon financial questions, and have had rather a distaste for such controversies. But his statements were so very plain that I understood every sentence; and my common sense and my moral sense cordially responded thereto. Everything I have read of his seems to me to have the ring of true metal. I am constantly reminded of the practical good sense and sturdy honesty of Francis Jackson.

I was especially pleased with the emphasis he places on the assertion that there was a right and wrong in the War of the Rebellion; I would not have one unnecessary word said that would hurt the feelings or wound the pride of the South. They acted just as we should have acted if we had been educated under the same institution. But their institution was bad, and the means they took to sustain and extend it were bad. I have been disgusted, and somewhat discouraged, by the "mush of concession" that has passed current under the name of magnanimity. The tendency to speak of both sides as equally in the right, because they both fought bravely, is utterly wrong in principle and demoralizing in its influence.

TO MRS. S. S. RUSSELL.

WAYLAND, September 23, 1880.

MY PRECIOUS FRIEND, — I have not answered your last kind letter as soon as my heart dictated, because I have waited in hopes to give a better account of myself. . . . At last, by the help of my friend Mrs. S., I have found a pleasant old doctor in Weston who has made rheumatism his specialty and been very successful in curing it. He is very positive that a cure will be effected in two or three weeks. Mrs. —— has been very kind and efficient, and the neighbors very attentive. It is a great blessing, also, that my general health has been and is extremely good. . . .

Some of my poor neighbors have been in trouble owing to protracted illness, and I shall make up to them the days when they have not been able to work. The worthy young man who comes here to sleep needs some help about learning a trade, and I am going to give him a lift. Divers other projects I have in my mind, and I expect to accomplish them all by the help of Aladdin's lamp. Oh, it is such a luxury to be able to give without being afraid. I try not to be Quixotic, but I want to rain down blessings on all the world, in token of thankfulness for the blessings that have been rained down upon me. I should dearly love to look in upon you at Newport, as you kindly suggest, but it is impossible. I once made a short visit to Dr. Channing there, and the loveliness of the scenery made an abiding impression on my memory. Your most grateful and loving old friend, L. MARIA CHILD.

APPENDIX.

REMARKS OF WENDELL PHILLIPS AT THE FUNERAL OF LYDIA MARIA CHILD, OCTOBER 23, 1880.

Mrs. CHILD's character was one of rare elements, and their combination in one person rarer still. She was the outgrowth of New England theology, traditions, and habits — the finest fruit of these: but she could have been born and bred nowhere but in New England.

There were all the charms and graceful elements which we call feminine, united with a masculine grasp and vigor; sound judgment and great breadth; large common sense and capacity for every-day usefulness; "endurance, foresight, strength, and skill."

> "A creature not too bright and good
> For human nature's daily food."

But lavishly endowed, her gifts were not so remarkable as the admirable conscientiousness with which she used them. Indeed, an earnest purpose, vigilant conscientiousness, were the keys to her whole life and its best explanation.

We shall better understand her life if we remember it was governed by the divine rule, "Bear ye one another's burdens." This, in fact, explains her courage, her economy, her painstaking industry, her interest and activity in reforms, and the scrupulous fidelity with which she cultivated every power.

How early her mind ripened and in what girlhood it opened to the most advanced thought of her times! And the first draught of fame, usually so intoxicating, never disturbed her clear judgment or tempted her to any undue compromise.

There were few women authors when, in 1821-22, she published her first novels. The success of these was so brilliant, and a woman's success then so rare, that the Boston Athenæum, — still the most fashionable and aristocratic, and then the only, public library — paid her the almost unique compliment of sending her a free ticket of admission. When, in 1833, she published her "Appeal in behalf of that Class of Americans called Africans," she of course sent that library a copy. Whether they ever placed the book on their shelves I do not know, but at any rate the directors immediately withdrew her ticket of admission. And a prominent lawyer, afterwards a notorious attorney-general of Massachusetts, is said to have used tongs to fling the obnoxious volume out of his window.

This is a sad record; but to recall it is only fair tribute to the young author, who never faltered; only gave to the hated and struggling cause a more public adhesion and a more liberal support. Hardly ever was there a costlier sacrifice. Few of us can appreciate it to-day. Narrow means just changing to ease; after a weary struggle, fame and social position in her grasp; every door opening before her; the sweetness of having her genius recognized.

No one had supposed that independence of opinion on a moral question would wreck all this. It was a thunderbolt from a summer sky. But confronted suddenly with the alternative, gagged life or total wreck, — she never hesitated.

One blow, and the spreading tree is dead. At the call of duty the young woman struck it without repining, and saw the whole scene change at once. Obloquy and hard work ill-paid; almost every door shut against her, the name she had made a talisman turned to a reproach, and life henceforth a sacrifice. How serenely she took up that cross, how bravely she bore it almost till life's close!

In religious speculation Mrs. Child moved in the very van. Her studies and friendships were with the foremost scholars. But it was not merely indifferentism, dissent, and denial — that negative and aggressive element to which Emerson has, of late, so strongly objected. She was penetrated with a deep religious fervor; as devotional, as profound and tender a sentiment as the ignorant devotee.

It has been my lot to find more bigotry and narrowness among free religionists than among their opponents. But Mrs. Child in her many-sidedness did not merely bear with other creeds; she heartily sympathized with all forms of religious belief, pagan, classic, oriental, and Christian. All she asked was that they should be real. That condition present, she saw lovingly their merits and gave to each the fullest credit for its honesty of purpose.

Her "Progress of Religious Ideas" was no mere intellectual effort. It was the natural utterance of a deep, kindly, and respectful sympathy with each. There was no foolish tenderness, no weak sentimentality about her. She held every one, as she did herself, strictly to the sternest responsibility. Still there was the most lovable candor and an admirably level fairness of judgment; always making every allowance and believing to the last in honesty of purpose.

She practised the most rigid economy always and in even the minutest particular. Her own hands ministered to her wants and those of her husband; waste was almost crime. But this hard and painstaking care with one hand was only that the other might be full for liberal gifts.

Franklin has had on one or two generations an evil influence that made them save only to accumulate, resulting in that despicable virtue "prudence;" despicable when it saps independence and shuts up the over-careful hand.

But Mrs. Child's prudence never held back one needed bold word, and was only to make her more able to give. There was a delicate shrinking from receiving too many favors; a pride of independence that never left her. To one who strove to do for her unpaid, she invented ways of remuneration until the balance of obligation was often on his side.

It was like her to refuse a gift of several thousand dollars, and, again when I suggested that the large-hearted friend who offered it had more than she could do to wisely distribute her income, and that Mrs. Child could and should help her in that, it was like her also to change her mind, accept the trust, portion out every dollar of income while she lived, and devise it, at her death, to the ideas and movements she loved.

And yet this princely giver kept till death the cheap, plain fashion of dress which early narrow means had enforced, — used an envelope twice, and never wrote on a whole sheet when half a one would suffice. "I do not think, Mrs. Child, you can afford to give so much just now," I said to her once, when, in some exigency of the freedmen's cause, she told me to send them from her a hundred dollars. "Well," she answered, "I will think it over, and send you word to-morrow." To-morrow word came, "Please send them two hundred."

Her means were never large: never so large that a woman of her class would think she had anything to give away. But her spirit was Spartan. When she had nothing for others, she worked to get it. She wrote me once, "I have four hundred dollars to my credit at my publishers for my book on 'Looking towards Sunset.' Please get it and give it to the freedmen."

"I want a dictionary," one said to her whom she was always importuning to allow her to give him something, "if you will insist on giving it to me; it will cost ten dollars." She sent the most valuable, costing double. But we who knew her cannot forget that this was not a hard life nor a harsh one. It bubbled up with joy. Threescore years and ten had still the freshness of girlhood, the spirits nothing could dull or quench; the ready wit, quick retort, mirthful jest. Her memory was a storehouse of fact, proverb, curious incident, fine saying, homely wisdom, touching story, brave act; and hence her conversation, fraught with all this treasure, was indescribably charming. Few scholars ever gave such fair play to their mother-wit; were so little overloaded and cumbered with massive accumulations. What variety of gifts! everything but poet. Narrative, fiction, journalism, history, sketches of daily city life, ethics, consolation for the evening of life, ennobling our nature by showing how, under all error, there lives the right purpose and principle. And she had nothing of the scholar's disease, timidity and selfishness. Her hand was always ready for any drudgery of service. It was she, as much as her lion-hearted husband, who, at their own cost, saved Boston from the crime and infamy of murdering the twelve pirates before they had even the mockery of a trial. The fallen woman, the over-tempted inebriate, she could take to her home and watch over month after month. And prison doors were no bar to her when a friendless woman needed help or countenance against an angry community.

Her courage was not merely intellectual. I remember well her resolute rebuke, spoken in the street, to the leader of one of the Sunday mobs of 1861, — so stern, brief, and pungent that it left him dumb. She was among the first to welcome John Brown. While anti-slavery senators and governors excused him as a "madman," and leading reformers smiled pityingly on the "fanatic," her sword leapt from its scabbard in his defence. While it yet hung in the balance whether the nation should acknowledge its prophet or crucify him, she asked to share his prison, and with brave appeal stirred the land to see the prophet vouchsafed to it.

She had much of that marvellous power which disinterestedness always gives. We felt that neither fame, nor gain, nor danger, nor calumny had any weight with her; that she sought honestly to act out her thought; obeyed the rule, —

"Go put your creed
Into your deed;"

was ready to die for a principle and starve for an idea ; nor think to claim any merit for it! What measureless power this has! With what hooks of steel this binds men to one! A dear lovable woman, welcome at a sick bedside ; as much in place there as when facing an angry nation ; contented in the home she made ; the loyal friend ; such ingenuity in devising ways to help you ; the stalwart fidelity of friendship, rare in these easy going, half-and-half, non-committal days ; such friendship as allowed no word of disparagement, no doubt of a friend's worth, to insult her presence. A wise counsellor, one who made your troubles hers and pondered thoughtfully before she spoke her hearty word : we feel we have lost one who would have stood by us in trouble, a shield. She was the kind of woman one would choose to represent woman's entrance into broader life. Modest, womanly, simple, sincere, solid, real, loyal ; to be trusted ; equal to affairs and yet above them ; mother-wit ripened by careful training, and enriched with the lore of ages ; a companion with the pass-word of every science and all literatures ; a hand ready for fireside help and a mystic loving to wander on the edge of the actual, reaching out and up into the infinite and the unfathomable ; so that life was lifted to romance, to heroism and the loftiest faith. May we also have a faith that is almost sight. How joyful to remember, dear friend, your last counsel, the words you thought spirit hands had traced for your epitaph : " You think us dead. We are not dead ; we are the living."

WITHIN THE GATE.

L. M. C.

WE sat together, last May-day, and talked
    Of the dear friends who walked
Beside us, sharers of the hopes and fears
    Of five and forty years

Since first we met in Freedom's hope forlorn,
    And heard her battle-horn
Sound through the valleys of the sleeping North,
    Calling her children forth,

And youth pressed forward with hope-lighted eyes,
    And age, with forecast wise
Of the long strife before the triumph won,
    Girded his armor on.

Sadly, as name by name we called the roll,
    We heard the dead-bells toll
For the unanswering many, and we knew
    The living were the few.

And we, who waited our own call before
    The inevitable door,
Listened and looked, as all have done, to win
    Some token from within.

No sign we saw, we heard no voices call;
    The impenetrable wall
Cast down its shadow, like an awful doubt,
    On all who sat without.

Of many a hint of life beyond the veil,
    And many a ghostly tale

Wherewith the ages spanned the gulf between
    The seen and the unseen,

Seeking from omen, trance, and dream to gain
    Solace to doubtful pain,
And touch, with groping hands, the garment hem
    Of truth sufficing them,

We talked; and, turning from the sore unrest
    Of an all-baffling quest,
We thought of holy lives that from us passed
    Hopeful unto the last,

As if they saw beyond the river of death,
    Like Him of Nazareth,
The many mansions of the Eternal days
    Lift up their gates of praise.

And, hushed to silence by a reverent awe,
    Methought, O friend, I saw
In thy true life of word, and work, and thought,
    The proof of all we sought.

Did we not witness in the life of thee
    Immortal prophecy?
And feel, when with thee, that thy footsteps trod
    An everlasting road?

Not for brief days thy generous sympathies,
    Thy scorn of selfish ease;
Not for the poor prize of an earthly goal
    Thy strong uplift of soul.

Than thine was never turned a fonder heart
    To nature and to art
In fair-formed Hellas in her golden prime,
    Thy Philothea's time.

Yet, loving beauty, thou couldst pass it by,
    And for the poor deny
Thyself, and see thy fresh, sweet flower of fame
    Wither in blight and blame.

Sharing His love who holds in His embrace
    The lowliest of our race,
Sure the Divine economy must be
    Conservative of thee!

For truth must live with truth, self-sacrifice
    Seek out its great allies;
Good must find good by gravitation sure,
    And love with love endure.

And so, since thou hast passed within the gate
    Whereby awhile I wait,
I give blind grief and blinder sense the lie:
    Thou hast not lived to die!

              JOHN GREENLEAF WHITTIER.

LIST OF MRS. CHILD'S WORKS,

WITH THE DATE OF THEIR FIRST PUBLICATION AS FAR AS ASCERTAINED.

Hobomok; a Tale of Early Times. Boston, 1824. 12°.
Evenings in New England. Intended for Juvenile Amusement and Instruction. Boston, 1824.
The Rebels; or, Boston before the Revolution. Boston, 1825. 12°.
The Juvenile Miscellany. 1826–1834.
The Juvenile Souvenir. Boston, 1828. 12°.
The First Settlers of New England; or, Conquest of the Pequods, Narragansets, and Pokanokets. As related by a mother to her children. Boston, 1829.
The (American) Frugal Housewife. Boston, 1829. 12°.
The Mother's Book. Boston, 1831. 12°.
The Girl's Own Book. Boston, 1831. 12°.
The Coronal; a Collection of Miscellaneous Pieces, Written at Various Times. Boston, 1831. 18°.

THE LADIES' FAMILY LIBRARY.
    Vol. I. Biographies of Lady Russell and Madame Guion. Boston, 1832. 12°.
    Vol. II. Biographies of Madame de Staël and Madame Roland. Boston, 1832. 12°.
    Vol. III. Biographies of Good Wives. Boston, 1833. 12°.

    CONTENTS. — Lady Ackland. — Queen Anna. — Arria, Wife of Poetus. — Lady Biron. — Mrs. Blackwell. — Calphurnia. — Chelonis. — Lady Collingwood. — Countess of Dorset. — Queen Eleanor Eponina. — Lady Fanshawe. — Mrs. Fletcher. — Mrs. Grotius. — Mrs. Howard. — Mrs. Huter. — Countess of Huntingdon. — Mrs. Hutchinson. — Lady Arabella Johnson. — Mrs. Judson. — Mrs. Klopstock. — Mrs. Lavater. — Mrs. Lavalette. — Mrs. Luther. — Queen Mary. — Countess of Nithsdale. — Mrs. Oberlin. — Panthea. — Baroness Reidesel. — Mrs. Reiske. — Mrs. Ross. — Mrs. Schiller. — Countess Segur. — Spurzheim. — Sybella. — Baroness Vonder Mart. — Mrs. West. — Mrs. Wieland. — Mrs. Winthrop.

Vol. IV.–V. History of the Condition of Women in Various Ages and Nations. Boston, 1835. 2 vols. 16°. Vol. I. The Women of Asia and Africa. Vol. II. The Women of Europe, America, and South Sea Islands.

An Appeal in Behalf of that Class of Americans called Africans. Boston, 1833. 12°.

The Oasis. Boston, 1834. 16°.

> CONTENTS. — CHILD, Mrs. L. M. Brief Memoir of Wilberforce; How to effect Emancipation; Malem Boo; Illustration of Prejudice; Joanna; I thank my God for my Humility; Safe Mode of Operation; Scipio Africanus; The Hottentots; Conversation with Colonizationists; Knowledge in Austria; Voices from the South; Scale of Complexions; Dangers of Emancipation; Knowledge in the United States; Old Scip; Derivation of Negro; Opinions of Travellers; Jamaica Mobs. — FOLLEN, Mrs. Remember the Slave; The Runaway Slave. — CHILD, D. L. Henry Diaz; Three Colored Republics of Guiana; Judicial Decisions in Slave States. WHITTIER, J. G. The Slave Ships. — WHITTIER, E. H. The Slave Trader. — BRADLEY, J. History of J. B., by Himself. — MAY, Rev. S. J. Miss Crandall's School. — FLORENCE. The Infant Abolitionist. — GOULD, H. F. The Land of the Free. — English Protest against the Colonization Society. — Alexander Vasselin. — Cornelius of St. Croix. — Ruins of Egyptian Thebes. — History of Thomas Jenkins. — A Negro Hunt.

An Anti-Slavery Catechism. Newburyport, 1836. 12°.

The Evils of Slavery and the Curse of Slavery. The first proved by the opinions of Southerners themselves; the last shown by historical evidence. Newburyport, 1836. 12°.

Philothea: a Romance. Boston, 1836. 12°.

The Family Nurse. Boston, 1837. 12°.

Authentic Narratives of American Slavery. Newburyport, 1838. 12°.

Rose Marian. Adapted from the German. 1839.

The Preaching of Whitefield. (In Boston Book, 1841.)

The Anti-Slavery Almanac. New York, 1843. 16°.

Letters from New York. First Series. New York, 1843. 12°.

Flowers for Children. First and Second Series. 1844.

Letters from New York. Second Series. New York, 1845. 12°.
Fact and Fiction. 1846.
Flowers for Children. Third Series. 1846.
Isaac T. Hopper; a True Life. Boston, 1853. 12°.
New Flowers for Children. 1855.
The Progress of Religious Ideas through Successive Ages. New York, 1855. 3 vols. 8°.
Autumnal Leaves: Tales and Sketches in Prose and Rhyme. New York, 1856. 16°.
Correspondence between L. M. Child and Gov. Wise and Mrs. Mason (of Virginia). Boston, 1860. 12°.
The Duty of Disobedience to the Fugitive Slave Act. An Appeal to the Legislators of Massachusetts. Boston, 1860. 12°. (Anti-Slavery Tracts, No. 9.)
The Patriarchal Institution, described by Members of its own Family. New York, 1860. 12°.
The Right Way the Safe Way, proved by Emancipation in the West Indies and elsewhere. New York, 1860. 12°.
The Freedmen's Book. Boston, 1865. 16°.
A Romance of the Republic. Boston, 1867. 12°.
Looking towards Sunset. From Sources Old and New, Original and Selected. Boston, 1868. 8°.
An Appeal for the Indians. New York (1868?). 12°.
Aspirations of the World. A Chain of Opals. With an Introduction by L. M. Child. Boston, 1878. 16°.

INDEX.

ABDY, EDWARD S., Mrs. Child's letters to, viii.
Adams, John Quincy, indebted to Mr. Child for facts on the Texas question, viii.; maintains the right to proclaim emancipation in war time, 151.
Adams, Samuel, Miss Whitney's statue of, 257.
Advertisements of fugitive slaves, 128, 129.
Alcott, A. Bronson, and family, 239.
Allen, Mr., of Alabama, testifies to horrors of slavery, 131.
Allyn, Rev. Dr., letter to, 9.
American Anti-Slavery Society, formation of, viii.
American Missionary Association, refuses to circulate Mrs. Child's "Freedmen's Book," 201.
Andrews, William P., sonnet to Mrs. Child, xxiii.
"An English governess at the Siamese Court," 210.
Animals, the treatment of, 214.
Anti-Slavery Society (Mass.), annual meeting of, mobbed, 148-150.
"Appeal in behalf of that Class of Americans called Africans," by Mrs. Child, ix., 48, 195.
Armstrong, General, and Hampton Institute, 241.
Arnold, Edwin, 257.
"Aspirations of the World," by Mrs. Child, xix., 246.
"Aurora Leigh," by Mrs. Browning, 87, 197.
"Autobiography of a Female Slave," 90, 132.

BANNEKER, BENJAMIN, 184.
Beecher, Henry Ward, magnetic power of, 193; defends the Chinese, 251.
Beethoven's music contrasted with Mendelssohn's, 76.
Benson, Edmund, 89.
Berrien, John McP., U. S. Senator, anecdote of, 179.
Bettine and Goethe, 50, 51.
Bible, anti slavery texts from, 123-125.
Bishop, Madame Anna, 140.
Bleby, Rev. Henry, 134.
Boston Athenæum, privileges of, given to, and withdrawn from, Mrs. Child, 195, 204.

Boutwell, George S., speech of, 168.
Bremer, Fredrika, meets Mrs. Child, 65; relates anecdote of Jenny Lind, 66; her estimation of Lowell and Emerson, 66.
Brisbane, Mr., 51.
"Broken Lights," by Miss Cobbe, 184.
Brooks, Governor, v.
Brown, John, letter of Mrs. Child to, 118; his reply, 119; martyrdom of, 137.
Browning's (Mrs.) "Aurora Leigh," 87.
Bryant, William C., writes to Mrs. Child, 186.
Buckle's "History of Civilization," 99.
Buddha, 257.
Burns, Anthony, returned to slavery from Boston, 72.

CARPENTER, E., letters to, 19, 22, 26.
Carpenter, Joseph, letters to, 41, 63.
Cassimir, a nephew of Kossuth, 162.
Chadwick, John W., 242.
Channing, William Ellery, discusses the anti-slavery movement with Mrs. Child, 24; letters of, to Mrs. Child, 44, 45; Mrs. Child's reminiscences of, 48; influenced by Mrs. Child's "Appeal," 77; her imagination of him in the spiritual world, 144.
Channing, William H., 188, 257.
Chicago "Tribune" has biographical sketch of Mrs. Child, 201.
Chapman, Maria Weston, 19, 147.
Child, letter to a, 36.
Child, David Lee, biographical sketch of, viii.; first meets Miss Francis, 8; his marriage, 10; letters to, from his wife, 10, 82, 86, 88, 96; his domestic happiness, xvi.; his death, xix., 229; Mrs. Child's reminiscences of, xvi.
Child, Lydia Maria, publishes her "Appeal" in behalf of the colored people, ix.; her consequent unpopularity, ix.; an advocate of individual freedom, 12; describes pro-slavery excitement in New York, 15; indifference to literary success, 21; on the prejudice against color among Friends, 23; converses with Dr. Channing on the anti-slavery movement, 24; hears Angelina Grimké speak, 26; life in Northampton, 29-41; discussions with slave-holders, 30; abusive letters

to, from Southerners, 41; edits the "Standard," in New York, 42; lives with Isaac T. Hopper's family, 43; interest in New Church doctrines, 43; letters of Dr. Channing to, 44, 45; her reminiscences of Dr. Channing, 48; life in New York, 50-60; characterization of, by Rev. Mr. Kent, 55; interview with Dr. Palfrey, 56; reads Emerson's essays, 57; her admiration of Domenichino's "Cumæan Sibyl," 57; has a birthday celebration, 59; her views on a salaried priesthood, 61; reads the "Countess of Rudolstaat," 62; dislikes letters of introduction, 63; her enjoyment of music, 64; at work on "The Progress of Religious Ideas," 65; meets Fredrika Bremer, 65; makes her will, 74; passes through strange spiritual experiences, 74, 75; spends a lonely winter at Wayland, 75; prefers Mendelssohn's music to Beethoven's, and Raphael's works to Michael Angelo's, 76; her labor in writing "The Progress of Religious Ideas," 78; her interest in the Fremont campaign and Kansas conflict, 79, 80; working for the Kansas emigrants, 83; writes a Free Soil song, 83; death of her father, 87; interviews with Charles Sumner and Henry Wilson, 88; her low estimate of worldly rank, 89; corresponds with Miss Mattie Griffith, 89; meets David A. Wasson, 91; her grief at Ellis Gray Loring's death, 95; meets J. G. Whittier, 97; her indebtedness to her brother, 98; her delight in works of art and in nature, 98, 99; reads Buckle's "History of Civilization," 99; lines in memory of Ellis Gray Loring, 101; correspondence with John Brown, Governor Wise, and Mrs. Mason, 103-137; attends prayer-meeting of colored people, 137; reads F. W. Newman's books, 139; reads "Counterparts," 140; visit to Whittier, 141; discusses a future state of existence, 143; attends an anti-slavery festival, 147; describes a mob at an anti-slavery meeting, 148, 149; denounces the return of fugitive slaves by U. S. troops, 150; her thoughts absorbed by the war, 153; meets old friends at the Anti-Slavery office, 155; visits at Mr. Sewall's, 156; her dread of a war with England, 163; reads "John Brent," 164; donations for the "contrabands," 165; working for the Kansas troops, 168; metaphysics her aversion, 169; her active winter life at Wayland, 170; her feelings about the Emancipation Proclamation, 171; death of her brother, 172; her indebtedness to him, 173; her sorrow at Colonel Shaw's death, 176; partial destruction of her house by fire, 177; reads Weiss's "Life of Parker," 179; meets George Thompson, 181; her happiness over Lincoln's reëlection, 183; success of her "Looking towards Sunset," 185; her enjoyment of winter scenery, 191; publishes "The Freedmen's Book," 192; her "Right Way the Safe Way," 192; on novels and sermons, 192, 193; not a loser, but a gainer, by her adherence to the anti-slavery cause, 194; her first meeting with Mr. Garrison, 195; the privileges of the Boston Athenæum given to, and withdrawn from, her, 195, 264; cultivates cheerfulness, 196; reads the "Spanish Gypsy," 197; her sixty-seventh birthday, 198; on Fourier and the labor question, 199; her jubilation over Grant's election, 200; reads Taine's papers on art, 200; her "Freedmen's Book" and the American Missionary Association, 201; her aversion to newspaper publicity, 201; her judgment of George Sand, 205; lines to George Thompson, 206; her appeal to Mr. Sumner in behalf of the rights of women, 208; on Grant's reëlection, 213; on the treatment of animals, 214; on the Indian question, xx., 218-221; in favor of the prohibitory law, 221; reads Mrs. Somerville's Life, and Mill's Autobiography, 222, and "A Princess of Thule," 223; her grief at Charles Sumner's death, 224; her reformation of a drunkard, 227; her views on "Sex in Education," 229; her loneliness after her husband's death, 230; passes the winter at Staten Island, 231; Christmas in New York, 232; returns to Wayland, 233; investigates "spirit-photography," 234; visits the Alcotts at Concord, 239; on the equality of the sexes, 243; reads Renan's "Life of Jesus," 245; publishes "Aspirations of the World," 247; her reminiscences of George Thompson, 248; her views on the Chinese question, 251; speculations on a future life, 252; on the death of Mr. Garrison, 254, 255; reads "The Light of Asia," 257; reminiscences of anti-slavery days, 258; her interest in Garfield's election, 260; her last days, 261; reminiscences of, xxi.; Mr. Phillips's remarks at her funeral, 263; Whittier's poem to her memory, 269.

Chinese in America, agitation against the, 251.

Choate, Rufus, employed to defend the slave child, Med, 20.

Christianity an accretion of all the antecedent religious aspirations of mankind, 202.

"Christian Register," The, 194, 201.

"Church of the Future," The, by Miss Cobbe, 184.

Clarke, Edward H., M. D., on "Sex in Education," 229.

INDEX. 277

Clarke, James Freeman, addresses an anti-slavery meeting, 149; Mr. Garrison's letter to, 243.
Cobbe, Frances Power, her "Broken Lights," and "Church of the Future," 184.
Colored people of Boston commemorate John Brown's death, 137.
Constantine, the Emperor, his conversion to Christianity, 187.
Constitution, U. S., passage of 13th Amendment to, 188.
"Contrabands," anecdotes of the, 158; donations for, 165.
Conway, Martin F., of Kansas, 168.
Correggio's "Diana," Toschi's engraving of, 70.
"Countess of Rudolstaat," The, a novel, 62.
Crawford, Mr., of London, 12.
"Cumæan Sibyl," by Domenichino, 57.
Curtis, George William, 79; oration of, 85; conducts Sunday services, 233; letter on caucus dictation, 252.

Davis, Jeff., 152.
De Staël, Madame, 247.
Devens, Charles, redeems Thomas Sims from slavery, 189.
Domenichino's "Cumæan Sibyl," 57.
Douglass, Frederick, 259.
Draft riots of 1863 in New York, 178.
Dresel, Mrs. Anna Loring, letter to, 191.
Dresser, Amos, publicly flogged at Nashville, Tenn., 184.
Dwight, John S., 29, 37, 50.

"Eclectic Review," The, viii.
Education of women in Egypt and India, the, 212, 213.
Elssler, Fanny, 35.
Emancipation Proclamation, 171.
Emerson, Ralph Waldo, attitude of the Unitarians towards, 34; sends Mrs. Child his Essays, 57; speaks at a mobbed anti-slavery meeting, 149.
Emerson and the Sphinx, 247.
"Eminent Women of the Age," vi.
Equality of the sexes, 243–245.

"Fable for Critics," A, by J. R. Lowell, xiv.
Faneuil Hall, meeting at, in behalf of Anthony Burns, 73.
"Fingal's Cave," Mendelssohn's overture of, 223.
Foote, Henry S., U. S. Senator, 179.
Fortress Monroe, fugitive slaves at, 150, 151.
Forten, R. R., 184.
Fort Pickens (Florida), fugitive slaves returned from, by U. S. officers, 150.
Fort Wagner, the attack on, 236; the grave of Colonel Shaw at, 238.
Fourier, François Charles Marie, 199.
Francis, Miss A. B., letters to, 231, 251, 258.
Francis, Convers, aids and encourages his sister, v., vi., 1; letters to 1, 2, 4, 5, 6, 7, 12, 16, 17, 29, 33, 39, 40, 50, 58, 63, 64, 65, 74, 89, 98; on the death of his wife, 163; death of, 172.
Francis, Lydia Maria, birth of, v.; her first schooling, v., vi.; ambitious to write a novel, vi.; reads "Paradise Lost," 1, 2; "Guy Mannering," 2; Gibbon's "Roman Empire," 4; "Shakespeare," 4; "The Spectator," 5; Johnson her favorite writer, 5; takes a school in Gardiner, Me., 5; her opinion of Byron, 7; discusses Paley's system, 7; her early literary successes, vii., 10; first meets Mr. Child, 8; her marriage, 10.
"Freedmen's Book," The, by Mrs. Child, 192, 201.
Free Religious Association, meeting of the, 239.
Fremont, John C., 79; his emancipation proclamation, 162.
Friends, the, degeneracy of, 22, 28.
Frothingham, Rev. O. B., 232.
"Frugal Housewife," The, vii.
Fugitive slaves, advertisements of, 128, 129; returned by U. S. troops, 149, 150.
Furness, Rev. William H., 81.
Future life, speculations on the, 252

Garfield, James A., 260.
Garrison, William Lloyd, interests Mr. and Mrs. Child in the slavery question, viii., 23; favors the dissolution of the Anti-Slavery Society, 190; his first interview with Mrs. Child, 195; mobbed in Boston streets, 235; letter to J. F. Clarke, 243; defends the Chinese, 251; the tributes to, on his death, 254; his belief in continued existence, 254; his influence on Mrs. Child's life, 255.
Gay, Mrs. S. H., 177.
Gibbons, James S., house of, gutted by rioters, 178.
Giles, Governor, message of, to Virginia Legislature, 132.
"Girl's Book," The, vii.
Goethe and Bettine, 50, 51.
Grant's (President U. S.) election, 199; reëlection, 213; his Indian policy, 229.
Griffith, Miss Mattie, emancipates her slaves, 89–91; her "Autobiography of a Female Slave," 90, 132.
Grimké, Angelina, addresses a committee of the Massachusetts Legislature, 26; her testimony against slavery, 130.
Grimké, Sarah M., her testimony against slavery, 129.

Hampton Institute and General Armstrong, 241.
Hedrick, Professor, expelled from North Carolina, 108.
Henry the Eighth and the Protestant reformation, 187.

Heyrick, Elizabeth, promulgates the doctrine of "Immediate Emancipation," 23.
Higginson, T. W., his biographical account of Mrs. Child, vi., xiii.; sermon to the people of Lawrence, Kans., 84; speech at an anti-slavery meeting, 149.
Hincks, Governor, of the West Indies, 134.
"History of Women," vii.
Hoar, Samuel, expelled from South Carolina, 108.
"Hobomok," Mrs. Child's first story, vii.
Hopper, Isaac T., 43; Mrs. Child's Life of, xiii.
Hosmer, Harriet, 68.
Hovey, Charles F., 82.

INDIANS, treatment of the, 218–220.

JACK, CAPTAIN, the Modoc chief, 220.
Jackson, General Andrew, and the Seminole War, 219.
Jackson, Francis, 260.
Jay, John, 188.
Jefferson, Thomas, testimony of against slavery, 133.
"John Brent," by Theodore Winthrop, 164.
"John Brown Song," the, 157.
Johnson, Andrew, speech of, at Nashville, 184.
Johnson, Oliver, 232.
Johnson, Rev. Samuel, 96, 214.
Julian, George W., letter to, 187.
"Juvenile Miscellany," vii., 10, 256.

KENT, REV. MR., characterizes Mrs. Child. 55.
King, Miss Augusta, letters to, 37, 52, 56.

LABOR QUESTION, the, 199.
Lafayette's observation of the change in color of the slaves in Virginia, 126.
Laws of the Slave states, against intermarriage, 126; against negro testimony, 126; in regard to punishment of slaves, 127; by which the master appropriated a slave's earnings, 128; prohibiting education of the blacks, 128.
Leonowens, Mrs. A. H., her book on Siam, 210, 216.
"Letters from New York," Mrs. Child's, xi., 45.
'Light of Asia," The, 257.
Lincoln, President, faith of the slaves in, 150; reëlection of, 183.
Lind, Jenny, anecdote of, 63.
"Linda," the author of, 204.
Lives of Madame Roland and Baroness de Staël, by Mrs. Child, xi.
Livingstone, Dr., and Stanley, 221.
"Looking towards Sunset," by Mrs. Child, success of, 185.
Loring, Miss Anna, letters to, 53, 94.

Loring, Ellis Gray, 21; letters to, 43, 65, 74; death of, 95; lines by Mrs. Child in memory of, 101.
Loring, Mrs. Ellis Gray, letters to, 15, 28, 82.
Lowell, J. R., tribute to Mrs. Child in his " Fable for Critics," xiv., xviii.; Fredrika Bremer's estimate of, 66.

"MARM BETTY," Mrs. Child's earliest teacher, v.
Married Women "dead in the law," 74
Martineau, Harriet, anecdote of, 19; her letter to the " Standard," 167.
Maryland, emancipation in, 184.
Mason, Mrs. M. J. C., letter of, to Mrs. Child, 120; Mrs. Child's reply to, 123.
Mason and Slidell, capture of, 162.
Massachusetts Anti-Slavery Society, annual meeting of mobbed, 148-150.
" Massachusetts Journal," the, viii.
May, Rev. Samuel, 72.
May, Rev. Samuel J., commends Mrs Child's " Progress of Religious Ideas," 77; meets Mrs. Child, 156; letters to, 192, 194; his " Recollections of our Anti-Slavery Conflict," 194; death of, 212; reminiscence of, 249.
Med, the slave-child, case of, 20.
Mendelssohn and Beethoven, their music contrasted, 76.
Mexico, the plot against denounced by Mr. Child, viii.
Michael Angelo and Raphael, 76.
Mill's (John Stuart) Autobiography, 222.
Milmore's (Martin) bust of Charles Sumner. 187.
Minute Man at Concord, the, 257.
Missouri Compromise, efforts to repeal the, 79.
Mobbing of the anti-slavery meetings, 148-150.
Modocs, persecution of the, 220; their assault on the Peace Commissioners, 221.
Montgomery, Col. James, 161, 162.
Morse, Professor, on Japan, 246.
" Mother's Book," The, vii.
Müller's (Max) " Science of Language," 201.

NEBRASKA BILL, passage of the, 72.
" Negro Boat Song," by Whittier, 159.
" New Chapter of Christian Evidences," in the " Atlantic Monthly, 202."
New Church doctrines, Mrs. Child's interest in, 43.
New England Anti-Slavery Society, formation of the, viii.
Newman's (Francis W.) works on " The Soul," and " Phases of Faith," 139.
New York draft riots of 1863, 178.
" North American Review " praises Mrs Child, vii.
Novels and Sermons, comparative value of, 192.

INDEX.   279

OLD TESTAMENT, the, injurious influence of parts of, 218.
"Oriental Religions," by Samuel Johnson, 214.
Osceola, the Seminole chief, 219.
Osgood, Miss Lucy, letters to, 61, 76, 80, 81, 84, 89, 91, 95, 99, 139, 143, 162, 169, 174, 179, 185, 188, 192, 200, 203, 204, 209, 211, 212, 214.
Paine, Thomas, grave of, 16.
Palfrey, John G., D. D., liberates the slaves bequeathed to him, 56; influenced by Mrs. Child's "Appeal," 77.
Parker, Theodore, his first return from Europe, 57; farewell note to Mrs. Child, 130; Weiss's biography of, 179; magnetic power of, 193.
Parsons, Mrs. S. M., letters to, 137, 229, 242, 243.
Paul, the Apostle, 201, 202.
Personal Liberty Bill of Massachusetts, effort to repeal the, 145.
Phelps, Elizabeth Stuart, 229.
Phillips, Wendell, confronts a mob, 147-149; defends the Chinese, 251; tribute of, at Garrison's funeral, 254; his remarks at Mrs. Child's funeral, 263.
"Philothea," by Mrs. Child, xi., 21.
Pierce, Mrs. E. C., letter to, 42.
Pierce, Senator, of Maryland, on "Uncle Tom's Cabin," 69.
Pocasset tragedy, the, 254.
'Princess of Thule," A, by William Black, 223.
'Progress of Religious Ideas," The, by Mrs. Child, xii., 65, 77, 265.
'Progressive Friends," meeting of the, 81.
Prohibitory law, aim and effect of the, 222.
Protestant reformation, the, helped on by base agents, 187.
Protestant reformation in England, the, 32.

QUINCY, EDMUND, presides at an anti-slavery meeting, 150; anecdote of, 173.

RANDOLPH, JOHN, on the insecurity of slave-holders, 133.
Raphael and Michael Angelo, 76.
'Rejected Stone," The, by M. D. Conway, 160.
Renan's "Life of Jesus," 245.
Richmond Enquirer," the, on the subserviency of the North, 73.
Ripley, George, 22.
'Romance of the Republic," A, by Mrs. Child, xix.
Rothschilds, the, compel the Emperor of Austria to repeal oppressive laws against the Jews, 141.
Russell, Mrs. S. S., letters to, 246, 262.

SAND, GEORGE, 205.
Sargent, Miss Henrietta, letters to, 24, 31, 54, 153, 156, 168, 206.

Savage, Rev. Minot J., 245.
Scudder, Miss Eliza, letters to, 174, 180, 182, 183, 196; her verses to Mrs. Child, 175.
Sears, Rev. E. H., 92.
Searle, Miss Lucy, letters to, 152, 155, 166, 167, 170.
Seminole war, origin of the, 218.
Sewall, Samuel E., letters to, 143, 232; Mrs. Child visits, 156.
Sewall, Mrs. S. E., letters to, 197, 234, 254, 257.
"Sex in Education," by Dr. E. H Clarke, 229.
Shaw, Miss Sarah, letter to, 12.
Shaw, Francis G., letters to, 30, 35, 37, 62, 70, 165, 177, 198, 205, 216, 218, 261.
Shaw, Hon. Lemuel, letter to, 145.
Shaw, Colonel Robert G., 172, 173, 235; death of, 176; proposed statue of, 190; sword of rescued, 236; opposed to burning of Darien, 237; his grave at Fort Wagner, 238; Whittier's tribute to, 240.
Shaw, Mrs. S. B., letters to, 68, 75, 73, 85, 87, 93, 98, 140, 141, 144, 147, 150, 164, 171, 172, 176, 180, 189, 190, 195, 199, 213, 218, 222, 224, 226, 229, 233, 239, 240, 241, 245, 246, 252, 258.
Sheridan's (Phil.) barbarities toward the Indians, 220.
Siam, abolition of slavery in, 216.
Silsbee, Mrs. Nathaniel, letters to, 59, 67.
Sims, Thomas, the fugitive slave, 144; his ransom secured by Mrs. Child, 145, 189.
Slaves, cruelties to, 126-132.
Smith, Gerrit, makes an anti-slavery speech in Congress, 70; his regard for Mrs. Child, 166.
Society for the Prevention of Cruelty to Animals, 213.
Somerville, Mary, Life of, 222.
"Spanish Gypsy," The, 197.
Sphinx, the Egyptian, 71.
Spirit-photography, 234.
Sprague, Charles, 235.
"Standard," the "National Anti-Slavery," edited by Mrs. Child, xiii., 43; letter to, 163.
Stowe, Harriet Beecher, and "Uncle Tom's Cabin," 69.
Suffrage for women, appeal to Mr. Sumner in behalf of, 207.
Sumner, Charles, speaks in Congress against Fugitive Slave Law, 69; influenced by Mrs. Child's "Appeal," 77; the assault on, 78; calls on Mrs. Child, 88; his position on the Mason and Slidell case, 163; Milmore's bust of, 187; letters to, 247.
Swedenborg and the New Church, 262.
Swedenborg's key of correspondences 75.

TAINE'S (H. A.) papers on art, 200.

Tappan, Arthur, threatened with assassination, 15.
Taylor, Father, anecdote of, 213.
Texas question, J. Q. Adams's speeches on, viii.
"The Rebels; a Tale of the Revolution," vii.
"The Right Way the Safe Way," by Mrs. Child, 192.
"The World that I am Passing Through," by Mrs. Child, x.
Thirteenth Amendment to U. S. Constitution, passage of, 188.
Thome, James A., denounces slavery, 131.
Thompson, George, threatened with abduction from New York, 15; speaks in the hall of the U. S. House of Representatives, 180; contrast between his first and last visits to the United States, 181; his explanation of England's attitude during the war, 181; lines to, 206; reminiscences of, 248.
Tubman, Harriet, *alias* "Moses," 161.
Tucker, St. George, testimony of, against slavery, 132.

"UNCLE TOM'S CABIN," success of, 69; read in Siam, 216.
Underwood, John C., expelled from Virginia, 108.
Unitarianism a mere half-way house, 189.
Unitarians, the, and R. W. Emerson, 34; convocation of, at New York, 189.

VENUS OF MILO, the, 172, 218.
Victor Hugo's tragedy of John Brown, 173.

WALLCUT, ROBERT F., 234.
War anecdotes, 158, 161, 180, 204.
Wasson, David A., 80, 91.
Wayland, Mass., Mrs. Child's home in xv.
Webster, Daniel, willing to defend the slave-child Med, 20; statue of, 190; "Ichabod," 269.
Weiss's (Rev. John) biography of Theodore Parker, 179.
Weld, Angelina Grimké, memorial of, 258.
Weld, Theodore D., letter to, 258.
"Westminster Review," The, 202.
White, Maria, 50.
Whitney, Miss Anne, letters to, 247, 256; her statue of Samuel Adams, 257.
Whittier, John G., biographical sketch of Mrs. Child, v.-xxv., 97; lines to Mrs. Child, on Ellis Gray Loring, 102; annoyed by curiosity-seekers, 142; letters to, 157, 159, 210, 215, 228, 235, 236; on the death of S. J. May, 212; his tribute to Colonel Shaw, 240; lines to Mrs. Child after her death, 269.
Wightman, James M., 149.
Wild, Judge, 20.
Willis, N. P., 58.
Wilson, Henry, 88.
Wise, Gov. Henry A., letter of Mrs. Child to, 103; his reply, 105; Mrs. Child's rejoinder to, 107; speech of, in Congress in 1842, 109.
Wright, Elizur, Jr., barricades his door against pro-slavery violence, 16.
"Woman Question," the, 208, 243–245.
Woman suffrage, Mrs. Child's letter to Mr. Sumner on, 207.

STANDARD AND POPULAR

Library Books

SELECTED FROM THE CATALOGUE OF

HOUGHTON, MIFFLIN AND CO.

CONSIDER what you have in the smallest chosen library. A company of the wisest and wittiest men that could be picked out of all civil countries, in a thousand years, have set in best order the results of their learning and wisdom. The men themselves were hid and inaccessible, solitary, impatient of interruptions, fenced by etiquette; but the thought which they did not uncover to their bosom friend is here written out in transparent words to us, the strangers of another age. — Ralph Waldo Emerson.

Library Books

OHN ADAMS and Abigail Adams.
Familiar Letters of John Adams and his wife, Abigail Adams, during the Revolution. Crown 8vo, $2.00.

Louis Agassiz.
Methods of Study in Natural History. 16mo, $1.50.
Geological Sketches. 16mo, $1.50.
Geological Sketches. Second Series. 16mo, $1.50.
A Journey in Brazil. Illustrated. 8vo, $5.00.

Thomas Bailey Aldrich.
Story of a Bad Boy. Illustrated. 16mo, $1.50.
Marjorie Daw and Other People. 16mo, $1.50.
Prudence Palfrey. 16mo, $1.50.
The Queen of Sheba. 16mo, $1.50.
The Stillwater Tragedy. $1.50.
Cloth of Gold and Other Poems. 16mo, $1.50.
Flower and Thorn. Later poems. 16mo, $1.25.
Poems. Complete. Illustrated. 8vo, $5.00.

American Men of Letters.
Edited by CHARLES DUDLEY WARNER.
Washington Irving. By Charles Dudley Warner. 16mo, $1.25.
Noah Webster. By Horace E. Scudder. 16mo, $1.25.
Henry D. Thoreau. By Frank B. Sanborn. 16mo, $1.25.
George Ripley. By O. B. Frothingham. 16mo, $1.25.
J. Fenimore Cooper. By Prof. T. R. Lounsbury.
(*In Preparation.*)
Nathaniel Hawthorne. By James Russell Lowell.
N. P. Willis. By Thomas Bailey Aldrich.
William Gilmore Simms. By George W. Cable.
Benjamin Franklin. By T. W. Higginson.
Others to be announced.

American Statesmen.

Edited by JOHN T. MORSE, Jr.

John Quincy Adams. By John T. Morse, Jr. 16mo, $1.25.
Alexander Hamilton. By Henry Cabot Lodge. 16mo, $1.25.
John C. Calhoun. By Dr. H. von Holst. 16mo, $1 25.
Andrew Jackson. By Prof. W. G. Sumner. 16mo, $1.25.
John Randolph. By Henry Adams. 16mo, $1.25.
James Monroe. By Pres. D. C. Gilman. 16mo, $1.25.

(*In Preparation.*)

Daniel Webster. By Henry Cabot Lodge. 16mo, $1.25.
Thomas Jefferson. By John T. Morse, Jr. 16mo, $1.25.
James Madison. By Sidney Howard Gay.
Albert Gallatin. By John Austin Stevens.
Patrick Henry. By Prof. Moses Coit Tyler.
Henry Clay. By Hon. Carl Schurz.

Lives of others are also expected.

Hans Christian Andersen.

Complete Works. 8vo.
1. The Improvisatore; or, Life in Italy.
2. The Two Baronesses.
3. O. T.; or, Life in Denmark.
4. Only a Fiddler.
5. In Spain and Portugal.
6. A Poet's Bazaar.
7. Pictures of Travel.
8. The Story of my Life. With Portrait.
9. Wonder Stories told for Children. Ninety-two illustrations.
10. Stories and Tales. Illustrated.

Cloth, per volume, $1.50; price of sets in cloth, $15.00.

Francis Bacon.

Works. Collected and edited by Spedding, Ellis, and Heath. In fifteen volumes, crown 8vo, cloth, $33.75.

The same. *Popular Edition.* In two volumes, crown 8vo, with Portraits and Index. Cloth, $5.00.

Bacon's Life.

Life and Times of Bacon. Abridged. By James Spedding. 2 vols. crown 8vo, $5.00.

Björnstjerne Björnson.
Norwegian Novels. 16mo, each $1.00.
Synnöve Solbakken.
Arne.
The Bridal March.
Magnhild.
A Happy Boy.
The Fisher Maiden.
Captain Mansana.

British Poets.
Riverside Edition. In 68 volumes, crown 8vo, cloth, gilt top, per vol. $1.75; the set, 68 volumes, cloth, $100.00.

Akenside and Beattie, 1 vol.
Ballads, 4 vols.
Burns, 1 vol.
Butler, 1 vol.
Byron, 5 vols.
Campbell and Falconer, 1 vol.
Chatterton, 1 vol.
Chaucer, 3 vols.
Churchill, Parnell, and Tickell, 2 vols.
Coleridge and Keats, 2 vols.
Cowper, 2 vols.
Dryden, 2 vols.
Gay, 1 vol.
Goldsmith and Gray, 1 vol.
Herbert and Vaughan, 1 vol.
Herrick, 1 vol.
Hood, 2 vols.
Milton and Marvell, 2 vols.
Montgomery, 2 vols.
Moore, 3 vols.
Pope and Collins, 2 vols.
Prior, 1 vol.
Scott, 5 vols.
Shakespeare and Jonson, 1 vol.
Shelley, 2 vols.
Skelton and Donne, 2 vols.
Southey, 5 vols.
Spenser, 3 vols.
Swift, 2 vols.
Thomson, 1 vol.
Watts and White, 1 vol.
Wordsworth, 3 vols.
Wyatt and Surrey, 1 vol.
Young, 1 vol.

John Brown, M. D.
Spare Hours. 3 vols. 16mo, each $1.50.

Robert Browning.
Poems and Dramas, etc. 14 vols. $19.50.
Complete Works. New Edition. 7 vols. (*In Press.*)

Wm. C. Bryant.
Translation of Homer. The Iliad. 2 vols. royal 8vo, $9.00. Crown 8vo, $4.50. 1 vol. 12mo, $3.00.
The Odyssey. 2 vols. royal 8vo, $9.00. Crown 8vo, $4.50. 1 vol. 12mo, $3.00.

John Burroughs.
>Wake-Robin. Illustrated. 16mo, $1.50.
>Winter Sunshine. 16mo, $1.50.
>Birds and Poets. 16mo, $1.50.
>Locusts and Wild Honey. 16mo, $1.50.
>Pepacton, and Other Sketches. 16mo, $1.50.

Thomas Carlyle.
>Essays. With Portrait and Index. Four volumes, crown 8vo, $7.50. *Popular Edition.* Two volumes, $3.50.

Alice and Phœbe Cary.
>Poems. *Household Edition.* 12mo, $2.00.
>*Library Edition.* Portraits and 24 illustrations. 8vo, $4.00.
>Poetical Works, including Memorial by Mary Clemmer. 1 vol. 8vo, $3.50. Full gilt, $4.00.
>Ballads for Little Folk. Illustrated. $1.50.

L. Maria Child.
>Looking toward Sunset. 4to, $2.50.

James Freeman Clarke.
>Ten Great Religions. 8vo, $3.00.
>Common Sense in Religion. 12mo, $2.00.
>Memorial and Biographical Sketches. 12mo, $2.00.
>Exotics. $1.00.

J. Fenimore Cooper.
>Works. *Household Edition.* Illustrated. 32 vols. 16mo. Cloth, per volume, $1.00 ; the set, $32.00.
>*Globe Edition.* Illust'd. 16 vols. $20.00. (*Sold only in sets.*)
>Sea Tales. Illustrated. 10 vols. 16mo. $10.00.
>Leather Stocking Tales. *Household Edition.* Illustrated. 5 vols. $5.00. *Riverside Edition.* 5 vols. $11.25.

Richard H. Dana.
>To Cuba and Back. 16mo, $1.25.
>Two Years Before the Mast. 16mo, $1.50.

Thomas De Quincey.
>Works. *Riverside Edition.* In 12 vols. crown 8vo. Per volume, cloth, $1.50 ; the set, $18.00.
>*Globe Edition.* Six vols. 12mo, $10.00. (*Sold only in sets.*)

Madame De Staël.
Germany. 1 vol. crown 8vo, $2.50.

Charles Dickens.
Works. *Illustrated Library Edition.* In 29 volumes, crown 8vo. Cloth, each, $1.50 ; the set, $43.50.
Globe Edition. In 15 vols. 12mo. Cloth, per volume, $1.25 ; the set, $18.75.

J. Lewis Diman.
The Theistic Argument as Affected by Recent Theories. 8vo, $2.00.
Orations and Essays. 8vo, $2.50.

F. S. Drake.
Dictionary of American Biography. 1 vol. 8vo, cloth, $6.00.

Charles L. Eastlake.
Hints on Household Taste. Illustrated. 12mo, $3.00.

George Eliot.
The Spanish Gypsy. 16mo, $1.50.

Ralph Waldo Emerson.
Works. 10 vols. 16mo, $1.50 each ; the set, $15.00.
Fireside Edition. 5 vols. 16mo, $10.00. (*Sold only in sets.*)
"*Little Classic*" *Edition.* 9 vols. Cloth, each, $1.50.
Prose Works. Complete. 3 vols. 12mo, $7.50.
Parnassus. *Household Ed.* 12mo, $2.00. *Library Ed.*, $4.00.

Fénelon.
Adventures of Telemachus. Crown 8vo, $2.25.

James T. Fields.
Yesterdays with Authors. 12mo, $2.00. 8vo, $3.00.
Underbrush. $1.25.
Ballads and other Verses. 16mo, $1.00.
The Family Library of British Poetry, from Chaucer to the Present Time (1350–1878). Royal 8vo. 1,028 pages, with 12 fine steel portraits, $5.00.
Memoirs and Correspondence. 1 vol. 8vo, gilt top, $2.00.

John Fiske.
Myths and Mythmakers. 12mo, $2.00.
Outlines of Cosmic Philosophy. 2 vols. 8vo, $6.00.
The Unseen World, and other Essays. 12mo, $2.00.

Goethe.
Faust. Metrical Translation. By Rev. C. T. Brooks. 16mo, $1.25.
Faust. Translated into English Verse. By Bayard Taylor. 2 vols. royal 8vo, $9.00; cr. 8vo, $4.50; 1 vol. 12mo, $3.00.
Correspondence with a Child. Portrait of Bettina Brentano. 12mo, $1.50.
Wilhelm Meister. Translated by Thomas Carlyle. Portrait of Goethe. 2 vols. 12mo, $3.00.

Bret Harte.
Works. New complete edition. 5 vols. 12mo, each $2.00.
Poems. *Household Edition.* 12mo, $2.00.

Nathaniel Hawthorne.
Works. "*Little Classic*" *Edition.* Illustrated. 24 vols. 18mo, each $1.25; the set $30.00.
Illustrated Library Edition. 13 vols. 12mo, per vol. $2.00.
Fireside Edition. Illustrated. 13 vols. 16mo, the set, $21.00.
New Globe Edition. 6 vols. 16mo, illustrated, the set, $10.00.

George S. Hillard.
Six Months in Italy. 12mo, $2.00.

Oliver Wendell Holmes.
Poems. *Household Edition.* 12mo, $2.00.
Illustrated Library Edition. Illustrated, full gilt, 8vo, $4.00.
Handy Volume Edition. 2 vols. 18mo, gilt top, $2.50.
The Autocrat of the Breakfast-Table. 18mo, $1.50; 12mo, $2.00.
The Professor at the Breakfast-Table. 12mo, $2.00.
The Poet at the Breakfast-Table. 12mo, $2.00.
Elsie Venner. 12mo, $2.00.
The Guardian Angel. 12mo, $2.00.
Soundings from the Atlantic. 16mo, $1.75.
John Lothrop Motley. A Memoir. 16mo, $1.50.

W. D. Howells.
Venetian Life. 12mo, $1.50.   Italian Journeys. $1.50.
Their Wedding Journey. Illus. 12mo, $1.50; 18mo, $1.25.
Suburban Sketches. Illustrated. 12mo, $1.50.
A Chance Acquaintance. Illus. 12mo, $1.50; 18mo, $1.25.
A Foregone Conclusion. 12mo, $1.50.
The Lady of the Aroostook. 12mo, $1.50.
The Undiscovered Country. $1.50.   Poems. $1.25.
Out of the Question. A Comedy. 18mo, $1.25.
A Counterfeit Presentment. 18mo, $1.25.
Choice Autobiography. Edited by W. D. Howells. 18mo, per vol. $1.25.
  I., II. Memoirs of Frederica Sophia Wilhelmina, Margravine of Baireuth.
  III. Lord Herbert of Cherbury, and Thomas Ellwood.
  IV. Vittorio Alfieri. V. Carlo Goldoni.
  VI. Edward Gibbon. VII., VIII. François Marmontel.

Thomas Hughes.
Tom Brown's School-Days at Rugby. $1.00.
Tom Brown at Oxford. 16mo, $1.25.
The Manliness of Christ. 16mo, gilt top, $1.00.

Henry James, Jr.
Passionate Pilgrim and other Tales. $2.00.
Transatlantic Sketches. 12mo, $2.00.
Roderick Hudson. 12mo, $2.00.
The American. 12mo, $2.00.
Watch and Ward. 18mo, $1.25.
The Europeans. 12mo, $1.50.
Confidence. 12mo, $1.50.
The Portrait of a Lady. $2.00.

Mrs. Anna Jameson.
Writings upon Art subjects. 10 vols. 18mo, each $1.50.

Sarah O. Jewett.
Deephaven. 18mo, $1.25.
Old Friends and New. 18mo, $1.25.
Country By-Ways. 18mo, $1.25.
Play-Days. Stories for Children. Sq. 16mo, $1.50.

Rossiter Johnson.

Little Classics. Eighteen handy volumes containing the choicest Stories, Sketches, and short Poems in English literature. Each in one vol. 18mo, $1.00; the set, $18.00 In 9 vols. square 16mo, $13.50. (*Sold in sets only.*)

Samuel Johnson.

Oriental Religions: India, 8vo, $5.00. China, 8vo, $5.00.

T. Starr King.

Christianity and Humanity. With Portrait. 12mo, $2.00.
Substance and Show. 12mo, $2.00.

Lucy Larcom.

Poems. 16mo, $1.25.   An Idyl of Work. 16mo, $1.25.
Wild Roses of Cape Ann and other Poems. 16mo, $1.25.
Childhood Songs. Illustrated. 12mo, $1.50; 16mo, $1.00.
Breathings of the Better Life. 18mo, $1.25.

G. P. Lathrop.

A Study of Hawthorne. 18mo, $1.25.
An Echo of Passion. 16mo, $1.25.

G. H. Lewes.

The Story of Goethe's Life. Portrait. 12mo, $1.50.
Problems of Life and Mind. 5 vols. $14.00.

H. W. Longfellow.

Poems. *Cambridge Edition complete.* Portrait. 4 vols. cr. 8vo, $9.00. 2 vols. $7.00.
Octavo Edition. Portrait and 300 Illustrations. $8.00.
Household Edition. Portrait. 12mo, $2.00.
Red-Line Edition. 12 illustrations and Portrait. $2.50.
Diamond Edition. $1.00.
Library Edition. Portrait and 32 illustrations. 8vo, $4.00.
Prose Works. *Cambridge Edition.* 2 vols. cr. 8vo, $4.50.
Hyperion. A Romance. 16mo, $1.50.
Outre-Mer. 16mo, $1.50.   Kavanagh. 16mo, $1.50.
Christus. *Household Edition,* $2.00; *Diamond Edition,* $1.00
Translation of the Divina Commedia of Dante. 3 vols. royal 8vo, $13.50; cr. 8vo, $6.00; 1 vol. cr. 8vo, $3.00.
Poets and Poetry of Europe. Royal 8vo, $5.00.
In the Harbor. Steel Portrait. 16mo, gilt top, $1.00.

James Russell Lowell.
Poems. *Red-Line Ed.* 16 illustrations and Portrait. $2.50
Household Edition. Portrait. 12mo, $2.00.
Library Edition. Portrait and 32 illustrations. 8vo, $4.00.
Diamond Edition. $1.00.
Fireside Travels. 16mo, $1.50.
Among my Books. 1st and 2nd Series. 12mo, $2.00 each.
My Study Windows. 12mo, $2.00.

T. B. Macaulay.
England. *New Riverside Edition.* 4 vols., cloth, $5.00.
Essays. Portrait. *New Riverside Edition.* 3 vols., $3.75.
Speeches and Poems. *New Riverside Ed.* 1 vol., $1.25.

Harriet Martineau.
Autobiography. Portraits and illus. 2 vols. 8vo, $6.00.
Household Education. 18mo, $1.25.

Owen Meredith.
Poems. *Household Edition.* Illustrated. 12mo, $2.00.
Library Edition. Portrait and 32 illustrations. 8vo, $4.00.
Shawmut Edition. $1.50.
Lucile. *Red-Line Edition.* 8 illustrations. $2.50.
Diamond Edition. 8 illustrations, $1.00.

Michael de Montaigne.
Complete Works. Portrait. 4 vols. crown 8vo, $7.50.

Rev. T. Mozley.
Reminiscences, chiefly of Oriel College and the Oxford Movement. 2 vols. crown 8vo, $3.00.

E. Mulford.
The Nation. 8vo, $2.50.
The Republic of God. 8vo, $2.00.

D. M. Mulock.
Thirty Years. Poems. 1 vol. 16mo, $1.50.

T. T. Munger.
On the Threshold. 16mo, gilt top, $1.00.

J. A. W. Neander.
History of the Christian Religion and Church, with Index volume, 6 vols. 8vo, $20.00; Index alone, $3.00.

C. E. Norton.
Notes of Travel and Study in Italy. 16mo, $1.25.
Translation of Dante's New Life. Royal 8vo, $3.00.

Francis W. Palfrey.
Memoir of William Francis Bartlett. 16mo, $1.50.

James Parton.
Life of Benjamin Franklin. 2 vols. 8vo, $4.00.
Life of Thomas Jefferson. 8vo, $2.00.
Life of Aaron Burr. 2 vols. 8vo, $4.00.
Life of Andrew Jackson. 3 vols. 8vo, $6.00.
Life of Horace Greeley. 8vo, $2.50.
General Butler in New Orleans. 8vo, $2.50.
Humorous Poetry of the English Language. 8vo, $2.00.
Famous Americans of Recent Times. 8vo, $2.00.
Life of Voltaire. 2 vols. 8vo, $6.00.
The French Parnassus. 12mo, $2.00; crown 8vo, $3.50.

Blaise Pascal.
Thoughts, Letters, and Opuscules. Crown 8vo, $2.25.
Provincial Letters. Crown 8vo, $2.25.

E. S. Phelps.
The Gates Ajar. 16mo, $1.50.
Men, Women, and Ghosts. 16mo, $1.50.
Hedged In. 16mo, $1.50.
The Silent Partner. 16mo, $1.50.
The Story of Avis. 16mo, $1.50.
Sealed Orders, and other Stories. 16mo, $1.50.
Friends: A Duet. 16mo, $1.25.
Dr. Zay. 16mo. (*In Press.*)
Poetic Studies. Square 16mo, $1.50.

Adelaide A. Procter.
Poems. *Diamond Edition.* $1.00.
Red-Line Edition. Portrait and 16 illustrations. $2.50.
Favorite Edition. Illustrated. 16mo, $1.50.

Henry Crabb Robinson.
Diary. Crown 8vo, $2.50.

A. P. Russell.
Library Notes. 12mo, $2.00.

John G. Saxe.
Works. Portrait. 16mo, $2.25.
Poems. *Red-Line Edition.* Illustrated. $2.50.
Diamond Edition. 18mo, $1.00.
Household Edition. 12mo, $2.00.

Sir Walter Scott.
Waverley Novels. *Illustrated Library Edition.* In 25 vols. cr. 8vo, each $1.00; the set, $25.00.
Globe Edition. 13 vols. 100 illustrations, $16.25.
Tales of a Grandfather. *Library Edition.* 3 vols. $4.50.
Poems. *Red-Line Edition.* Illustrated. $2.50.
Diamond Edition. 18mo, $1.00.

Horace E. Scudder.
The Bodley Books. 6 vols. Each $1.50.
The Dwellers in Five-Sisters' Court. 16mo, $1.25.
Stories and Romances. $1.25.
Dream Children. Illustrated. 16mo, $1.00.
Seven Little People. Illustrated. 16mo, $1.00.
Stories from my Attic. Illustrated. 16mo, $1.00.
The Children's Book. 4to, 450 pages, $3.50.
Boston Town. Illustrated. 12mo, $1.50.

J. C. Shairp.
Culture and Religion. 16mo, $.125.
Poetic Interpretation of Nature. 16mo, $1.25.
Studies in Poetry and Philosophy. 16mo, $1.50.
Aspects of Poetry. 16mo, $1.50.

Dr. William Smith.
Bible Dictionary. *American Edition.* In four vols. 8vo the set, $20.00.

E. C. Stedman.
Poems. *Farringford Edition.* Portrait. 16mo, $2.00.
Victorian Poets. 12mo, $2.00.
Hawthorne, and other Poems. 16mo, $1.25.
Edgar Allan Poe. An Essay. Vellum, 18mo, $1.00.

Harriet Beecher Stowe.
Agnes of Sorrento. 12mo, $1.50.
The Pearl of Orr's Island. 12mo, $1.50.
Uncle Tom's Cabin. *Popular Edition.* 12mo, $2.00.
The Minister's Wooing. 12mo, $1.50.
The May-flower, and other Sketches. 12mo, $1.50.
Nina Gordon. 12mo, $1.50.
Oldtown Folks. 12mo, $1.50.
Sam Lawson's Fireside Stories. Illustrated. $1.50.
Uncle Tom's Cabin. 100 Illustrations. 12mo, full gilt, $3.50.

Bayard Taylor.
Poetical Works. *Household Edition.* 12mo, $2.00.
Dramatic Works. Crown 8vo, $2.25.
The Echo Club, and other Literary Diversions. $1.25.

Alfred Tennyson.
Poems. *Household Ed.* Portrait and 60 illustrations. $2.00
Illustrated Crown Edition. 48 illustrations. 2 vols. $5.00.
Library Edition. Portrait and 60 illustrations. $4.00.
Red-Line Edition. Portrait and 16 illustrations. $2.50.
Diamond Edition. $1.00.
Shawmut Edition. Illustrated. Crown 8vo, $1.50.
Idylls of the King. Complete. Illustrated. $1.50.

Celia Thaxter.
Among the Isles of Shoals. $1.25.
Poems. $1.50.   Drift-Weed. Poems. $1.50.

Henry D. Thoreau.
Walden. 12mo, $1.50.
A Week on the Concord and Merrimack Rivers. $1.50.
Excursions in Field and Forest. 12mo, $1.50.
The Maine Woods. 12mo, $1.50.
Cape Cod. 12mo, $1.50.
Letters to various Persons. 12mo, $1.50.
A Yankee in Canada. 12mo, $1.50.
Early Spring in Massachusetts. 12mo, $1.50.

George Ticknor.
History of Spanish Literature. 3 vols. 8vo, $10.00.
Life, Letters, and Journals. Portraits. 2 vols. 8vo, $6.00.
Cheaper edition. 2 vols. 12mo, $4.00.

J. T. Trowbridge.
A Home Idyl. $1.25. The Vagabonds. $1.25.
The Emigrant's Story. 16mo, $1.25.

Voltaire.
History of Charles XII. Crown 8vo, $2.25.

Lew Wallace.
The Fair God. 12mo, $1.50.

George E. Waring, Jr.
Whip and Spur. $1.25. A Farmer's Vacation. $3.00.
Village Improvements. Illustrated. 75 cents.
The Bride of the Rhine. Illustrated. $1.50.

Charles Dudley Warner.
My Summer in a Garden. 16mo, $1.00. *Illustrated.* $1.50.
Saunterings. 18mo, $1.25.
Back-Log Studies. Illustrated. $1.50.
Baddeck, and that Sort of Thing. $1.00.
My Winter on the Nile. 12mo, $2.00.
In the Levant. 12mo, $2.00.
Being a Boy. Illustrated. $1.50.
In the Wilderness. 75 cents.

William A. Wheeler.
Dictionary of the Noted Names of Fiction. $2.00.

Edwin P. Whipple.
Works. Critical Essays. 6 vols., $9.00.

Richard Grant White.
Every-Day English. 12mo, $2.00.
Words and their Uses. 12mo, $2.00.
England Without and Within. 12mo, $2.00.
Shakespeare's Complete Works. 3 vols. cr. 8vo. (*In Press.*)

Mrs. A. D. T. Whitney.
Faith Gartney's Girlhood. 12mo, $1.50.
Hitherto. 12mo, $1.50.
Patience Strong's Outings. 12mo, $1.50.
The Gayworthys. 12mo, $1.50.

Leslie Goldthwaite. Illustrated. 12mo, $1.50.
We Girls. Illustrated. 12mo, $1.50.
Real Folks. Illustrated. 12mo, $1.50.
The Other Girls. Illustrated. 12mo, $1.50.
Sights and Insights. 2 vols. 12mo, $3.00.
Odd or Even. $1.50.
Boys at Chequasset. $1.50.
Pansies. Square 16mo, $1.50.
Just How. 16mo, $1.00.

John G. Whittier.
Poems. *Household Edition.* Portrait. $2.00.
Cambridge Edition. Portrait. 3 vols. crown 8vo, $6.75.
Red-Line Edition. Portrait. 12 illustrations. $2.50.
Diamond Edition. 18mo, $1.00.
Library Edition. Portrait. 32 illustrations. 8vo, $4.00.
Prose Works. *Cambridge Edition.* 2 vols. $4.50.
John Woolman's Journal. Introduction by Whittier. $1.50.
Child Life in Poetry. Selected by Whittier. Illustrated. $2.25. Child Life in Prose. $2.25.
Songs of Three Centuries. Selected by J. G. Whittier. *Household Edition.* 12mo, $2.00. *Illustrated Library Edition.* 32 illustrations. $4.00.

Justin Winsor.
Reader's Handbook of the American Revolution. 16mo, $1.25.

A catalogue containing portraits of many of the above authors, with a description of their works, will be sent free, on application, to any address.

HOUGHTON, MIFFLIN AND COMPANY, BOSTON, MASS

www.ingramcontent.com/pod-product-compliance
Lightning Source LLC
Chambersburg PA
CBHW030741230426
43667CB00007B/797